Strategies for
Success

AN EFFECTIVE GUIDE FOR TEACHERS
OF SECONDARY-LEVEL SLOW LEARNERS

Strategies for Success

AN EFFECTIVE GUIDE FOR TEACHERS OF SECONDARY-LEVEL SLOW LEARNERS

Gloria Wilkins
Susanne Miller

ONEIDA SENIOR HIGH SCHOOL
ONEIDA, NEW YORK

TEACHERS COLLEGE PRESS

TEACHERS COLLEGE, COLUMBIA UNIVERSITY
New York and London   1983

Published by Teachers College Press, 1234 Amsterdam Avenue,
New York, New York 10027

Library of Congress Cataloging in Publication Data

Wilkins, Gloria, 1947–
   Strategies for success.

   Bibliography: p.
   Includes index.
   1. Reading—Remedial teaching. 2. English language—
Remedial teaching—Curricula. 3. Slow learning children
—Education—Curricula. 4. English language—Study and
teaching (Secondary) I. Miller, Susanne, 1934–
II. Title.
LB1050.5.W488   371.92′64   82-5438
ISBN 0-8077-2701-6   AACR2

Manufactured in the United States of America

87 86 85 84 83   1 2 3 4 5 6

To Bob and Ed
with our love
for their patience
and understanding

Contents

vii

Introduction

"Are you sure you have the patience to work with me?" is the cry of many high school students. It may not be expressed in these words, but it is reflected in the slouching posture of a boy trying to hide in the last row, in the refusal of a young girl to read a part in the play ". . . because I didn't bring my glasses," and in the restlessness of a junior high school student counting cinder blocks on the classroom walls. None of these students may actually say "I can't read," but all have developed compensatory mechanisms for surviving in an educational system that *assumes* its students can read. If they don't invent their own devices for survival, they soon join the ranks of dropouts.

Kenny was an enthusiastic eighth-grade American history student. Highly verbal and anxious to please, he participated in all discussions and seemed to be very involved in all classroom projects. On the day of the first quiz, the teacher asked Kenny to number on his paper from one through ten. He started with ten at the top of the page and in descending order wrote all of his numbers backwards, a talent that several of his classmates tried to imitate. He knew the capitals of all the states when questioned orally, but when faced with writing the words, he could not spell a single one of them. None of his spellings indicated any attempt to use phonetics. He always became physically ill and developed a headache when given a written test.

At eighteen years of age, Gerry was entering his sophomore year of high school. A large, hulking boy, he disliked sports, was a loner, and remained in school only because it was ". . . more peaceful than at home." He had never read through an entire book in all his thirteen years of schooling. His answer to a teacher questioning him about why he slept through most of her class reveals much about Gerry: "I'm hung over. I drink a lot because that's the only thing I'm good at."

Most enthusiastic new teachers of junior and senior high school students are not prepared to teach the Kennys and Gerrys of our society. First of all, it's difficult for new college graduates to believe they exist. As graduates of college preparatory programs in high school, they did not have a Kenny or a Gerry in their own classes or among their circle of acquaintances. Certainly, when they arrived at college, they did not find Kenny or Gerry there. These problem students never made it, and as a result, many new teachers begin their teaching careers prepared to teach only students like themselves.

PURPOSE

Strategies for Success provides content-trained teachers with insight into how secondary-level students can have reached adolescence without learning to read, diagnostic and prescriptive aids, practical teaching devices, and realistic suggestions for establishing more effective curriculum for this type of student within the traditional school framework. We are hired to teach content to *all* students, not only to those who can read.

Although the strategies suggested on the following pages are directed primarily to secondary English and reading teachers, other content area teachers will be able to glean helpful information as well. This text is *not* meant to be a handbook for teachers who wish to investigate theories of education and the reading process. These theories have merit, of course, but by themselves they do little or nothing to help a teacher stranded in a classroom with twenty-eight nonreading, unmotivated, apathetic students. This is an invitation to classroom teachers to pick up a book about reading without the fear of having to wade through the "jargon" of reading specialists. Our book is for average dedicated teachers who were given no instruction in how to teach reading because they were preparing to teach on the secondary level.

When you finish this book, what do we hope you will have learned? First, we hope you will have an understanding about the kinds of students who have reading problems. What kind of fifteen-year-old girl makes it to the tenth grade without knowing that *hit* is a verb? Why does she read only on a fourth-grade level? Why does she think of herself as a failure? Why does she not have very high goals for her life?

Second, we hope you will realize that a teacher of this kind of student must have a very thick skin. If you are teaching because *you* need the ego-building, then you should certainly stick to teaching only the scholarship seniors who will stay after class with curious questions about the day's discussion. The teacher of the adolescent who can't read and who has a poor self-concept, however, will rarely receive any ego-building from the students. This teacher must be able to ignore such comments as "I hate English"; "This class is boring"; and "I won't never see why we have to know what a verb is."

The rewards of teaching this type of student are few and far between. You must be the one who is strong, who gives support even when it isn't wanted, who can bolster a student's sagging self-concept. You can hardly expect these students to do all this for you, even though you want outward assurances from your students that you are doing a good job. Teachers of the low achiever will have rewards also, but they will have to be satisfied with helping one or two pupils a year. They'll have to be content with a certain look in a student's eye or even with noticing that John has finally washed his only shirt and jeans after three months.

Third, we hope you will realize the priorities of the students. An eleventh grader may consider Shakespeare or *A Tale of Two Cities* unimportant when he knows he will be a mechanic at eighteen or be married and have a child at seventeen. Especially for the low-achieving adolescent who is not going on to higher education or who may even drop out before graduation, we must remember the basics. Instead of spending week after week on creative composition, let's spend some weeks on writing complete sentences for job applications and learning how to spell the common words in life. Remember who your students are; choose materials from *their* life style, not yours; and concentrate on skills that they can use in the world after graduation.

HOW TO USE THIS BOOK

Strategies for Success is divided into two parts. Chapters 1–3 deal with background, process, and diagnosis; chapters 4–10 deal with concrete and practical suggestions for organizing your classroom and developing your curriculum. In addition, we have prepared a book of duplicating masters containing material for class use to accompany the main text.

If you wonder how it is possible for a Kenny or a Gerry to have made it as far as high school, we suggest that you start with chapter 1, which will help put Kenny and Gerry in perspective. What factors in teacher training, parenting, school administration, and society contributed to their problems? What effect have poor attendance, failure to individualize instruction, the failure syndrome, poor self-image, cultural deficits, and assumptive teaching had on our students with learning problems?

Chapter 2 discusses why reading is difficult for some people. For those who have had little formal training in reading instruction, chapter 2 provides the background and theory behind the reading process itself. If you have done recent graduate work in the reading attributes of intelligence, vision, auditory skills, motor, tactile, and kinesthetic skills, and word attack skills, you may wish to skip this chapter, but the occasionally technical information presented here is essential as the basis for decisions on curriculum suggested later in the text.

The first section of *Strategies for Success* concludes with chapter 3, which provides practical advice on how to determine reading levels and skill levels of the students. Methods covered include group and individual screening devices, informal reading inventories, class inventories of strengths and weaknesses, and suggested composites for charting diagnostic information. Since you cannot write prescriptive materials until you know what is wrong with a student's learning process, this chapter is very important.

Chapters 4–10 move into the concrete areas. Where do we go from here? How do we do what has been suggested? Along with the thorough explanations, suggestions, and descriptions in the text of these chapters, there are many figures that present material that can be used for class use. Some of these are simply examples of material that we have found useful; you should adapt them to your program. Others you could easily use as they are; in that case, they are repeated (along with many other activities) in *Strategies for Success Duplicating Masters*, also available from Teachers College Press.

Chapter 4 covers prescription to match diagnosis, an analysis of the heterogeneous classroom, and practical strategies designed to meet some of the off-beat problems not usually considered in a book of this scope. Multilevel texts, thematic units, multilevel study guides, individualizing, grouping, journals, uninterrupted sustained silent reading, individual interest units, contracts, and varied levels of grammar instruction are among the survival strategies included in chapter 4. Much of the material suggested for class use in this chapter is included in the book of duplicating masters.

Moving into the realm of an ideal classroom, chapter 5 provides specific information on establishing a class in English or some other content area *specifically* for students with poor reading skills; it explains the criteria for selecting the students, the teachers, and the necessary training for developing materials especially for this type of class.

Probably the single most important factor in turning older students on to learning is affective concerns: all the things that make students feel good about themselves and motivate them to think that they can learn. Chapter 6 discusses methods of getting through this obstacle to learning. The major thrust of this chapter is improving student self-image through the techniques of peer tutoring, positive grading, built-in rewards, behavior modification, few (but enforceable) rules, effort grading, seating arrangements, positive conditioning, partners, establishing specialists, and motivating for original and creative work.

Chapter 7 focuses on the most basic element of reading instruction:

vocabulary, the essence of content subjects. This chapter takes you through the steps in writing varied vocabulary material, from simple to complex. The chapter considers the criteria by which words are selected and taught, but the main emphasis is the need for constant reinforcement. We have included a wide range of examples from vocabulary exercises, with detailed explanations of their structure. The book of duplicating masters contains many complete vocabulary worksheets.

On the other hand, what good are words if the students can't understand what the author means or the implication of those words to the reader's life? Chapter 8, "Comprehension," discusses the differences in literal, interpretive, and applied levels of comprehension. This chapter takes you through the step-by-step process of writing study guides for different kinds of students. Again, many of the study guides excerpted in this chapter are offered in their entirety in the book of duplicating masters.

With the current emphasis on competency testing, no text would be complete without a section on writing. The material in chapter 9 follows the "simple-to-complex" formula: from writing complete sentences, through paragraphing, to writing compositions. Sections on writing business letters, reports, and persuasive compositions incorporate some of the more advanced-level techniques, but this chapter stresses the importance of daily journal writing and includes suggestions for creative writing.

The final chapter of the book deals with curriculum. Chapter 10 provides criteria for sequencing various units in a four-year program, and stresses moving from oral emphasis to written emphasis and from simple to complex. This chapter promotes the concept of starting with students at the point where their skills and interests are, not where they are supposed to be. It offers guidance in developing material with built-in "crutches" carried through to the gradual elimination of some of these supportive devices. One of the strengths of this chapter is that it meets the needs of traditionalists as well as those concerned with a more modern curriculum.

The Appendices include our Individual Secondary Skills Inventory (a group screening device providing diagnostic information for classroom teachers) and a sample of our Informal Reading Inventory (a tool for quickly assessing whether a student can handle material at a given level). These are presented as a model of what you can develop using your own textbooks. There are also examples of management materials and a glossary. In addition, we have provided an extensive bibliography.

The last appendix contains thirty-four study guides, worksheets, and tests, to be photocopied or Thermofaxed for students to use in five reading curriculum units. These exercises illustrate the ideas presented throughout the text.

As you join us in *Strategies for Success*, keep in mind that our text was written out of desperation. We are desperate for the new teachers entering our classrooms each fall prepared to teach Mediterranean literature, Greek drama, and Keats but not prepared to teach a Kenny or a Gerry. We are desperate for the Kennys and Gerrys who enter those same classrooms each September daring to anticipate that ". . . maybe this year I'll catch on." We are desperate for our system of education which remains committed to learning via the printed page. We are desperate for the content area teachers wondering, "How did he ever get up here if he can't read?" We hope that in sharing our experiences we can ease some of your desperation as you evolve a teaching style that will make curricular content meaningful to readers and nonreaders alike.

Part One
THE THINKING BEHIND THE STRATEGIES

Why Secondary Reading Instruction? 1

Many teachers, administrators, school board members, and parents are at a loss to explain why some adolescents reach junior and senior high school without being able to read or to cope with everyday life. Brenda is typical of this kind of adolescent.

Brenda lives in a rural area. She is the third of five children born to parents who are on welfare. Brenda's father works occasionally, but he is in debt and finds it difficult to "get ahead." Neither her father nor her mother completed high school. Her father dropped out in the tenth grade to join the army. Her mother married at eighteen after waitressing for several years.

Brenda began elementary school with several strikes against her. Because her early home life lacked cultural opportunities, Brenda did not have the experiential background necessary for reading readiness. Not having much money, her family did not travel. Most of the social contacts Brenda had were with her immediate family, grandparents, and aunts and uncles. Brenda watched television, usually police and crime dramas. Rarely did she see educational programming such as "Sesame Street." Brenda's early language development was impeded because her parents did not spend much time conversing with her. Usually family members all were talking at once, and no one was listening to anyone else. With all this noise, Brenda learned to tune out most conversation. Consequently, her language skills were weaker in first grade than those of the average student.

Nevertheless, in first grade, Brenda was reading fairly well and was assigned to the middle reading group. However, she missed several weeks of school and fell behind. Because her parents did not feel education was very important, they did not encourage Brenda to try to catch up. They did not show much interest in any of her school work. As a result, by second grade, Brenda was in the low reading group, was an

3

occasional discipline problem, and was absent regularly. She repeatod second grade.

By the time Brenda reached the fifth and sixth grades, she had become a member of the low achiever group. She spent much of her time doing "busy work" because her teachers were not able to give her the individual attention needed to bolster her skills. They tended to promote her because they didn't want to have too many low achievers the next year.

Brenda was thirteen when she entered seventh grade. She was still reading on the third-grade level. Since she had missed much school, she had also missed the basics of geography, math, and science. Her teachers in junior high school were ill equipped to handle a student lacking in such basic skills. Most of the textbooks were written on the sixth- or seventh-grade level, so Brenda could not even begin to fathom their content. Becoming more and more discouraged and falling further and further behind, Brenda stopped trying in school and became content with Ds and Fs. By now, her self-image was very poor. She received little support from her parents. Her teachers had given up trying to motivate her, and no one had the time to work with her individually; therefore, Brenda turned to outside activities to gain the self-confidence and esteem she so desperately wanted. She began to "hang around" in the streets and skipped school frequently. She was out late at night. Most of her social contacts were with other low achievers. They also had poor self-images and turned to misdemeanors, drugs, alcohol, and sex for fulfillment.

Somehow, Brenda made it to senior high and ninth grade. She continued to hang out with the drug crowd and now began to fantasize about her future. Because she could see no relationship between school and her future, she began looking for a means of escape from school. To a sixteen-year-old, romance and marriage, babies and family seemed to be the ideal solution.

Brenda had met Joe in junior high school. He was a year older than she was, but he was also a student who could not read and who was unsuccessful in school. By the time Brenda was a sophomore, she was pregnant. She and Joe decided to get married before he went into the army. They both dropped out of school. The prospect of marriage and children seemed much more exciting than staying in school and struggling with rules, regulations, textbooks, teachers, and assured failure.

Brenda lived with her parents while Joe was in basic training. They rented a small apartment later and began raising their family.

The cycle was beginning all over again. Brenda had a ninth-grade education, and her husband had completed tenth grade. Their basic skills were on an elementary school level, and they would have difficulty coping with day-to-day living. Soon they would be on welfare.

Perhaps they would have three or four children before anyone could convince them to use birth control. There would be tension in the home as a result of the economic problems, job setbacks, and poor self-images. The children would be left much on their own and would not receive the cultural and educational enrichment needed to develop reading readiness. They would likely have reading problems throughout their school careers and follow in the footsteps of their parents.

Brenda's story, sad as it is, is one that repeats itself all too often. The problem is born, feeds on itself, and perpetuates another problem. Let's think about some of the major stumbling blocks that Brenda encountered.

HOME ENVIRONMENT

Brenda did not receive the attention she needed at home. The preschool years are very important for preparing a child to get ready to read. Conversation in the home contributes greatly to language development. Travel and cultural inputs broaden the experiences of the child and provide a wider frame of reference for reading and learning. There is much parents can do to expand their children's intelligence. If a child receives love, attention, and adequate stimulation in the home during the preschool years, he will probably begin first grade on equal footing with the average student.

Language Development

A child needs to be talked to and listened to. Parents need to *talk* to one another, not yell. If a child sees his parents reading often, he will wish to imitate them and will want to read also. Very few children will develop good language patterns if they are not given the model to follow. Parents who watch television passively for hours or who are too busy to take time to talk to their child are giving the example that "nontalking" is the normal thing to do. A child cannot learn language patterns unless he has a chance to practice them.

Cultural Experience

A preschooler also needs to have cultural experience. A child who has never been more than ten miles from his home town is not prepared for the experience of first grade. He will not understand many of the words in the primer readers. For example, if he has lived in the city all his life, he will not know what an author means by *farm* unless his parents have read him farm stories, discussed life on a farm, or visited one with him. By the time a child is three, he is old enough to be taken to museums and on sight seeing trips to familiar places around his town. Most firefighters will go out of their way to give a small child a tour of the fire department. Other places a child can have visited by the time he has entered first grade are a bank, a library, a store, a hospital, a newspaper office, and a school. If a child has a wide enough range of experiences before he enters first grade, he will be more ready to read. He will then have the experiential background necessary to help him understand the meanings of the words he is learning to read.

SCHOOL ENVIRONMENT

When Brenda began school, she was already lacking in reading readiness skills. This caused a problem for her overworked teachers. They had too many students in their classes to be able to cope with special problems. Students like Brenda were shunted off into the puzzle corner while the teacher taught the majority of the class.

Teachers

By the time Brenda was promoted into junior high school, she was so far behind in her basic skills that she was discouraged, and so were her teachers. Her secondary teachers had received little training during their college preparation in how to instruct the thirteen-year-old who cannot read. In addition, the more experienced teachers did not teach the low achievers. They were looking for the more challenging classes of the college-bound seniors.

Usually the teachers who are given the slower classes are the brand new graduates full of idealism and untested discipline theories. Other teachers who are given these classes are the older teachers whom the administrators are trying to push into early retirement. They may hope that the dull or frightening experience of teaching slow learners will cause these teachers to make a hasty exit. Obviously, such teacher selection often does not help slow learners. They need experienced, dedicated teachers who are willing to give them the time they need to catch up on their skills.

The fact that you are taking the time to read this book and explore new ideas shows that good teachers are always trying to improve their teaching techniques and to look for the best possible methods of helping their students. Unfortunately, many teachers are not as conscientious. Instead of helping the poor readers, these teachers perpetuate their students' problems with poor teaching, inadequate preparation, and little motivation.

Teacher Preparation

It may be beneficial to consider the college preparation of the average teacher in order to understand why some—not all—professional people become uninspired teachers of the slow learner. In the past, college students have chosen to follow an educational career for several possible reasons. Exciting jobs in big cities where an English degree will be the ticket to an executive position in a publishing firm are few and far between. The safer career often appears to be in education. This is where college graduates feel they can succeed because the territory is familiar to them. Didn't they spend twelve years in the public school system? Certainly they can do as good a job as many of the elementary and secondary teachers they had. So they take a few education courses. Those preparing for elementary education degrees also take two or three reading courses. Whereas most colleges require that their English and social studies candidates also take one or two reading courses, the students may doubt the need for these courses. After all, they themselves could read long before they reached seventh grade. Why should there be any problem with their future students?

Besides seeing education as a "safe" career, college students sometimes look forward to the fringe benefits received by the teaching profession. Look at all those vacations! See all the money and the easy raises given every year for standing in front of a class five times a day lecturing. Who can beat that?

What happens to these naive "rookies" when they begin teaching in a junior or senior high school? Experienced teachers will attest to the fact that the first-year teachers are given the most difficult assignments. They often receive what is left over after the tenured teachers have finished dividing up the classes. This may mean five or six classes plus a study hall, at least three preparations, and, of course, most of the slower students. Almost every teacher with more than two years' experience wants to teach the college-bound senior or upper-level junior classes. These students provide rewards and are self-motivated. The teachers simply pour out the information, and the students absorb it. Not so the lower-level students. They are "turned off" to begin with and require extra preparation and motivation. Because of heavy teaching loads, new teachers fresh out of college do not have the time to prepare exciting lessons or to worry about individual motivation. Worrying about the students' reading levels is next to impossible. So what do the "rookies" do?

New teachers generally follow one of three patterns. Some teach as if they really had the upper-level juniors and the college-bound seniors. They close their eyes to the actual problem and blame the failure of the students on laziness and skipping of classes. For teachers who have little or no conscience, this is the easiest escape route. The loss of the students can be rationalized a thousand different ways. By ignoring the basic problem, usually lack of reading skills, new teachers also avoid making extra work for themsleves. They remain in the school, receive tenure, and continue to turn off students by their lack of conscience and their dull classes.

Another possible avenue open to the beginning teacher is to give up and quit. We have seen several teachers who tried to be pals to low achievers. Being friends is all right, but that relationship usually emerges after several months or years of strict discipline and realistic expectations. When the students see that you care enough about them to believe that they are able to achieve instead of fail, then they understand that you are their friend, and you are trying to help them. The teachers who try to be "good guys" during the first months of the school year are often not respected. Students take advantage of the good intentions of the teachers to gain their own goals, which are most likely the breaking of some rule: getting out of detention, skipping gym, or walking the halls. The "good guy" teachers don't last. They become disillusioned easily, and sense the disrespect of their students. They resort to yelling, making threats, and detaining students after school. None of this will win the respect they are frantically seeking. Without this form of "stroking," young teachers often resign prematurely. With their high ideals and aspirations dashed, they see themselves as failures. If they don't quit themselves, the school system may sense that they don't have the qualifications for teaching. The unsuspecting "rookies" will be given notice several weeks before their names were to be mentioned for tenure. The only good thing about this solution to the problem of unprepared teachers is that it spares the low-achieving students from more inadequate teaching.

The third, and most frustrating, alternative is to try to find a way to help the poorly prepared, nonreading student. Unless the "rookies" have a lot of willpower, stamina, and sheer guts, this alternative is the most discouraging. The new teachers will feel as though they are up against a blank wall with no place to turn for help. None of their college courses explained what to do with Mark, the tenth grader who can't spell any words except the, and, and is. Some of the less motivated and less conscientious teachers may give up unless encouraged by the older, more experienced teachers and the department head. Unfortunately, many times, the new recruits are left to flounder and only get a few sage words of advice on observation days. Getting angry is another result of this alternative. This does not help unless the anger is channeled into constructive searches for new methods and new knowledge, especially knowledge of reading skills. We hope the new teachers will be creative enough and strong enough to withstand all the initial setbacks and disappointments. The first year may be difficult, but the second year will be easier.

Assumptive Teaching

One of the most damaging aspects of the educational system is assumptive teaching. This, more than anything else, causes students to fail and fall further behind. Assumptive teaching means instructing the student as if he has actually assimilated all the material presented to him in preceding years. The assumptive teacher does not take the time to give students diagnostic tests and seems to ignore the obvious signs that a student is lost in the class. These symptoms may vary from disruptive behavior, to skipping class altogether, to falling asleep in the back of the room.

The snowball effect of assumptive teaching begins as early as first grade. A few first-grade teachers assume all the students are ready to learn to read. Even if they don't make this assumption, most elementary school teachers have too many children in their rooms to be able to deal individually with each. The slow learner or the child who needs a little more preparation before being given a book, may be put aside in favor of the student who is average or above average. Teachers don't do this intentionally, of course, but they are only human. Their days are only so long. They have too few aides. So the slower learner receives sporadic attention throughout the year. He makes slow progress, and he never graduates from the low to the middle reading group. What happens at the end of the year? This child is promoted along with the majority of the class. He is not retarded and certainly has the very basic skills. With a little extra work at the beginning of second grade, he should be able to catch up or at least become low average.

In second grade, assumptive teaching may again take place. The second-grade teacher also has too many students and would rather put emphasis on the students who are reading above grade level than dwell on the 25 percent who are below grade level. So the slower student again receives only occasional attention and is left to plod along as best he can. He picks up some more skills, but he falls further behind the majority of his classmates. He is promoted into third grade largely for reasons of social promotion. (Fortunately, the pressure imposed by competency testing has begun to have an impact on elementary schools, and we are beginning to see a reversal of this irresponsible social promotion. In many schools, however, social promotion still continues throughout the elementary school years.)

Inadequate preparation is not as noticeable in grades 1 through 6 as it becomes once the pupil enters seventh grade, the traditional beginning of junior high school. In the seventh and eighth grades, the student is expected to take on more responsibility. He is considered a young adult. This means more homework, which means more reading. He has heavier loads in school and more classes to keep straight. Most junior high school students must also learn to deal with a variety of teachers.

Instead of having to "psyche out" only one teacher, the low-achieving student must understand the whims of three or four teachers who all are different and who all expect different things. This is a lot to expect from the average student, but for the slow learner, who is ill prepared in the first place, it is a monumental task. He may be able to learn about his teachers, but he is unable to cope with the added homework and reading assignments. If he couldn't read the simple books in fifth and sixth grades, the science and literature texts in junior high will seem as if they're written in a foreign language.

Many junior and senior high school teachers again assume students come to them with the skills needed to complete more advanced work. They may come to realize that some of their students are painfully behind in skills, but they don't have the time or the preparation to provide adequate help. Also, the student is so far behind in his skills that the teacher does not even have materials to cover such basic areas.

Curricular Material

By the time a student reaches junior or senior high school, a new problem arises—curricular material. There is plenty of material, but most of it is not on the interest level of the low-achieving ninth grader. Teachers are forced to make their own materials or to search madly through catalogs for high-interest, low-vocabulary books. (In all fairness though, we must say that more and more of this kind of material is being published.)

Administrators

Administrators include superintendents, assistant superintendents, business managers, principals, and assistant principals. What do they have to do with the problems of the low achiever? Certainly, family and teachers seem to have the most influence on the slower student, but administrators also play a role because they are the men and women who develop and maintain school policy. If that policy is geared toward the college-bound student, then the remaining student population may not receive priorities.

An administrator may have begun his job with the best of intentions. He may have had high, idealistic goals for the school system. He may have started his professional educational career as a teacher. This probably only lasted a few years, during which time his sights were set on higher goals. While teaching, he was taking courses toward a master's degree. He then got a job as an assistant principal while working on his doctorate. Within ten or fifteen years, this former teacher became superintendent and may have lost touch with the average teacher in the classroom. He spent so much time getting degrees and developing theories of educational philosophy that he forgot the needs of teachers and students. Obviously, this doesn't apply to all administrators, but far too many fall into this category. Certainly ambition is a commendable quality, but it is very difficult to advance one's career and still remain sensitive to the problems of the lower echelon.

The administrator soon realizes that he has to compromise many of his idealistic plans in order to make a few changes. There are too many people to please—the teachers, the public, the school board, and in some communities the students. Ideally, all of these people are working for the betterment of the school system and higher quality education, but often they don't seem to be working together. The person in charge soon finds that he is not totally "in charge." He must not "rock the boat" with too many radical ideas. Creativity is not encouraged; in fact, it may be suspect. The administrator, like the politician, is forced into a position of neutrality.

Faculty members who are most successful at influencing administrators are the forceful teachers and department heads. As in many areas of life, "the squeaky wheel gets the grease!" The department heads or teachers who make the most noise about instituting new programs may be discouraged at first, but persistence pays off, and the programs they fight for inevitably are developed.

Also, new programs for non-college-bound students are not as popular as the upper-level science and math courses. For some reason, it is much easier to support programs for the brighter students. When a rare program is developed for the low-achieving students, the students and parents don't flock to praise the teachers. On the contrary, the public doesn't seem to care.

There is another stumbling block to developing programs to help the poor reader in secondary schools besides the lack of forceful teachers and the unpopularity of remedial programs. This is money. All programs cost money, and with today's economy, not many school systems have the extra money for the development of a special curriculum. Where do administrators look for money? To the federal government. Ah, but there are two catches here! First, current fiscal policies indicate that the well of public funding is drying up. Education appears to be the victim of not only the old "guns versus butter" argument but also the federal government's decision to place more responsibility for education on local governments. Should any money for federal programs be available, however, you will immediately find yourself faced with the second obstacle, red tape. In addition to knowing how to deal with red tape, the persons writing the proposal must be familiar with the special jargon in which all requests are made. If a school system does not have teachers willing to put up with the jargon, red tape, and forms in order to apply for federal money, then the programs never get off the ground.

Here again, the administration can be a help or a hindrance. Teachers need to know when the *Federal Registry*[1] announces prospective grants, so applications can be prepared. Administrators need to be aware of the various avenues open to obtain money for innovative programs. Inexperienced teachers may need help with the special language of grant applications.

Although the administrators of a school system do not have direct contact with the students, the decisions made at the higher levels often make the big difference. If the administration is not sympathetic to the needs of slow learners, they will probably be ignored in favor of more popular curriculum projects involving the average and above-average students.

SELF-CONCEPT

In addition to Brenda's problems with home environment and school environment, her self-concept was poor. Her attitude and constant failure "turned off" most people working in the school system. She was not eager for knowledge and was not trying to earn "brownie points." A teacher or other adult had to attempt over and over again to win her confidence and trust. Too often, the adult was rejected several times and stopped trying. Some teachers expect slow learners to show signs of gratitude in return for a few crumbs of attention.

The very people who were in a position to help Brenda may not have been inclined to do so. The teacher did not take time to help improve skills. The administrator did not give good recommendations for a job. The adult in the community pressed charges instead of taking the time to understand and try to help out.

Brenda's peers also did nothing to enhance her self-concept. The "smart" kids wanted nothing to do with the "dummies." Socially, Brenda was restricted to other potential dropouts. She learned how to forge absence notes, smoke pot and cigarettes in the girls' room without getting caught, and skip school frequently. Her associates also had low self-concepts and expected to fail at most everything adults hold dear. They did not help each other; rather, they contributed to each other's downfall.

[1]The *Federal Registry* is a list of projects that the federal government states it is willing to fund if selected through competitive bidding. The *Registry* is updated several times a month and is available to teachers through their central office or in public libraries.

The Reading Process 2

Definitions of reading vary according to author and are too numerous to mention in a text designed to help the content area teacher function in the classroom. Highly technical theories aren't much help to a teacher faced with twenty-eight fidgety teen-agers, fourteen of whom read more than two years below grade level. For our purposes then, let us define reading as *that process by which a person receives and interprets a message from a printed page.* This definition may be too general for the reading specialist, but it provides a flexible framework within which the classroom teacher may operate.

Reading is more than decoding letters into words. It is more than linking words into sentences. It is more than structuring sentences into paragraphs, paragraphs into chapters, or chapters into books. It is so much more, in fact, that when one considers the complexity of the reading process, it is baffling that any of us can read at all!

INTELLIGENCE

When an author writes a book, his first assumption is that the reader will have the intelligence to infer his message from the text. Of all the components of the reading process, however, intelligence may be the least important. While intelligence is very significant in determining a reader's ability to draw abstract principles from a written page, it is not essential to the decoding process. It is interesting to note here that some special education students who have been identified as retarded on an individually administered Wechsler Intelligence Scale for Children[1] (WISC) can read at a functional (fifth-grade) level, while other students

---

[1]New York: Psychological Corporation, 1949.

identified by the same test as not being retarded may be reading at far less than fifth-grade level.

When you suspect that a student may be having difficulty with your assignments, we suggest that you begin your inquiries by checking with the guidance office for an overview of his past performance and test scores. It is extremely important, however, that you treat his I.Q. scores with caution. Many school districts administer the Lorge-Thorndike Intelligence Tests[2] or the California Test of Mental Maturity[3] (CTMM) to measure students' intelligence. *Both tests are administered in a group situation and require that a student be able to read in order to perform.* If your student has a reading problem, his score on such a test will not be a reflection of his intelligence so much as of his reading ability. If, however, you find an I.Q. score as measured by the WISC or the Stanford-Binet Intelligence Scale,[4] you can consider it a more reliable reflection of his intelligence. Both of these tests are individually administered by trained personnel and do not require the student to read, thus removing his reading ability as a factor in the measuring of his intelligence. Do keep in mind, however, that because they are administered individually, usually by a school psychologist, they are expensive, and it is not practical for a school district to administer them to every pupil. They are usually reserved for the testing of students for possible placement in special education classes. Should you find that a student has taken a WISC, a WAIS (Wechsler Adult Intelligence Scale[5]—a test administered to adults over the age of fifteen) or a Stanford-Binet, it will be helpful to you to note his performance on the subtests related to visual and auditory memory. They may provide you with some clues related directly to his ability to read.

Let us suppose that your pursuit of background information on a student only provides you with an intelligence score from a group-administered test. If you have reason to be seriously concerned about his intelligence and have no school psychologist available to you, we suggest that you obtain The Slosson Intelligence Test.[6] The Slosson is administered individually and may be given by a classroom teacher who has not had specialized training in test administration. The directions are clear, and the results correlate highly with those of the Stanford-Binet.

It is especially important to keep in mind that intelligence scores are best used as a guide to the type of instruction to offer your student, not as a reason for having him removed from your classes. Intelligence scores can indicate the amount of reinforcement and repetition of class-

---

[2]Boston: Houghton Mifflin, 1962.
[3]New York: CTB/McGraw-Hill, 1963.
[4]Boston: Houghton Mifflin, 1960.
[5]New York: Psychological Corporation, 1955.
[6]Available from Slosson Educational Publishers, 140 Pine Street, East Aurora, N.Y. 14052.

room material that may be necessary. They are not an excuse for not working with a student.

VISION

After intelligence, the author next assumes that his reader has adequate vision. Vision, however, is more complicated than just the ability to see the printed page. We will consider three components of vision: visual acuity, visual perception, and visual memory.

Visual Acuity

Visual acuity refers to the eye's capability of sighting an object at both near point and far point. Normal classroom activities provide you with an opportunity to observe students who may be squinting, rubbing their eyes, or suffering from frequent headaches or watery eyes. If you suspect a visual acuity problem, check with your school nurse. School districts customarily use the Snellen Chart[7] to measure visual acuity. Since this test measures acuity at a distance of twenty feet, it is not helpful for identifying those students who are farsighted. It may be necessary for you to request that the nurse also administer the A.M.A. Rating Card[8] to obtain a more complete assessment of a student's visual acuity at the customary reading distance of sixteen to twenty inches.

Visual Perception

If acuity refers to the student's ability to "sight" or take a visual "photograph" of an object, what is visual perception? Visual perception, sometimes called visual discrimination, refers to the mental translation or interpretation of the object sighted. Your student may sight the shape of the letter *d*, but his brain interprets this shape as a *b*. Students who read *was* for *saw* or *no* for *on* show signs of whole-word reversal difficulty. Some students may reverse only letters appearing in the medial position: *paly* for *play, dorp* for *drop*. Sometimes it is a problem of phrase reversal: *once there was* for *there once was*.

Don't assume, however, that all students who have difficulty reading completely through a word have reversal difficulties. A student who reads *democracy* for *democratic* and *experience* for *experiment* may be showing signs of lazy decoding techniques rather than a perceptual problem.

Visual training as a possible solution for a child suffering from a

[7]Southbridge, Mass.: American Optical Company.
[8]Chicago: American Medical Association.

perceptual handicap is currently a controversial issue. Professionals in the fields of medicine, optometry, and learning disabilities have published much material in support of, and in opposition to, the use of developmental lenses, binocular fusion exercises, and perceptual motor training. We do not wish to add fuel to this heated argument, but our experience indicates that there is no transfer of skills from visual training to the actual process of reading. While young children may profit from some outside support in hastening the maturation of the focusing process, we find no evidence that this training is beneficial to students of junior and senior high school age. At this age level, it becomes more important to use the printed page rather than exercises having nothing to do with reading.

Visual Memory

The term visual memory, as used here, refers more to the student's preferred method of learning than his ability to see. Does he retain items taught visually as well as, or better than, those taught orally? Can he look at spelling words and remember them? Or does he have to look at them, say them out loud, and write them in order to retain them? Can he close his eyes and recall the items of clothing worn by other students in the room? If your student has a poor visual memory and was taught to read primarily by the look-say method, you have a clue as to why he may now be a poor reader. In the look-say method, the teacher introduces new words to the students by holding up cards with new words printed on them. The teacher pronounces the word and asks the class to repeat it. This is reinforced through a variety of techniques, including extensive use in context, but essentially, the retention of the new word depends on a student's ability to grasp the word visually and retain that image as the major clue to the word in the future.

Visual memory, however, is trainable, and while it may never be your student's preferred modality for learning, there are games and devices you can use to improve this important aspect of reading (see chapter 4).

Before leaving the area of vision and its role in the reading process, we should point out that high school students may be reluctant to wear glasses that have been prescribed. The older the student, the more important vanity becomes! Take note of empty glass cases used as bookmarks and pockets bulging with unworn glasses.

HEARING

Normal hearing is important for students learning to read in the typical elementary school classroom. Like visual skills, auditory skills have three components: auditory acuity, auditory perception (or discrimination), and auditory memory.

Auditory Acuity

Auditory acuity refers to the ear's capability for hearing high- and low-frequency sounds. With the noise of industrial equipment and the volume at which rock music is frequently played, it is not uncommon to discover adolescents with newly-emerging hearing problems. Unusual posture, a turning of the head, insistence that you face him when speaking, some difficulties with speech, or frequent requests that you repeat something may be clues that a student has a hearing problem. (One note of caution—the quiet child who never asks to have anything repeated may have a possible hearing loss. Over the years, students develop their own ways of compensating for hearing problems and may prefer not to draw attention to themselves by asking questions.)

Acuity is usually tested by the school nurse with an audiometer. Sounds are produced at varying frequencies through earphones worn by the student who raises his hand to indicate that he has heard a sound. A student whose auditory acuity is at 25 decibels or below is considered to be within the normal range. A referral to a hearing specialist should be made for auditory acuity above 30 decibels. From the classroom teacher's point of view, the most important item to note is whether the difficulty is in the high-frequency area or low-frequency area. If there is high-frequency loss, it may explain why the student has problems with consonant sounds. A loss in the low-frequency area provides a clue to difficulty with vowel sounds.

Auditory Perception

Auditory perception, or discrimination, refers to the brain's interpretation of what the ear receives. If, for example, your student appears puzzled when you say *they*, it may be because he has understood you to say *Faye*. If you have a reading specialist available to you, ask to have your student tested on the *distorted* version of the Wepman Audial Discrimination Test.[9]

If this is not possible, you can improvise a test yourself. Begin by compiling a list of pairs of words or pseudowords with the same or different *final* sounds (*they:say, rag:rat, light:light, high:thigh*). Next, add to your list pairs of words that have the same or different *initial* sounds (*slap:clap, fairy:very, berry:berry*). In constructing this test, keep in mind that the goal is to end up with ten pairs that are exactly alike (*bug:bug, said:said, pay:pay*) and thirty pairs that are different

[9]Available from Language Research Associates, 175 East Delaware Place, Chicago, Ill. 60611.

(*they:vey, try:cry, bog:box*). When selecting words for the pairs that are different, try to have fifteen of them differ in *initial* sound (*flug:clog, fairy:scarcy, they:suy*) and fifteen of them differ in *final* sound (*bug:but, rag:rat, pot:pop*). Randomly disperse the ten pairs that are alike throughout the thirty pairs that are different. Read each pair of words to the student and ask him to tell you if they are the same or different. As you present the pairs to the student, it is important that you keep your voice in a montone, so that voice inflection does not reveal the answer. Record the student's answer next to each pair. A student who is unable to tell you that *say:say* are alike has more of a problem than a student who tells you that *berry:very* are alike. In fact, if the student misses any of the pairs that are alike, the test is considered invalid and unreliable. If he scores less than 90 percent on the remaining thirty pairs, you should consider that this student has immature auditory discrimination.

Auditory Memory

Auditory memory presents an entirely different problem. A student who cannot follow directions given to him orally or who cannot recall a lesson taught orally the previous day is not necessarily demonstrating an unwillingness to try. Rather, he may simply have difficulty recalling information administered orally. Auditory memory, like visual memory, is trainable, and we shall consider diagnostic-prescriptive techniques in chapter 3.

In concluding this section on the auditory aspects of the reading process, we want to point out that the technical point of view of the audiologist and the reading specialist may cause us to overlook one very simple point. If your student suffered from tonsil and adenoid or allergy problems at the time he was being taught to read with phonics, he may have missed much basic reading instruction, simply because these common childhood ailments can cause temporary hearing problems. In addition, his frequent illnesses may have caused him to miss much essential instruction. While his hearing as an adolescent may test in the normal range, he may have had difficulty hearing at a very important phase of his reading development.

MOTOR, TACTILE, AND KINESTHETIC SKILLS

One parent, irritated with her child's elementary school report card, complained, "Of all the ridiculous things! 'Skipping—Unsatisfactory.' Who cares whether or not a child can skip? What does that have to do with intellectual development?" Actually, skipping is an important indicator of another skill area the author assumes his reader has mastered. A young infant gropes with two hands for the mobile over the crib. This

Figure 1. Handwriting of Student Unable to Use Dominant Hand

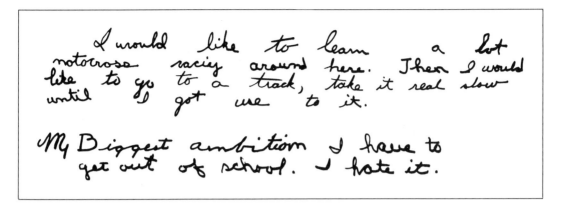

bilateral development is the first step of a very complicated neurological process of acquiring motor skills. The next phase involves the development of *alternating laterality*, including the ability to grasp things with one hand or the other. The final stage is called *integrating laterality* and can be measured by a child's ability to skip. All three stages must be acquired in sequence in order to insure smooth motor skill development. A high school student who has difficulty in motor skills will often have trouble holding his pen properly, walking down an aisle without knocking over books, shifting gears in drivers' education, and performing elementary exercises in gym class. This classroom "klutz" is often the victim of the sarcastic remark, "Coordinated much?" No one wants him on the team in gym class, and a boy with this problem is the least likely candidate to carry a girl's books home because he can barely carry his own!

Often the most obvious sign of motor difficulties is handwriting. Harold is a student born with multiple birth defects. One of these defects was the absence of a right hand. He has had fourteen plastic surgical procedures to create a right hand that is satisfactory for the performing of large motor skill tasks. He is not, however, able to write, button, zip, or cut with his right hand. He is right-footed, and he prefers to use his right eye. The sample of his handwriting in figure 1 is evidence of his difficulty after thirteen years of writing with his left hand. The angle of the letters is not consistent, and the awkwardness of his stroke is seen in the wavering lines.

Many studies have been done on left-handedness, but few support the theory that left-handed people are poorer readers.[10] Several studies do indicate that while left-handed students may have more difficulty

---

[10]See C. C. Bennett, *An Inquiry into the Genesis of Poor Reading* (New York: Bureau of Publications, Teachers College, Columbia University, 1938), and Karen J. Tinker, "The Role of Laterality in Reading Disability," *Reading and Inquiry*, Conference Proceedings of International Reading Association 10 (1965): 300–3.

initially in acquiring a skill, eventual mastery is equal for both "lefties" and "righties." Problems do arise, however, when a child is prevented from using a dominant side. Harold is an example of this. Apparently born with a neurological preference for his right side, he was forced by a physical handicap to use his left hand for fine motor work. In spite of the fact that he has had years of experience at this, writing with his left hand is still awkward and tension producing.

Fred has a different problem. He suffered minimal brain damage as the result of a particularly violent epileptic seizure. All of his motor skills, including handwriting, have been impaired as a result. Unlike Harold, Fred is a true "leftie," preferring to use left eye, hand, and foot. Lacking a sense of spacing, Fred writes each word as an extension of the previous word (see figure 2). Note also that he employs little distinction between upper- and lowercase letters. One of our suggestions to Fred was that he try writing on graph paper, leaving one empty space after each word or punctuation mark. As handwriting and spacing improve, such a student is gradually weaned from graph paper to standard ruled paper.

Another neurological problem (not necessarily motor in origin but appropriate to this section since it is manifested in handwriting) is that of *perseveration*. Perseveration is seen in both reading and writing when a student repeats indefinitely an idea, word, or concept. He may read, "The quick brown fox jumped over the, jumped over the, jumped over the, ..." His reading sounds like a "broken record." Perseveration, however, is more frequently seen in handwriting. A student writes a phrase over and over, unaware that he is doing so. (See the example in figure 3.)

Be sure that you can distinguish between the student actually suf-

Figure 2. Handwriting of Student with Impaired Motor Skills

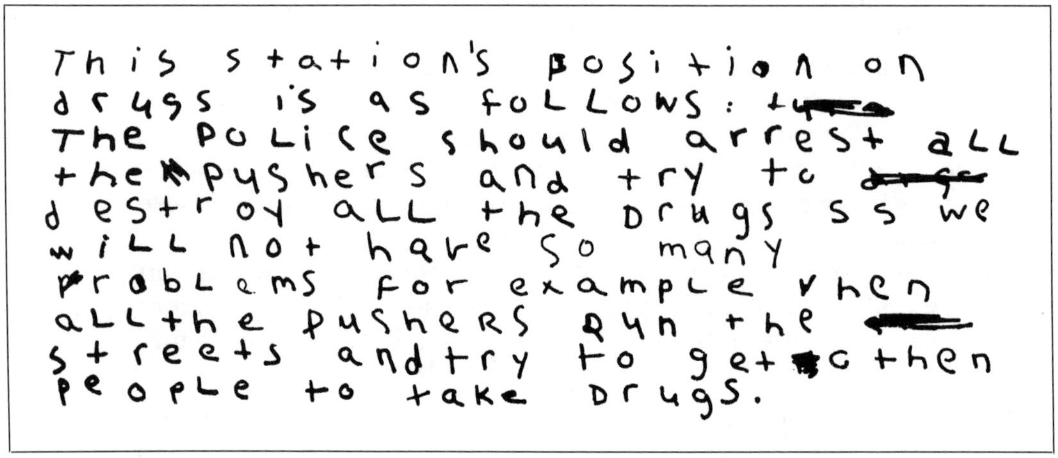

Figure 3. Handwriting of Student with Perseveration

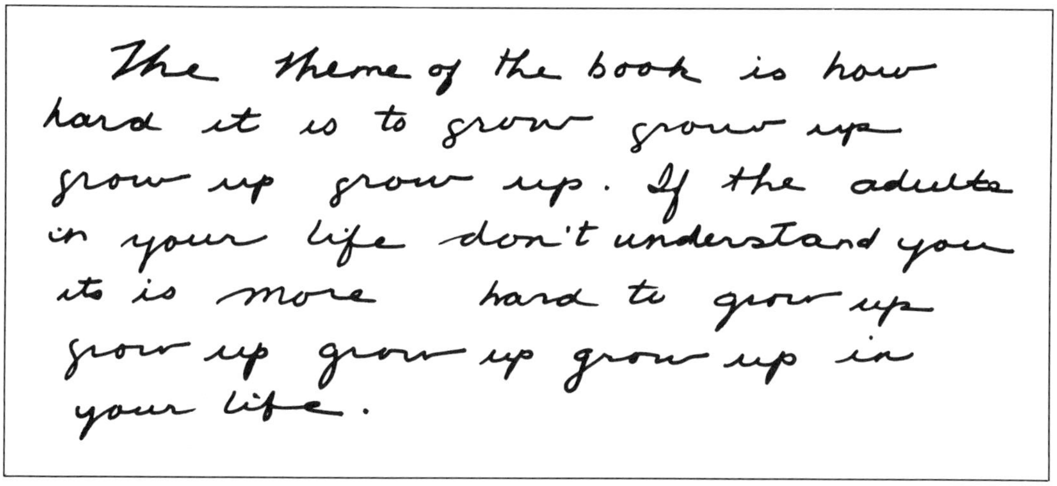

fering from perseveration and the student who has developed a gimmick for taking up space in compositions.

A student with motor problems may have difficulty moving from left to right across a printed page, dropping one line of print instead of two, working with test tubes in science class, following graph lines, and performing daily tasks most of us take for granted.

WORD ATTACK SKILLS

Probably the most elementary assumption which our author makes is that his reader is comfortable with words. For those of us who have worked with slow learners, this is the classic example of assumptive teaching! When an author sees his words in print, he assumes that even if a person has difficulty in pronouncing some of those words, he can eventually decode them and come to understand their meaning. If you were to come across the word *sesquipedalian* in a text and could not use a dictionary or ask a friend, you would automatically fall back on tried-and-true elementary school skills. First, divide the word into syllables (ses-qui-pe-da-li-an) . . . a-ah! You remembered them! Next, look for a familiar root (*ped*—yes, that has something to do with *foot*). Now, look at the prefixes and suffixes (*sesqui* and *ian,* which means one who does something). Oops! Don't you remember your Latin? (Well, *sesquicentennial* means one and one-half centuries. Maybe *sesquipedalian* means something that is one and one-half feet long.) Now use the word in context. (When you get through studying the Miller Analogies book, you should be able to cope with *sesquipedalian* words.) Foot-and-a-half-long words are multisyllabic words! Such a structural analysis required you to have knowledge of and skill in using profixes, suffixes, roots, syllabication, and context. Pity the poor reader who comes across *ferroequestrologist* without a bright friend or a good dictionary!

VOCABULARY

It is easy to see how the author can assume that his reader has the ability to decode the words on a printed page. But the author may not realize what a monumental task it is for the poor reader to develop an extensive vocabulary. Give him the word *apathy*, and you have the classic case of irony. This student, more than any other, has experienced apathy, but he has had no experience with this particular word. "Why bother to look it up? If I just skip over it, she won't know because I don't read too good anyway." The vocabulary of the adolescent is dependent on his family, friends, teachers, reading, and experiences. If swearing is used frequently in the home, or in peer groups in which gutter slang is the vernacular, how can we expect sesquipedalian words? These students read little, have limited experiential opportunities, and are taught by teachers who mistakenly "talk down" to them. Result: limited vocabulary.

TEACHING

Our author also assumes that his readers have had good teaching in school. Good teaching would certainly have *guaranteed* proficiency in word attack skills and vocabulary. The adage "There's a rotten apple in the barrel" is unfortunately far too common in teaching. Like any other profession, teaching has its good, mediocre, and poor members. Poor training, weak or no supervision, laziness, and lack of imagination and patience all can combine to produce certified teachers who have no business in the classroom. We recognize, of course, that some teaching situations are so bad that even the most talented teacher could not reach the Brendas, Kennys, and Gerrys of this world. Nevertheless, the poor student, falling further and further behind in skills, requiring more individual attention and receiving less, and regarding himself constantly as a failure, is not going to be motivated to struggle through our author's work.

AFFECTIVE CONCERNS

Motivation brings us to perhaps the most important part of the reading process. By the time our students have experienced years of failure and have reached a wide disparity in skill achievement from that of their peers, the single most important factor contributing to that escalating failure lies in the area of affective concerns. Affective concerns can be broken down into three areas: motivation, emotional stability, and self-concept.

Motivation

Without models of reading in the home, young people are not motivated to pick up a book. We are now working with children of the television generation, the "boob-tube illiterates." They see reading as much too taxing compared to the passivity of being entertained by the television. Our kids have become good listeners and have learned how to use this skill quite effectively to avoid reading tasks. What motivation is there to read *Swiss Family Robinson* when they can turn on channel 9? Television has done a good job in providing wider exposure to experiential background, but we can't say that it has motivated young people to pick up a book. With the constant cry that "nothing we do in school is relevant," there is little that turns students on to reading.

Emotional Stability

Current formulas used to establish guidelines for the writing of federal projects on learning disabilities choose to avoid the terminology that might include students with emotional problems. Our experience shows, however, that students who have reached high school and are functioning with learning disabilities have a larger problem with the emotional difficulties they have acquired than with the original learning problems. It is unreasonable to expect that a student who has been told for eleven years that he is "dumb" can possibly have strong emotional health. Anyone who has worked with the adolescent slow learner is well aware of the variety of compensating devices these students have acquired over the years. We have met the master con-artists. We have met the "super attention-getters." We have met the best "task-avoiders" in the business. "This is stupid." "Who wants to know that anyway?" "I don't feel like doing this anymore." "I have a headache." All of these are the cop-out pleas of the students who are unable to handle their failures.

Self-concept

Of the three areas of affective concerns, self-concept has the most impact. The image-makers of Madison Avenue could have a full-time job trying to sell these slow learners to themselves! The years of failure, coupled with the awkwardness of adolescence, tend to deliver to the high school a batch of insecure, defeated, frustrated poor readers. The years of remediation have not paid off—one more session with phonics, and these kids might quit school. The high instance of motor problems makes physical education requirements a nightmare. They are not good at sports. They are not good at school work. They are not asked to join the clubs, because they are not "in." They are not good at "playing school." They just don't belong! More significant than how others see them is how they see themselves. They see themselves as losers, and so does society. Like most of us, these students tend to meet the expectations of society. So they continue to be losers.

All of these aspects of the reading process are then put through a filter of experience. The cultural background and experiential opportunities discussed in chapter 1 are an essential part of reading readiness and progress. Without wide frames of reference against which to measure new knowledge, there can be little application of a written message. Our author may be amazed at the narrow scope of the poor reader's experience. Literary terms such as *herculean task* are incomprehensible to a reader who has never heard of Hercules. The author would be chagrined to discover that phrases he takes for granted have no meaning for his reader.

In conclusion, the reading process is a highly complicated process requiring the smooth functioning of several skill areas. An electric sign looks great at night with all the bulbs functioning. But let one bulb burn out, and the message of the sign may be distorted. So it is with the reading skills of slow learners. With the complexity of the reading process in mind, we can repeat that it is truly a miracle that any of us read as well as we do.

DYSLEXIA

In any discussion on the reading process and specific strengths and weaknesses, we would be remiss if we did not refer to dyslexia. Like many concepts in the field of reading education, however, dyslexia is very controversial and is sometimes used indiscriminately to categorize all reading difficulties. Articles have appeared describing famous world leaders as dyslexic, and it is on their successes as adults that anxious parents have hung their hopes for their own slow learners.

Dyslexia is defined as an *inability* to obtain a message from the written word. When you consider the complexity of the reading process, it is easy to see how anyone struggling with the frustration of a learning problem could feel better about himself by identifying himself as a dyslexic. Some people may even feel that the term relieves them of the responsibility of struggle. "I can't read. I have dyslexia." Certainly individuals who are truly dyslexic will attest to the pain of being "the class dummy." But no label can make the road to becoming a good reader less painful.

In our opinion, true dyslexics are rare, and the term is greatly overused. This is why we are reluctant to spend too much time in a discussion. If you think your student is a dyslexic, by all means refer him to your school's learning disabilities team for an in-depth diagnosis, but do not simply accept a diagnosis of dyslexia that has been suggested in reports passed down through the years without updating reevaluations. A diagnosis of dyslexia relieves parent, school, and student of the responsibility for patient repetition, hard work, and slow reward. Our job is to encourage hope and the possibility of success, not to provide an excuse.

3 Diagnosis for Classroom Teachers

For the content teacher, the brief introduction to the reading process in chapter 2 provides necessary, though perhaps not very exciting, background for the rest of this book. This short description of the reading process will help you diagnose and prescribe, and develop the materials you will need to survive! This chapter and the next two are devoted to survival skills. Before you can acquire the confidence, experience, and ability to make worthwhile changes, you have to be able to survive. These three chapters will present techniques you can use to operate effectively in the classroom when you are confronted with students with wide disparity in reading levels, inadequate materials, administrative concern that you "keep them quiet," and guidance office platitudes such as "I didn't know where else to put them."

GROUP AND INDIVIDUAL SCREENING DEVICES

Remember the adage "Take them from where you find them to where they ought to be"? You may never have students functioning at the where-they-ought-to-be end of the spectrum, but certainly you can't make much progress unless you know where they are when you start. If you don't have a high school reading teacher to provide you with information on your students' reading strengths and weaknesses, you will need an efficient method of assessing the ability range of your class. Unfortunately, there is no one perfect *secondary* reading test that we can recommend.

For want of a perfect test, we recommend the Gates-MacGinitie Reading Test[1] for a one-period classroom assessment. This test yields

[1]New York: Teachers College Press, 1969 (now available exclusively from Riverside Publishing Co.).

scores from three subtests: speed and accuracy (three minutes); vocabulary (fifteen minutes); and reading comprehension (twenty-five minutes). All raw scores are easily converted to grade levels ranging from fourth grade to college. This test provides fifty multiple choice questions, and is easily hand scored with a scoring template.

We recommend that you eliminate the speed and accuracy subtest. The results are not particularly helpful in choosing materials, and don't really provide you with any significant diagnostic information. You'll probably want to begin with the reading comprehension subtest. This subtest actually measures a student's ability to use vocabulary in context, rather than his ability to answer questions about the passage he has read. The student is provided with three- to four-sentence paragraphs containing two or three blanks. He has to choose one of four alternatives to complete the sentence so that it makes sense. Some interpretation of reading passages is needed, but a student's score is heavily dependent on his vocabulary as well. The vocabulary subtest gives the teacher an understanding of the student's rote knowledge of vocabulary. When the teacher compares the vocabulary and reading comprehension subtests, the discrepancy between the student's actual knowledge of the meanings of vocabulary words and his ability to use context to guess meanings becomes clear. As with all tests to which graded reading levels are assigned, remember that scores on either end of the spectrum are less valid than those in the center. In addition, it is important to remember that a student's score may vary on any given day because of extenuating circumstances: fatigue, state of health, emotional problems, or attitude toward testing. As always, graded reading scores should be interpreted with some degree of flexibility. Be careful to use them only as an indicator and *not* as an absolute.

You may wish to consider an individual screening device for students who score in the lowest ranges—fifth grade level or below. If you have only two or three students who fall into this category, we recommend the Spache Diagnostic Reading Scales.[2] This test has a variety of subtests including word recognition, silent reading, oral reading, listening comprehension, and several phonics subtests. Don't try to administer this test to everyone, because it takes roughly two classroom periods per student. It does, however, provide very useful diagnostic information about your most troubled readers and is well worth the time in severe cases. If you have had no experience in administering this test, however, plan to spend considerable time studying the manual prior to testing, because the results are interpreted in a manner peculiar to this test.

If you have classes of average and above-average students, and you would like to obtain a reading level for them, you may wish to use the

[2]Monterey, Calif.: CTB/McGraw-Hill, 1963.

Nelson-Denny Reading Test.[3] This test provides three scores: vocabulary, speed, and comprehension. The comprehension passages tend to bo highly literary and rather remote from students' interests. Because the content of the passages is more difficult than that of the Gates-MacGinitie, we hesitate to recommend the Nelson-Denny except for use with above-average students. The lowest grade level obtained on this test is seventh grade.

A compromise between the Nelson-Denny and the Gates-Mac-Ginitie may be the California Achievement Tests.[4] This achievement battery offers subtest scores in vocabulary, reading comprehension, math problem solving, computation, spelling, reference skills, and English language usage. The reading comprehension subtest consists of passages followed by comprehension questions. While the subject matter of these passages is less literary than that of the Nelson-Denny, the content still is not of high interest to students. As a true test of reading comprehension, however, this test still is closer to the actual classroom requirement of teachers, while the Gates-MacGinitie is closer to the "degrees of reading power" format of state competency tests. The "degrees of reading power" format consists of a series of nonfiction prose passages, presented in order of difficulty, starting with an easy text and increasing to the most difficult. Seven words are deleted from each passage. The student must choose the most appropriate word from the five options provided for each deletion.

To investigate the more subtle types of comprehension problems plaguing your average and above-average readers, you might wish to consider administering the Sequential Tests of Educational Progress (STEP).[5] This series includes tests for measuring comprehension in reading, writing, listening, social studies, and mathematics. The scoring instructions identify the type of skill each question is intended to measure, so that you may obtain a composite of the skill strengths and weaknesses of your students. Unfortunately, these tests are designed for students reading at a specific grade level. For example, if you have a tenth-grade class in social studies, it is presumed that you would give the social studies test for grade 10. If the results of the Gates-MacGinitie show that you have a wide disparity of reading levels in your class, the STEP is probably not appropriate for your lowest level groups. For average and above-average readers, though, this test remains a helpful device for identifying specific comprehension difficulties.

In the past, if the class scores on the Gates-MacGinitie indicated more basic skill testing was necessary, we administered a Spache to each student. We were not satisfied with the time-consuming task of

---

[3]Boston: Houghton Mifflin, 1960.
[4]New York: McGraw-Hill, 1970.
[5]Princeton: Cooperative Test Division, 1956, rev. ed. 1963.

group testing with the Gates-MacGinitie followed by individual testing with the Spache, so we developed our own group screening device for class administration. Our Individual Secondary Skills Inventory (ISSI) is reprinted as Appendix A. This diagnostic screening device is designed to be used in place of the individually administered Spache. The only part of the test that must be administered individually is Test 1. The remaining subtests may be completed by the class as a whole in one class period.

The ISSI subtests cover long and short vowels, initial blends and final consonants, syllabication, simple prefixes, basic spelling, punctuation (capitalization, commas, periods, and quotation marks), and simple paragraph writing. This test is easy to administer and score. You can develop a class composite from the resulting information that can help you formulate prescriptive goals for your students.

Since the Individual Secondary Skills Inventory yields diagnostic information on basic skills deficiencies, it is best used with a lower-track group. The vocabulary and comprehension scores obtained from the Gates-MacGinitie are sufficient for your college-bound classes.

For a heterogeneous class of average to above-average ability, you might wish to use an informal reading inventory. Appendix B presents an informal reading inventory for students in grades 7 through 12. These better students have mastered the basic skills, and you may wish to measure a student's competence at a particular task without reference to other students. An informal reading inventory consists of passages at varying levels of difficulty followed by questions that require the student to make inferences, draw conclusions, determine causes and effects, contrast and compare, and find main ideas. The student reads at levels of increasing difficulty until he is no longer successful. Though informal inventories are time consuming, they do allow you to see how the pupil functions in a practical situation. This test is adaptable to any content area subject where the teacher wishes to measure students' application of reading skills to specific areas such as social studies, math, or science.

For ideas on how to develop your own informal reading inventory, we suggest that you refer to *Informal Reading Inventories*[6] by Margorie Seddon Johnson and Roy A. Kress. You will have to decide for yourself if an inventory will provide you with enough worthwhile inormation to justify the time involved in writing and administering it. We feel that in the hands of a conscientious teacher who is willing to follow up on the information obtained, an inventory does serve a useful purpose.

Acting on the information obtained from testing can be a problem, particularly for the inexperienced teacher. First things first. Now you know the reading levels of your students. Next, check the reading levels

---

[6]Newark, Del.: International Reading Association, 1965.

of the books you have been asked to use. (You can use the Fry Graph—see chapter 4 and figure 9—to determine reading levels of books.) If the texts are inappropriate, discreetly shelve them. Imagine the frustration of a tenth grader reading at the third-grade level and using a twelfth-grade-level text!

LATERALITY TESTING

In addition, you may wish to do some laterality testing to determine the right or left preferences of your students. We suggest that you use at least two informal tests each for hand, eye, and foot. For testing the preferred hand use, start by having the student sign his name. You will note immediately whether he prefers to write with his right or left hand. Next, have the student cross his arms at the wrist. You cross your hands also and squeeze his hands. You are looking for the stronger grip to determine hand preference. Since the student does not know what you are looking for, he concentrates on the grip. The hand which has the stronger squeeze is the preferred hand.

For the eye, hand the student a small cardboard tube such as the inside of a paper towel roll. Ask him to look through the tube at a mark you have placed on the opposite wall. He will place the tube at his preferred eye. The fact that he is able to see the mark is irrelevant. You are interested in which eye the student chooses to use. A second test for determining eye preference involves having the student look at the same mark through a small hole punched in a piece of paper. Ask the student to move the piece of paper around until he is able to see the mark on the opposite wall through the hole with both eyes open. When he is able to do this, have him hold both his head and the paper still. Cover one eye at a time, asking him if he can still see the mark. The eye he is using when he says he can still see the mark is his preferred eye.

For testing foot preference, wad up a piece of paper and place it between the student's knees. He is to look at you, drop the wad to the floor, and kick it toward you. Since he is not able to look at it while he is kicking it, he will rely on the foot he trusts the most. A second test involves having the student lean on a wall with his arms against the wall as if he were being searched. His feet should be about three and a half feet out from the base of the wall. This way he is slightly off balance. Ask him to step back quickly as if the wall on which he is leaning were about to collapse. He will again rely on his most trusted leg.

The next step is to draw up a class composite of skill strengths and weaknesses (see Appendix A for a sample form). For example, the Individual Secondary Skills Inventory would have told you who needed help in punctuation, syllabication, writing, spelling, and word attack skills. Determine the areas in which many of the students need work, and you have your starting point. If you find that half of your students really need help in paragraph writing, you have a legitimate beginning, a starting point that meets two main requirements of most secondary school teaching: skill development and curricular need.

Part Two
CLASSROOM STRATEGIES

The Heterogeneous Classroom

SKILL DEVELOPMENT AND CURRICULAR NEEDS

Most secondary school content area curricula have two simultaneous goals: to provide each student the opportunity for (1) the development of the basic skills necessary for (2) the mastery of the specific content requirements of the course. In this chapter we will discuss the heterogeneous classroom, in which the students have a wide range of skill abilities and reading levels. The first part of the chapter will emphasize what you can do for the students' skill development, using the results of the diagnostic tests discussed in chapter 3. All of the suggestions dealing with skill development can also be used successfully with homogeneous classes and for individual tutoring.

The second part of this chapter covers curricular needs of the content area course. We explain several methods of organizing and managing the heterogeneous class so that students, regardless of their varying abilities, will all receive adequate content instruction.

SKILL DEVELOPMENT: PRESCRIPTIVE TEACHING

The basis for any prescriptive teaching is diagnosis and matching of materials to the problem. This is easy when a majority of the class has the same problem. The real dilemma arises when you have only one or two students who have a severe learning deficit or handicap in a particular area. This is where the concept of individualizing comes in. While the selection of skills to be taught depends on diagnostic test results, the secret of individualizing is good management materials. Examples of these can be found in Appendix C, and individualization is discussed in detail in chapter 10.

Meanwhile, what can you do with a student who has visual, auditory, or motor problems? You are aware of his problem, but you have a classroom full of students without similar handicaps. There are some teaching strategies you can use to help such an individual without taking away from the teaching time needed for the other members of the class.

Visual Problems

Kathy is a ninth-grade student with visual perception problems. She still displays reversals in her oral reading. When she means to write words like *experiment,* she actually writes *experience.* She randomly interchanges the letters *b* and *d.* Written spelling words "don't look right" to her. Her approach to visual tasks is fragmented. Tracking through words, phrases, and sentences is difficult for her. What can you do to help?

You can use visual perception puzzles to reinforce vocabulary for the entire class. Everyone will enjoy them, and at the same time, you will be helping Kathy with her particular problem. (See figure 4.) In these puzzles, the vocabulary or spelling words are hidden in a maze of extraneous letters. The student has to track through the letters to find the vocabulary or spelling words. You can vary this technique by providing written clues to go along with the puzzle. Figure 39 (page 112) is an example of this type of puzzle.

Note that in these examples students are only asked to track through the letters from left to right and from top to bottom. Students who have grave visual perception problems should not be asked to track

---

Figure 4. Visual Perception Puzzle

Name: _____

The following vocabulary words from the unit on the rise of parliament appear <u>vertically</u> or <u>horizontally</u> in the puzzle below. Find the words and circle them.

rise	monarch	bail	assemble
lord	grant	guarantee	session
oppress	revolt	warrant	parliament
tax	consent	petition	wealth
approve	execute	funds	antagonize
depose	king	divine	war
true	law		

O	P	P	R	E	S	S	A	D	K
P	E	T	I	T	I	O	N	I	I
T	W	A	R	R	A	N	T	V	N
D	E	P	O	S	E	D	A	I	G
E	X	E	C	U	T	E	G	N	R
M	O	N	A	R	C	H	O	E	E
R	W	G	W	G	R	A	N	T	V
A	A	U	E	L	A	W	I	C	O
P	R	A	A	D	B	O	Z	O	L
P	A	R	L	I	A	M	E	N	T
R	F	A	T	S	I	E	L	S	R
O	U	N	H	P	L	N	O	E	I
V	N	T	R	U	E	T	R	N	S
E	D	E	A	T	A	X	D	T	E
L	S	E	S	E	S	S	I	O	N
D	R	A	S	S	E	M	B	L	E

diagonally. The closer the task is to actual reading, the higher the transfer of skills, so don't complicate the assignment by adding the diagonal element. Puzzles can be very time consuming to design, but we've found them to be worth it, since they provide an enjoyable change of pace for the other students while they help students like Kathy.

Every once in a while you might wish to introduce some "fun" exercises to stimulate critical thinking. Collect several different pictures, such as the one shown in figure 5. Divide your class into groups of four or five students and have each group move around the room together to see if they can identify the hidden element in each picture. This is an exercise in visual perception that is fun for everyone.

For variety, you can have a game day, when you adapt familiar games such as dominoes or concentration to reinforce spelling, vocabulary, or characters from plays and novels. Establish several game stations around the room. At each station, set up games that provide an opportunity to review or practice a skill associated with your content material.

You can use word dominoes to help lower-track ninth-grade students who have difficulty with the *wh* and *th* words. Make cards that resemble dominoes, except that instead of having two sets of dots, each of your cards will contain a pair of words such as *who, what, when, where, they, then, there, that.* Deal out five cards. Students take turns matching the words just as they would in dominoes. (See figure 6.) Each student matches the words on his cards with those left on the end by his opponent. For example, if one student has a card with *where* and *what,*

Figure 5. Illustration for Visual Perception Exercise

Figure 6. Word Dominoes

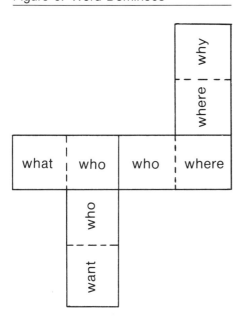

he will be able to match the last card played by his opponent if it left a *where* or a *what* exposed. Each card should have an arbitrary number of points written on the reverse side. A *what/where* card might be worth, for example, five points. For each card a student is able to play he adds that card's points to his running score. As a student plays a card, he draws a replacement card from the remaining dummy pile. The student having the highest number of points when the last card is played wins.

The game of concentration, adapted to meet the curricular and skill needs of your students, can help improve visual memory. Use spelling or vocabulary words, or words difficult for your students to remember. Write each word on two cards. Make up a deck of pairs of problem word cards. Deal out the cards face down on the desk in several rows. The game is played by two students who take turns turning up cards two at a time. If the cards don't match, turn them face down again. Both students should try to remember where those cards are. When a student turns up a pair, he gets a point. The student with the most points at the end of the game wins. (See figure 7.)

When you are individualizing with a student who is having extreme difficulty distinguishing between visually similar words, you may wish to try a visual perception sheet. (See figure 8.) These take time to write, so you may want to prepare them on duplicating masters. Keep them in a folder, since over the years you are bound to have other students with the same problems. The sample visual perception sheet in figure 8 uses the word in context, visual tracking for spelling reinforce-

Figure 7. Concentration with Vocabulary Words

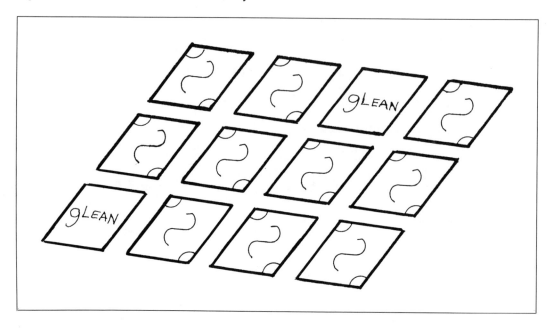

ment, visual recognition among words similarly shaped, and a final spelling reinforcement. Obviously, it would not be wise to overwork this technique by using it with every difficult word; save it for the hard-core words.

There are several commercially prepared games and puzzles that aid in visual reinforcement while providing a break in structured classroom procedure.[1] You can also make up some of your own. Our only advice is to create games that are as close to the reading process as possible. For example, use words rather than a code. Use sentences and phrases rather than geometric shapes. Keep the rules simple, and be sure to build in the possibility of winning.

Auditory Problems

Although more emphasis has been placed on visual perception and memory in the improvement of reading, it is important not to overlook the development of auditory skills. Auditory learning is very important to poor readers at the secondary level. While most students depend on

---

[1]Some of these are: *Probe* (Parker Brothers), *Word Links* (Creative Teaching Associates), *Password* (Milton Bradley), *Language Arts Box* (Educational Insights), *Sentence Cube Game* (Selchow & Righter), *Vocabulary Builder* (Curriculum Associates), *Triad* (Creative Teaching Associates), *Synonym and Antonym* (Creative Teaching Associates), *Add a Word* (Curriculum Associates), *New Word Puzzles* (Gerald L. Kaufman), and *Word Games* (Niles Grant).

Read these directions to the student.

1. Trace the model word at the top of the sheet with your finger. Repeat, tracing with your pencil.
2. Look at the sentence that follows the word. Read it and circle the correct word.
3. Next look at the group of letters. Moving from left to right, circle the model word letters sequentially as they appear in this random collection of letters.
4. Circle the model word each time it appears in the twelve words provided.
5. Using the model word as a guide, insert the missing letter.
6. Using the individual spaces as a clue, write the letters of the model word.
7. Now using the solid line, write the model word.
8. Finally, use the model word in a sentence of your own.

---

from

We heard (form, from) Mary last week.

---

abpfhgunreaodtlqnumv

---

form	from	frame
farm	frame	from
from	form	farm
frame	farm	form

---

f___om   fr___m   ___rom   fro___

— — — —

_____

Use in a sentence of your own. _____

reading for learning, many poor readers may do all their learning via auditory intake.

The key here is to draw attention to listening as an important learning tool. On a "fun" day, try an exercise that forces the class to concentrate on auditory skills. Make a tape recording of ten sounds heard around school: a student typing, a locker slamming, the coach's footsteps on the asphalt tile, the squeaking auditorium door, and so forth. Have the students number from 1 to 10 on their papers. Then play the tape, and ask them to write down what they think they hear.

Another method is to use your voice in the teaching of grammar. You can demonstrate punctuation clearly by your hesitation and breathing. When you think the students have understood your lesson, read the sentence to them in a monotone, asking them to write in the necessary punctuation on their worksheets. This is particularly effective in teaching the difference between complete sentences and fragments or run-ons.

It's best not to have your slow learners in an open-classroom situation, as the auditory distraction in "rooms without walls" is considerable. If, however, circumstances thrust you into a "circus" situation, then you might wish to develop some exercises that will help your students attend to their tasks in spite of all the noise around them. Provide background music while teaching a lesson. It is important to use music of their choice, since you wish to draw their attention away from what's going on in the other open areas. Decrease the volume a little each day until you have trained them to pay attention to you and not the surrounding stimuli. Of course, this might result in better learning taking place with music than without it. If this happens, what is wrong with reading to music?

For a realistic analysis of your students' ability to function and learn with noise as a background, provide your students with one half of a list of vocabulary words, spelling words, steps of a plot, or whatever you want them to learn. Play music while they study the material for ten minutes. Provide immediate testing of this material. Next, give them the second half of the material, and this time, have them study in silence. Again, give an immediate feedback quiz, to measure the percent of comprehension or retention during study without music. Compare the two scores, and you will have a rough idea which of your students learn better to music, and which learn better in silence. You may actually wish to set up a music corner in your room where those students who do better with music could listen to music on headsets, leaving the rest of the room in the traditional silence. Don't, however, let them con you into thinking that some of them study better in front of a television. While there are some surveys indicating that certain people retain more information if it is learned against a background of music, there are *no* studies showing that learning improves against a background of both auditory and visual distraction!

There are a variety of other gimmicks you can use to improve auditory attention. For example, provide rhyming clues for vocabulary reinforcement. After the students have studied the vocabulary lists, give them a homework assignment of clues containing a word that rhymes with the vocabulary word. "When I feel squished like a pear, I am lost in d e s p a i r." Recordings of famous people's voices can provide games on "fun" days.

While many of these suggestions are on the order of fun and games, the lesson behind them is a serious one that cannot be ignored. Listening and paying attention are skills that are essential to learning on the secondary level. By taking time to work on developing auditory skills, you give them the necessary image of importance. Keep in mind that what you think is important your students will also think is important.

Motor Problems

Take another look at the composite of skill strengths and weaknesses that you have developed. Having taken into account your students' visual and auditory problems, you should now pay some attention to possible motor difficulties. The older a student with motor problems becomes, the more difficult it is to help him. It is important that you recognize why writing assignments and even just sitting still may be difficult for some students. Being aware that there is a motor skill problem can help you empathize with them. To the student accustomed to teachers complaining about his handwriting, your sensitivity to his problem is the first step in the right direction.

You'll want to try any little trick possible to aid in correcting a well-established motor pattern. The writing assignments of your students will provide the best evidence of motor impairment. The way they approach writing tasks will give you some clues. Watch for the student who grasps his pen or pencil with such pressure that his knuckles are white. With that much physical tension, he certainly is not going to enjoy writing. Downplay neatness, which, after all, is not your prime goal. You can work on legibility and neatness after you have the confidence of your students.

The adolescent who grips his pen between his first two fingers instead of his thumb and first finger (while resting it on the second finger) has developed his own style for compensating. He has probably been writing that way for years, and you don't want to dwell on it as the wrong way to write. Try to help him with a modeling technique. Get some caulking compound, Playdough, or potter's clay and make yourself a pen holder. Place a wad of the pliable clay around your pen, and hold your pen in the correct manner, pressing in to make a comfortable grip. Use this pen as you walk around the class making corrections on individual papers. Obviously, someone is going to ask you why your pen looks that way. Tell him that you build up a callous on your third finger knuckle, and your hand gets tired writing all day. You use this as a way to relax while writing. Would he like to try it? Your grip won't help him, since everyone has a personal preference in holding a pen. Get some clay for the students who are interested in copying your pen, be sure they grip the pen correctly while making the mold, and you're off to a start. Keep in mind that this should be done in a very positive way. Never force a student to make himself a grip. Just use yours and hope the idea rubs off!

Look back at the sample of Fred's handwriting in figure 2. Fred is an example of a student who has severe motor problems. He can't walk down an aisle without knocking over books. Getting a piece of notebook paper from the rack under his seat is a major task. Buttons pop off when he buttons his coat; pencil points break whenever he tries to write. He approaches all motor tasks with tension and overcontrol. By over-control, we mean too much muscle tension and overconcentration. This proverbial "bull in a china shop" doesn't know how to ease up. He has a compelling motor thrust. Initially, we had Fred write on graph paper, as described in chapter 2. This method didn't work with Fred, though it is effective with some students.

What did work with Fred was typing. We had him scheduled into basic typing. During one of his study halls, we introduced him to the typewriter and gave him a pass to the reading room where he could practice. The formally scheduled typing class taught him the basics of the machine and the correct procedure, while the private sessions gave him confidence. He approached the typewriter with the same zeal as he had his pen, but soon he learned that the machine had some limits! He did have to use the space bar between words, and the machine forced him to think about his spelling. Most important, however, was the praise he received in shop and social studies for the effort and time it took him to type his assignments. The positive "strokes" plus the read-ability of his assignments made all the work worth it.

Consistency of format is another aid you can build into your curricular materials. The sameness of presentation provides necessary structure for students with motor difficulties. These students will also benefit if you give them plenty of white space to write in. The less visual distraction on a page, the more likely the student will be able to limit his attention to the task at hand. When you are preparing an assignment, keep in mind that use of lines to divide tasks on the same page is another helpful gimmick for the student with motor or visual perception problems. Youngsters with motor problems may read a question and record the answer in some totally irrelevant space. By providing lines to separate assignments, you help the student focus attention on the appropriate area.

Testing situations generally provide additional anxiety for the pupil with motor problems. You and I may take the separate answer sheet for granted. It certainly is easier for us to take home a single answer sheet per student instead of an entire test booklet, but the very process of reading a test item, locating the answer, and then shifting to a separate answer sheet to record the answer may be enough to thwart a student with motor problems. It is much better if you write the stem of the question, list the alternatives vertically beneath the stem, and then provide answer spaces on both sides of the question—one for the righties and one for the lefties—as follows:

_____ 1. The first president of the United 1._____
       States was
       a. George Washington.
       b. John Adams.
       c. Thomas Jefferson.
       d. James Madison.

Without blanks on the left side, the left-handed student is covering up the question and alternatives with his hand in order to write in the space provided by a right-handed teacher. If the teacher is left-handed and puts the blanks on the left-hand side, the righties are faced with the same predicament. Something as simple as this avoids a lot of the tension associated with testing.

Very often, students with motor difficulties develop their own compensatory devices. For example, take a second look at the student who reads with his finger. After third grade, using a finger while reading has always been a real "no-no." Nonsense! Whatever works should be okay with you. In fact you will find it easier yourself to use your finger when trying to read a newspaper column rapidly. The same goes for bookmarks! If they work, use them! Never force these gimmicks on your students. Again, however, you may wish to try modeling as you did with the pen holder. Use a bookmark while reading and have a small pile of bookmarks available nearby. When the students ask you what you are using, show them, and offer them bookmarks too.

Initially, diagnosing and prescribing may seem very time consuming, but after you have had some experience behind you, you will find that matching strengths and weaknesses to appropriate materials becomes almost second nature. You will just *know* what to do for specific problems.

Good diagnosis isn't something that only takes place in the fall. It continues all year long and throughout high school. Daily journal entries (see chapter 9) provide you with a great deal of information on spelling, motor, and visual problems. Note *how* students approach a task, methods they use to avoid a given job, speaking and writing styles, facial expressions, tilt of the head, posture, and casual comments made to friends sitting nearby—all these things may reveal your students' learning difficulties. Formal testing can provide you with specific diagnostic data, but daily observations also contribute a wealth of information. Use formal instruments when possible; be observant and alert; trust your own intuition; and then use all of these to plug your students into a realistic and functional prescription!

CURRICULAR NEED: ORGANIZING THE HETEROGENEOUS CLASSROOM

Now you are in charge of a roomful of students. Where do you begin? Probably the first and most important step is diagnosis. Chapter 3 discusses diagnostic materials and techniques that the novice teacher can use.

So . . . you have the statistics of the class before you, and you are horrified. Of the twenty-three students in this tenth-grade class, five read on the tenth-grade level or better, six read on the seventh- to ninth-grade levels, six read on the fifth- and sixth-grade levels, and six scored below the fifth-grade level. The students' writing samples indicate abilities ranging from exquisite creative efforts and attempts at poetry to incomprehensible incomplete sentences and garbled spelling. As a well-meaning, newly-trained teacher, you wish to meet the needs of all your students. How do you do this and still cover the curriculum prescribed by your department head?

Textbooks

If you were given hardbound textbooks along with the curriculum, put them on a high shelf in your room and try to use them sparingly. With such a varied class it is impossible to begin on page 1 of an anthology the first week of school, plow faithfully through all four hundred pages before the end of May, and still think you are meeting the individual needs of the students. The ideal way to teach a class with a wide range of reading levels is to have a wide range of reading material on all levels also.

Suppose you are given a single hard bound textbook in the fall with explicit instruction that it *must* be used. There is no money for frills. How can you teach students at the various reading levels in the class if you're using a book that is probably suitable for only the upper third of the class? One way of approaching this problem is through the use of study guides. Chapter 8 contains many examples of study guides and explains how to develop them. You might decide to develop a single study guide with several types of questions geared to different reading levels. The students can then be asked to answer only those questions that are within their range of ability. For example, when using a study guide for class discussion on an essay or short story, ask the slower students to answer the literal questions (perhaps numbers 1, 4, 6, and 7). The average students can answer the more interpretive questions (perhaps numbers 2, 3, 8, and 9). The better students can answer the applied-level questions that require making a judgment based on reading and using critical thinking (perhaps numbers 5 and 10). This method allows each student to feel that he is contributing to the class.

Choosing alternatives to the given text and making sure these alternatives are on grade levels equal to the ability of the students is one of the most important tasks of a new teacher. Since reading is a major part of any junior or senior high school curriculum, a teacher's first concern should be finding proper reading material. On the other hand, don't feel that most of the material in the curriculum has to emphasize reading. You may find it impossible to depend mainly on reading with a large heterogeneous class. Consider other avenues to reaching the objectives set by the curriculum. These may include mass media, oral language skills, and drama or poetry.

You can plan a thematic unit on an interesting topic you think will motivate the class. Then select reading material on your topic at various reading levels. Such material can include essays, short stories, or poetry taken from other books that are around the school. Television, records, magazines (from the school library) may be used also. This does not have to be expensive or time consuming on your part. You might decide to teach a unit using all novels (see the section in this chapter on individual novels), or you might use other genres such as poetry, short stories, or mass media. The important thing is to have enough reading levels represented so that all the students can succeed. Some means of sharing information among the students is necessary, so that each student can feel that he is making a valuable contribution to the class. After the students have read selections near their reading levels, they can make reports, either to the class or in groups. If each member of the class provides information on a different aspect of the topic, all the students will be able to play a role in developing the final concepts of the unit.

Fry Graph   The Fry Graph (figure 9) may be used to evaluate the reading level of any piece of prose. This is a fairly reliable formula, and once you have used it a few times, you will wonder what you ever did without it.

To use the Fry Graph, randomly select three 100-word passages from the reading material you wish to evaluate, one from the beginning, one from the middle, and one from the end. Count the total number of sentences and the total number of syllables in each of the three passages and average the results. Plot the average number of sentences and syllables on the graph. The point at which the two meet represents the approximate grade level of the material.

Figure 9. Fry Graph for Estimating Readability

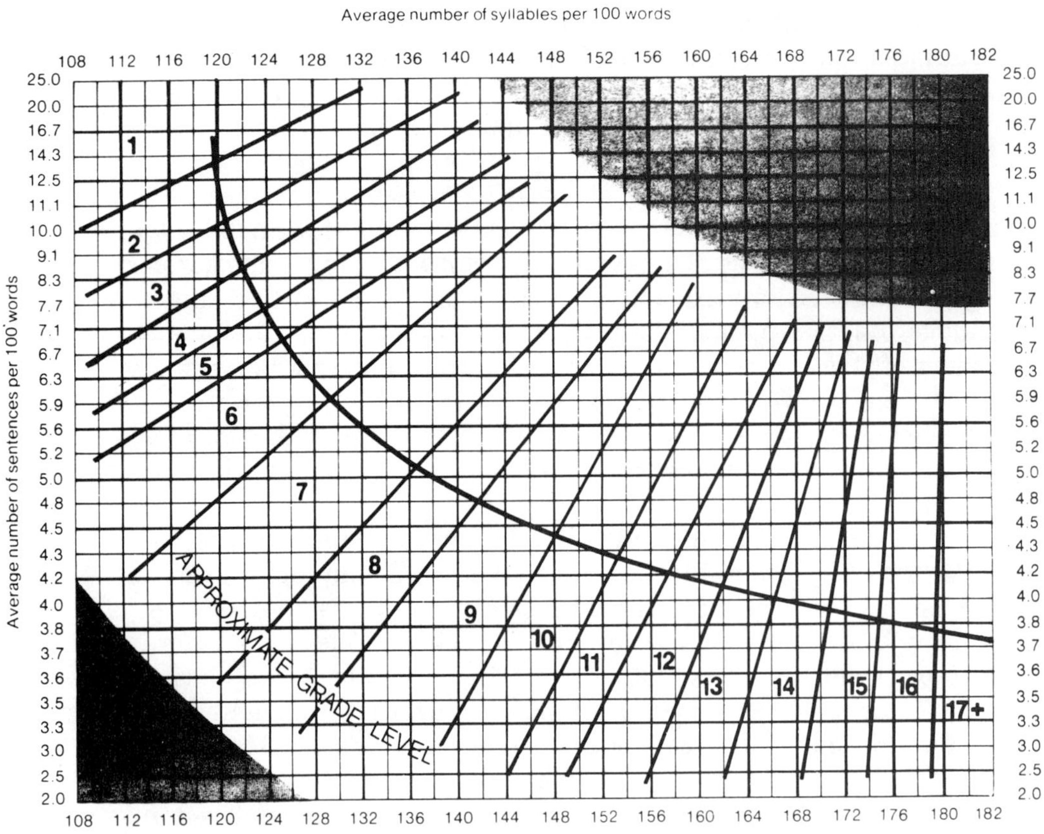

Average number of syllables per 100 words

SOURCE: Edward Fry, Rutgers University Reading Center, New Brunswick, N.J. Reprinted by permission.

Hooked-on-Books

Another strategy to use with heterogeneous classes is Hooked-on-Books. This program was first implemented by Daniel Fader at a penal institution in Michigan, and it was so successful that he wrote *Hooked-on-Books*,[2] a well-known book that describes the program.

Essentially, Hooked-on-Books is a structured free reading period. Reading material such as paperback novels, magazines, comic books, and newspapers should be provided for the students. Then, everyone, including the teacher, reads silently. During the last ten or fifteen minutes of the period, the students write in their journals. (See chapter 9 for a discussion of the value of journals.) The slower students may simply copy a passage from what they have read; the better students may write an original paragraph expressing their opinion. This is an excellent

[2]Daniel Fader and Elton B. McNeil (New York: Berkley, 1977).

program for heterogeneous classes because each pupil can be guided to reading material at his grade level. Since the material should also be on his interest level, he will be motivated to read. Usually, we use Hooked-on-Books every day for one to two weeks.

If you use this program periodically throughout the year, you should see some improvement not only in the students' attitudes toward reading, but also in their writing.

Although we discuss journal writing in detail in chapter 9, perhaps a few comments about managing the grading of journals should be interjected here. When we first started having the pupils keep journals, we were very enthusiastic and looked forward to reading them every night. We had told the students that if they wished, we would grade their journal entries. All they had to do at the end of each writing session was write "Grade" at the top of the page. As you may guess, it wasn't long before the pressure of grading journals every night became more than we could handle. We had to find a happy medium between the number of times the students wrote and the number of entries we graded. Journal writing is a good idea; however, be sure you manage it so that both teachers and students are motivated, not overburdened.

Uninterrupted Sustained Silent Reading

A method similar to Hooked-on-Books is Uninterrupted Sustained Silent Reading (USSR). Each student chooses his own reading material and brings it to class. The students and the teacher read for a certain period of time each day. The length of reading time may range from ten minutes to the entire class period. The main difference between Hooked-on-Books and USSR is that in USSR the students do not write in their journals. The idea is to encourage a love of reading by exposing the students to written material on a regular basis.

Individual Novel

Earlier in this chapter we spoke about individualizing when you had only *one* book or anthology to use with the whole class. We suggested that you develop study guides with questions at various levels to accommodate the differences among the students. Another technique is to use *several* books at all levels on a central theme, so each student may choose a book that fits his ability and interest. For example, for a unit on death and dying you might choose five or six novels with the central theme of death. These novels would have various reading levels and you would guide each student to the book which he could read most easily. For each book, prepare a study guide, a vocabulary list, reinforcement worksheets, and quizzes or final test. (See chapters 7 and 8 for examples of the first three items.) Each student will be able to work with the study guides and worksheets at his own pace, allowing time for you to walk around the room giving assistance where needed.

As with many other suggestions in this book, an integral part of the success or failure of a method is the management materials. It is essential that you have some kind of chart for keeping track of the progress of each student. These students need to see their progress nearly every day. Don't wait until a student has finished the entire study guide before you look it over or grade it. As you walk around the room while they are reading, grade each chapter of the study guide as a student finishes it.

These management materials are simple to construct. For each novel the class is reading, write the students' names down the left-hand column of a sheet of paper. Divide the remaining space into columns for each of the chapters in the book. Subdivide each column for any worksheets and quizzes that apply. This way you can mark the grades for each chapter in the appropriate boxes. Sample management materials can be found in Appendix C.

Scholastic Book Services offers good alternatives to the individual novel format. The *Action Libraries*[3] consist of many short teen-age novels that are written on the second- to sixth-grade reading levels. They are excellent for the slower reader because they are usually on his interest level, and although the print is larger than usual, the books themselves do not look "babyish." Each of the books comes with a set of duplicating masters for vocabulary and word attack skill worksheets. The student can use these worksheets to increase his understanding of the book. The *Action Libraries* do not come with comprehension guides for the reading material, but chapter 8 explains in detail how to write these guides.

INDIVIDUALIZED GRAMMAR

Although the thought of grammar horrifies most students, nearly every English teacher must, at some time or another, cross over into this forbidden territory. Many of the students who can't read also can't write. Many of them don't understand such concepts as complete sentences and good paragraphs. For this reason, the basic rules of grammar (What is a verb? What is a subject? A paragraph must have more than one sentence.) must be reviewed every year. As with reading levels, the grammatical abilities in a heterogeneous class will be extremely varied.

Traditionally, there have been two ways of dealing with grammar problems in the classroom. One method does not involve any formal grammar instruction. The aim here is to approach each student's grammar problems through his writing. As the students write compositions,

---

[3]*Action Libraries, I, II, IA, IIA* (New York: Scholastic Book Services, 1972, 1975).

the teacher becomes attuned to the particular grammatical weaknesses of each student. Then, as time permits, each pupil has an individual conference with the teacher or is given worksheets that address his particular problems. The trick to this system is time. We have found that there is not enough time to have the students write as often as they should. In order for the teacher to keep on top of grammar problems by reinforcing strengths and correcting weaknesses, the pupils should be writing at least once every two weeks. Writing once a week would be ideal, but what teacher has the time to correct one hundred or so essays, diagnose grammar problems, develop strategies to help individual students, and work on still other areas of the English curriculum? Teaching grammar through the students' writing may not be the most efficient or effective method.

We have found that spending a block of time, usually two weeks, on the mechanics of grammar works better in the long run. Like books, the study of grammatical principles can be individualized so that each student is able to study the areas relevant to his weaknesses. We have developed an individualized grammar unit based on diagnostic testing. (See the section on grammar in chapter 9 and figures 42 through 44.) Prescriptive materials, which are written on index cards, consist of groups of sentences at each level that reinforce a grammatical rule. A student can go to the set of cards for his assignment and work independently through the exercises, checking from time to time with the teacher, and taking quizzes when he feels he has mastered the material. Each pupil is working on his particular weakness, and none of the class time is wasted. The teacher still gives writing assignments, but they can be given as time permits, and they can be used to reinforce grammatical principles developed during the intensified grammar study.

CONTRACT PROJECTS

Another method for dealing with students of varying levels in the heterogeneous classroom is the use of contracts. This can be particularly effective for several reasons. First, each pupil will be working on a topic that interests him. Where there is student interest, the teacher will have to do less to motivate him. Second, because the student has chosen the grade he wishes to receive and knows how much work he has to do to earn it, he will be better able to allocate his time so that he can complete all the requirements. We all know that even the *average* student has difficulty avoiding last-minute pressures, so it's unrealistic to expect that a *below-average* student will magically begin to turn in all his work on time. With the contract method, however, we have experienced less difficulty in getting the students to work, and we have had fewer complaints about grades. Each student understands how his grade will be computed, and he understands due dates. Procrastination and failure to turn in assignments result in zeros.

The student chooses a topic ranging from mystery stories to snowmobiles. Next, he signs a contract specifying the grade he wishes to receive at the end of the unit and the work required for that grade. He knows that he will have to read a few more magazines or conduct a personal interview to get an A. In general, each student contracts to complete several steps before finishing the unit. He reads a book on his topic and then writes a book review. He reads two magazine articles and compares them. Because we hold most of the classes in the media center, he can look at filmstrips or other audiovisual materials pertaining to his topic. During the reading, listening, and writing sections of the unit, he is required to make a list of at least ten unfamiliar vocabulary words. He has to look up the definitions and use the new words in sentences, and he is encouraged to use the words frequently in his review writing and oral report.

Next, the student conducts a personal interview with a resource person. For some topics, like snowmobiling, several of the students might go on a short field trip to a local snowmobile dealer and ask him questions. For other topics, like mystery stories, a local mystery buff might come to the school to be interviewed by the students. When possible, we find a resource person and arrange for the interview, since it can be difficult for the lower-level student to track down such a person on his own.

As a final project the student prepares an oral report. The form of this presentation may vary quite a bit. One student may draw a graph, while another may actually build a model and discuss it in class. We have had students bring in their motorcycles or snowmobiles and discuss the various parts of the machines and the advantages of their models. The students enjoy these presentations, probably because they are speaking about something they understand and like.

At the end of the unit, the student's work is evaluated. If he has met all the requirements of his contract, he receives the grade he wanted. If, on the other hand, he did not do one or more of the sections expected for his grade, he is given a lower grade more in keeping with his performance.

These are just a few ideas on how to handle the classroom where the students' activities vary widely. Of course, there are many other possible ideas that could be used in this situation. You may wish to combine some of the methods suggested here or to develop new ones. The heterogeneous classroom is a definite challenge, but these techniques and your own innovative teaching ideas provide a sensible beginning to helping all your students.

How to Set Up a Homogeneous Class 5

The merits of heterogeneous and homogeneous classrooms have long been debated. Wherever you find retired teachers, current teachers, or prospective teachers, there will be opinions on the subject equal to the number of people present! Rather than become victims of the semantics of debate, we make no apologies for the simplicity of our answer: Put the *right students* with the *right teachers* using the *right materials*. For us the definition of *right students* is definitely students with similar strengths and weaknesses. Yes, we favor homogeneous grouping in order to avoid the ludicrous situation of trying to teach Dickens to a classroom with both a National Merit Scholar and a learning-disabled student as members.

Obviously there will be cries of "No kid wants to be in the 'dumb' class! You'll ruin him for life!" Doubting parents claim that their child will be stigmatized by being scheduled into a class with students of similar ability. Somehow, the same parents cannot grasp the image of their youngster, reading at the fourth-grade level, struggling through *Julius Caesar* toward ultimate frustration. The parents must think that their child will improve by osmosis. Put him in a room with bright students, and he will become bright! It just doesn't work that way. Initially, a weak student may have some good feelings about being in a class with strong achievers, but those feelings vanish with the first test. Often it is the students who become realistic before the parents. Students are much quicker to admit that the work is too hard for them than some parents are to accept that their child is inappropriately placed. The key to parent and student acceptance of proper placement is making the appropriate scheduling attractive. If the student understands what his weaknesses are, then the chances are that he will recognize that his opportunity for success lies in the placement you propose.

It is important to note that we recommend homogeneous classes in the major academic subject areas only. Placing students with similar strengths and weaknesses in the same English, social studies, science, and math classes does not preclude their placement with students representing a wider range of abilities in physical education, drivers' education, home economics, industrial arts, business subjects, art, and health.

Homogeneous grouping in the academics makes it possible to teach at a student's instructional level rather than his frustration level; it allows you to use material appropriate to his reading level and to provide reasonable, not impossible, competition. The student has a chance of success, rather than guaranteed failure. If the student progresses to the point where he is no longer challenged in his homogeneous class, he can only profit from a move upward. It is important to keep this in mind when working on the scheduling of your slower students with guidance counselors who are wont to say, "Let him try the harder class. We can always reassign him." It is always much better to elevate a student's placement rather than demote him for failing to succeed at the original placement. While incorrect placement may be the real culprit, it is homogeneous grouping that often incurs the blame if a student is unable to succeed or appears to have a poor self-image.

In order for a homogeneous class of slower students to achieve its purpose, the class should be kept small, and the main teacher should have some help; otherwise, the remedial workload can become overwhelming. In our school, the classes (one per grade level) for the poorer students are limited to eighteen students, and the classroom teacher teaches with the full-time assistance of the reading teacher. As the content area teacher conducts the class, the reading teacher moves about the room helping students individually. (If a reading teacher is not available to you, perhaps an aide is.) This additional help provides a nine-to-one student-to-teacher ratio which means that a student is going to be noticed. He cannot hide in the back of the room and sleep, because there is a teacher right there to help him catch on to a new concept or make up back work he may have missed.

CONVINCING GUIDANCE COUNSELORS AND ADMINISTRATORS

After you decide that it would be best to group the students with basic skill deficiencies in one class, you may have to convince both the guidance office and your school administration that homogeneous grouping is a good idea. How can you show them that the students will be more likely to succeed; the parents will be happy with their children's success; and, therefore, the administrators' lives will be easier?

Your best ammunition will be statistics about attendance and discipline.[1] When you write curriculum built on students' interests and needs and offer materials on their reading levels, school suddenly won't seem so bad! Since the emphasis is on the positive, and the poor learner has a chance of succeeding for the first time, he is more willing to come to school. It's amazing how class attendance can improve. Our own classes show an average 64 percent better attendance than comparable attendance records prior to homogeneous grouping. For the same reasons that these classes have good attendance, they also have very few discipline problems. If poor learners see the possibility of achieving, getting individual attention, and doing something interesting, they don't need to tear the room apart while you are putting their self-images back together.

Another reason you can give your administrators for supporting this type of program is the current requirements for accountability under federal and state education laws. If a school district accepts funds from Title I, Title IV, or any other special programs, the school must show proof that it has established a program specifically to meet the needs of those students as stated in the project request. A homogeneous class set up for students with basic skill deficits can be the answer to your counselors' and administrators' needs. Schools are very quick to obtain maximum publicity for scholarship winners, hero athletes, and winning debate teams. In today's federal funding market, schools must also obtain good press for their programs for the youngsters with skill deficits. Our schools must show that they meet the needs of all young people, not just the favored few. With the emphasis on *selection* rather than assignment of both teachers and students for this class, administrators will not have teacher complaints. Since only teachers who choose to teach this class have remedial students, the complaints are rare.

SELECTING TEACHERS

Certainly the key to success is the staff selected to work with basic skill students. Since responsibility for improving self-concept, attendance, attitudes toward school, reading ability, and a host of other educational maladies is the specific charge of these teachers, we suggest that these tasks only be entrusted to very special people. In a teaching situation in which every child is exceptional, "exceptional" must be the hallmark of the teacher as well.

Of primary consideration is the word *volunteer*. Every teacher in this program should have requested the assignment, since only people

---

[1]You could obtain this data from us. However, a compilation of your own statistics based on your local student population is generally more convincing.

who are committed to working with this type of student have a chance of making the program succeed. If there are not enough volunteers, the administrator should consider the staff carefully and approach the best candidate in a positive manner. "We have *selected* you because we think you have special qualities to contribute to the program." Since most classes are assigned, it is important that the teacher feel he has the opportunity to refuse this request. At least the teacher does not feel he has been forced into an untenable position.

After the desire to teach this class, the most important qualification is a sense of humor. Without the ability to laugh *at* himself and *with* others, the teacher would be doomed to failure. Teachers who work with students weak in skills must guard against becoming stuffy, boring, or rule conscious, and against taking themselves too seriously. In order to establish a successful relationship with these youngsters, a teacher must enjoy life, himself, and the students. He must consider the students worthy of his attention. As a model for improvement of self-concept, the teacher must show some pride in self along with the ability to laugh at his weaknesses.

Along with the idea of sense of humor comes the quality of "hamminess." There is no substitute for that precious gift of being a stand-up comic, a Bill Cosby of the high school set, a ham! No one acquires this trait in graduate institutions; in fact, many of them encourage the adoption of *teacher posture*—highly structured, orderly, serious demeanor, the very qualities that turn kids off. Many young teachers have a natural quality of "hamminess" but have learned to conceal it during their student teaching and have deferred to the more classic teacher image. It is possible to be a ham without losing control of the classroom. The freedom of spirit and lack of inhibitions that allow a teacher to roar up and down the aisles while reading a dramatic part in a play or to characterize the Hunchback of Notre Dame in great leaping strides around the room, endear these literary characters to students rather than detract from the story. To bring literature alive, you have to be alive. So while structure and order are necessary in the classroom, don't forget to bring along your vitality and pizzaz as well!

The teacher of lower ability students must also have an inexhaustible supply of energy. Any teaching is exhausting, but teaching kids with learning difficulties can be paralyzing! Frustration and the never-ending dilemma of how to do something that others have failed at tire even the hardiest person. To maintain a high level of student motivation, it is necessary to grade papers immediately and return them the following day. To keep up with the work to be corrected while, at the same time, creating new structured worksheets requires a person who uses time well and just doesn't tire easily.

Round out this perfect teacher with generous doses of sensitivity, empathy, intelligence, and patience. It should be obvious that we want to get the *best* teachers assigned to these classes. It is time that these students have the best that a school district has to offer.

TRAINING TEACHERS

Once the right teachers have been identified and brought into the program, the next important step is the training of this staff. If these teachers are to be able to put the right material into the hands of these students, your program must allow *the time to train them* to develop this curricular material. It is wrong to assume just because certain staff members have said they would be willing to teach these classes that they know *how* to do so. Training should include at least some of the following:

Descriptions of learning deficits and their symptoms
Physical and psychological backgrounds of students with learning impairments
Importance of avoiding assumptive teaching
Becoming aware of gaps in students' knowledge
Diagnosing and prescribing
Writing material based on prescriptions
Recognizing the sequencing necessary in developing comprehension skills
Improving affective domain while developing student skills
Writing appropriate vocabulary reinforcement
Devising writing assignments with the necessary high degree of structure
Developing consistency in evaluation procedures

Much of the material in this book is based on the kind of training we feel these teachers need. We've found that well-intentioned people are not automatically good classroom teachers of slow learners. One is not a good teacher of poor readers merely because one is a graduate of an accredited institution. One has to *learn* how to write curriculum for this type of student. It's also important for these teachers to know when to push a student and when to proceed with restraint.

In our school, after we select the staff to work with the basic skills classes, we put the teachers through a training workshop to teach them how to develop good materials and to be sensitive to the needs of youngsters with learning problems. This workshop is followed immediately by work days devoted to writing the kind of material demonstrated in the workshop. Follow-up sessions are used to help reinforce some of the concepts included in the training. This training and reinforcement can contribute to the success rate of your program.

PLACING STUDENTS

And now for the third essential ingredient, the right students. We are looking for the student who has learning problems, not the student who is a discipline problem. We are not looking for the lazy kid who just doesn't feel like the hassle of a college-preparatory program. We are not looking for the youngster who has conned his family and teachers into not asking the most of him. We are looking for that special youngster who tries to succeed but has difficulty, the student who has had the same spelling words for years but has not been able to master them, the pupil who wants desperately to pass but continues to fail. This student may or may not have turned off school because of the frustration of failing. We exclude the cut-ups who are bright but bored. We exclude the wise guy who is immature but not stupid. We exclude the lazy one, the con artist, and the troublemaker who have skills but don't use them. We are after the youngster deficient in basic skills, the one who *wants* to learn but *can't*.

For purposes of scheduling, we do our screening in the spring of eighth-grade year, but depending on the structure of your high school, you could do the same type of identification at the end of sixth or ninth grade.

Our initial screening is directed toward paring down the grade as a whole to a workable list of students, appropriate in need. For this purpose, we use the New York State Pupil Evaluation Program (NYSPEP) test administered in grade 6. (If this test is not available to you, any standard achievement or reading test that yields a vocabulary and silent reading comprehension score would be fine.) Every pupil who scores in the third stanine or below is placed on a special screening list. (A bell curve reporting test scores can be divided vertically into ten sections. These sections are known as stanines. Students whose scores appear in the lower three stanines are assumed to be the weakest, as indicated by their performance on that particular test.) To this information, we add the seventh- and eighth-grade results of the reading comprehension section of the Iowa Test of Basic Skills. (Results of the California Achievement Test or the Metropolitan Achievement Test would be equivalent to those of the Iowa.) In addition, we also use comprehension and vocabulary scores from the most recent Gates-MacGinitie reading test. The Differential Aptitude Test (DAT) administered in eighth grade also provides screening information. The final objective data are provided by the California Test of Mental Maturity. In this instance, we record the Total Language I.Q. scores from the *two* most recent administrations. The purpose of this is not to add I.Q. information, but to note specifically a decline of ten points or more in score between the first and second administrations of the test. Since the reading passages used on the CTMM become progressively more difficult, a significant decline in scores can confirm that a student has a reading problem rather than a deterioration of intellectual aptitude.

To this objective data, we add the subjective referral of classroom teachers (English, social studies, science, and reading), and support personnel such as speech teacher, school nurse, physical education teacher, school psychologist, and guidance counselor. We are looking for the youngster clearly identified by objective testing information that is reinforced by subjective personal recommendations.

Figure 10 shows a sample form that you can use to compile the results. Across the top of the form, write the names of the objective and subjective criteria you will be using. Don't forget to include columns for the totals. List the names of your potential students in the left-hand column, and write in the scores for each student under the appropriate column headings. Determine cut-off points for each of the objective tests. Then circle the scores that fall below their cut-off points and all of the "yes" recommendations.

On the form we use, the first column refers to the NYSPEP reading results from the test given in sixth grade. If a student scores in the third stanine or below, his name appears on the list; therefore, most of the students on this list have the first box circled. The only exception, as you will note, is Mike Edwards. Mike scored in the fourth stanine on the NYSPEP in reading, but he is on the list because of his third-stanine score in math. (Note that reading screening and math screening are done separately. The first ten columns on the form are the basis for selection of students with reading impairment. The next six columns are for math screening. This allows us to identify students who need help in reading, math, or both areas but frees us from placing students in a total remedial program if it is not necessary.)

The second column refers to the reading comprehension score derived from an eighth-grade administration of the Gates-MacGinitie Reading Test (Form E). We circle the name of any student who scores at two or more years below current grade placement (in this case, sixth grade or below).

The third column refers to the reading comprehension score obtained from the Iowa Test of Basic Skills administered in seventh grade. Again on the Iowa, we circle the scores that are two or more years below grade level. Keep in mind that this means 5.0 or below since this test was administered in seventh grade.

The next column refers to the Differential Aptitude Test, which

Figure 10. Sample Form for Screening Students

Student	Reading Screening NYS Reading Test Grade 6 stanine	Gates-MacGinitie Grade 8 Form E (Comprehension)	Iowa Grade 7 Rdg. Comp. Gr. Level	DAT—Verbal Percentile Grade 8	CTMM Grade 3 IQ Language Total	CTMM Grade 6 IQ Language Total	English Teacher	Social Studies Teacher	Science Teacher	Reading Teacher	Math Screening NYS Math Test Grade 6 stanine	Iowa Grade 7 Math Grade Level	DAT—Numerical Grade 8	CTMM Grade 3 Non-Lang. Total IQ	CTMM Grade 6 Non-Lang. Total IQ	Math Teacher	School Psychologist	School Nurse	Physical Education Teacher	Speech Teacher	Guidance Counselor	Total Reading Referrals (9 maximum)	Total Math Referrals (5 maximum)	Total Extra Personnel Referrals (5 maximum)	Total Referrals
Brown, Alan	2	3.6	5.2	25	75	71	yes	yes	yes	yes	4	4.8	25	86	91	?		yes			yes	7/9	2/5	2/5	
Cole, Matt	3	2.9	4.6	3	102	66	yes	yes	yes	yes	4	6.6	45	109	105	yes		yes			yes	9/9	1/5	2/5	
Dennis, John	3	7.0	4.6	40	93	85	No	No	No	No	3	7.0	50	93	87	No						2/9	1/5		
Edwards, Mike	4	8.6	6.0	35	111	110	No	Ni	No	No	3	7.7	3	111	109	No							2/5		
Finn, Tony	3	4.1	4.8	20	89	74	yes	yes	yes	yes	3	5.3	15	85	61	yes		yes			yes	9/9	4/5	2/5	

measures a wide range of potential areas of strength and weakness. In this column, we are looking for the scores that reflect the twenty-fifth percentile or lower on total *verbal* aptitude measure.

The adjacent two columns are to be treated as one entry. As we have pointed out, the California Test of Mental Maturity is a paper-and-pencil I.Q. test that requires reading ability, so it may measure reading skill more accurately than I.Q. Here we are looking for the youngster whose score dropped ten points or more from the third grade to the sixth grade.

The remaining columns for individual teacher referrals speak for themselves. This is the opportunity for teachers to agree or disagree with the objective screening done by standardized testing. When you have finished circling the data for the reading referrals, total the circles for each student and record the number of items circled in the column at the right where nine possible referrals are suggested.

Now, go back and do the same thing for math. Record the number of circled referrals in the math column. Do the same with the extra personnel referrals. These are used primarily to reinforce or double-check the students referred via the reading screening. If, for example, you have a borderline pupil where the screening might indicate five out of nine referrals, and all the extra personnel who knew the student recommended him for the class, then those additional referrals would provide the necessary impetus to make a defensible decision. If on the other hand, you have five out of nine referrals, and none of the extra personnel who know him recommend him, you would probably be safe in assuming that he may just have had a few poor test scores but probably doesn't belong in the program.

Your school may use an entirely different set of standardized instruments; however, the principle is the same. Use a combination of objective measures and subjective input to select the students. Once this data is tabulated, choose the students with the highest numbers of referrals. A nine out of nine, for example, would be certain placement in the program. Then move on to those with eight out of nine, and so on. We try to aim for about eighteen students, no more, in one class. If necessary, we form a second class. One of the secrets of success is keeping the class size manageable.

Now that you have selected the students, use the Individual Secondary Skills Inventory discussed in chapter 3 to diagnose each student's areas of strength and weakness. Once that is done, follow the prescriptive techniques presented in chapter 3 to match your students to material written specifically for their needs.

Once this is done, you have the essential ingredients for the simple formula we suggested at the beginning of this chapter: Put the *right students* with the *right teachers* using the *right materials*. The simplicity of this suggestion may not be well received by other educators, but we can attest to the fact that it works. We have had students improve as much as two years in reading comprehension during a nine-month school year. There is nothing magic about selecting the right teachers and the right students; it's a logical and methodical process used to weed out the cut-up students and the inappropriate teachers. It matches students with severe learning deficits to teachers who have the stamina and creativity to wrestle with learning impairments. A tough road at best. At least you will have created the right learning environment for achievement.

Building Affective Concerns 6

Good morning, class! Today I will prepare
you for the future. Listen carefully, and
don't interrupt! Are there any questions?
. . . None? Good![1]

Up to this point, we have been talking about *you*: the harassed new teacher, struggling to survive. We have worried about how you could diagnose the problems your students have. We have been concerned that you wouldn't know how a student could reach senior high school and still not be able to read. We have introduced suggestions to help you cope with a heterogeneous classroom as well as initiate a homogeneous one. This chapter will focus on the most important person in your classroom: the student. If you don't do a good job of teaching, you will survive, but your student may not. You obviously have something going for you, or you wouldn't have gotten through college, but your student may have nothing going for him, or no one rooting for him. You are accustomed to having friends with interests and capabilities similar to yours. Your students have friends with similar interests, but capabilities will differ widely. What it comes down to is the fact that you will have students who are not like you; therefore, you can't teach them the way you were taught.

We're talking about a very special breed of child. The oddball who is not wanted in his neighbor's yard because he steps on the tulips and teases the dog. As a teen-ager, he is unable to keep lawn-mowing jobs because he isn't thorough. He's even unpopular in Sunday school. He is the child of desperate parents; tranquilizers didn't work on him, so his

[1]Albert Cullum; *The Geranium on the Window Sill Just Died, But Teacher You Went Right On* (Belgium: Houlen Quist, 1971), p. 60.

parents took them! He is the child whose reputation preceded him from grade to grade. He was the object of much teachers' room speculation: "Just wait until you get Kenny next year. What'll you pay me to retain him?" The only thing he has done consistently in his whole life is remain in the lowest reading group. He is the kind of student who was probably overlooked during your practical preparation for teaching. He is, by all standards, a loser.

SELF-IMAGE

By the time a student reaches junior and senior high school, the biggest single obstacle to learning is self-image. In spite of what you may say to him, he sees himself as retarded, slow, or brain damaged.

Unless this student's affective concerns are met, no content-oriented program, including one for poor-achieving high school students, will be effective.

Let's consider one particular young man as an example. The following comments are taken directly from his folder:

Grade 1:   "Gerry has not caught on to reading."
Grade 3:   "Gerry has no idea what reading is all about."
Grade 4:   "Gerry's reading skills are so bad, I send him down to the first-grade room twice a day for extra help."
Grade 5:   "Gerry is too busy causing trouble to learn to read."
Grade 6:   "Gerry is quiet and prefers the puzzle corner to reading."
Grade 7:   "Gerry was placed in an SRA program in reading class."
Grade 8:   "Gerry requires individual help, something that is not available in this building."
Grade 9:   "Gerry can't read."

Perhaps comments from Gerry himself tell us more about him than these comments from his student folder. "I just sit in the last row, and she don't call on me to read." "I'm a loser. I don't know why I haven't quit before this. Guess it's cause this is better than being home." "Why not drink? It's the only thing I do good." "You sure you got the patience to work with a dumbhead like me?"

In doing a case study on this boy, we discovered that he had had remedial reading since he was eight years old. When we contacted his former teachers and tutors, we discovered that no one could tell us about Gerry as a person. None knew his interests, family background, or goals. No one could name even one thing at which the boy might excel! He was described to us by a former classroom teacher and a reading tutor as being "dumb" and "disinterested." All teachers questioned knew that he had had remedial instruction, but no one knew the boy or how he felt about himself. Up to this point, he had experienced little or no success in remediation. He was eighteen years old, reading on the first-grade level, and assigned to the tenth grade. He described himself to us as "possibly retarded."

We developed a program for Gerry based essentially on improving his self-concept. His I.Q. on a Slosson Intelligence Test was 125, in contrast to the 64 recorded on his ninth grade California Test of Mental Maturity. We shared this information with Gerry to help him see that his problem was reading, not intellect. Next, we set up a tutoring program in English and social studies. The main purpose of the tutoring was to increase his grades so that his self-image would improve. He began using a tape recorder to tape lectures in class and started to talk about his reading problem freely with teachers and other students. After work on employment application vocabulary words and interviewing techniques, Gerry went out and obtained a part-time job on his own. He was assigned a hall monitoring job in school, and was made the prime counseling assistant for students who wanted to drop out of school. In two months he retested on an informal reading comprehension test at fifth-grade level. No formal reading instruction, other than that with the application sight words, had taken place. Gerry won the Most Improved Junior Award at the end of his junior year. He graduated from high school after having been on the honor roll for three of the six marking periods of his senior year. Once his academic survival had been assured, we did work him into a structured reading program. During the two years he was in the reading program, his grade level went up five more years, to tenth grade on Gates-MacGinitie Form F. (Form E of the Gates-MacGinitie is used with students in seventh, eighth, and ninth grades. Form F is used with students in tenth, eleventh, and twelfth grades.) We remain convinced that his success was a direct reflection of the attention paid to affective concerns in his program.

It is interesting to note that affective concerns are rarely mentioned in the suggested designs of proposed secondary reading programs. Experts do occasionally mention self-pacing and self-selection when they are discussing individualization of instruction. The closest Bond and Tinker in their *Reading Difficulties* come to mentioning affective concerns is when they say, "Emotional disturbances are likely to accompany reading disability. In many cases, such maladjustment is due to frustration in the learning situation. The need of successful achievement is fundamental at all educational levels."[2] Daniel Fader is more explicit when he suggests that self-destruction is ". . . the only self-

2Guy L. Bond and Miles A. Tinker, *Reading Difficulties* (New York: Appleton-Century-Crofts, 1967), p. 6.

expression left to people who don't have anything else to say that anybody will listen to."[3] From these students come our discipline problems, dropouts, and societal rejects. "You're dumb. You can't say it right, so don't say it at all."[4] How can a young man or woman like this possibly see himself or herself as anything but a loser?

After a few months of teaching experience, you will have noticed many things that schools unconsciously do to reinforce the poor self-image of weak students: allowing unsupervised study halls and more freedom for the students earning high marks, choosing the better students for the fun things like ushering at concerts, working backstage, hosting foreign exchange students, and sending the better students on errands. Teachers don't deliberately decide to "put down" kids who have trouble with academics. "Rewarding" the faster and brighter students is simply more efficient: a teacher needs something done and so sends the first student who has free time. The students with the least ability are obviously not the first ones done, so they don't ever get to take attendance slips around or introduce the new student to the cafeteria. Students who get good grades probably don't need as much time in study halls to do their homework, right? The less able students, then, need more time to spend on more work since they don't master it the first time around! That's the theory. However, if you ask any experienced teacher which students use study halls less wisely in actual practice, he'll probably tell you the poorer students. While schools don't set out to dehumanize the weaker students, they may unwittingly contribute in subtle ways to these pupils' poor self-concepts.

The Influence of Home Environment on Self-image

It's not difficult to see why some students come to school with a poor self-image when the home environment is considered. Our experience tends to reinforce the notion that academically weaker students often come from economically and culturally deficient backgrounds. The parents may be separated. The mother may work and be too tired to chat with her children at night. The children represent responsibility and may be considered a burden. There may be constant hassles over money. Nutrition and appearance may be low on the priority list. There may be little control over the children at home. Since the only kind of discipline they know may be the physical kind, it is often difficult for them to accept discipline by reason at school. The parents of these students rarely call school; if they do, it may only be to give blanket permission to punish a child as necessary because "I can't handle him any more."

---

[3]Daniel Fader, *The Naked Children* (New York: Macmillan, 1971), p. 13.
[4]Fader, p. 13.

Since these children frequently come from homes where little emphasis is placed on values and where their personal opinions are not held in esteem, one of our biggest jobs as classroom teachers is to show that while we recognize they are deficient in skills, we do value their opinions. This rapport is difficult to establish because poor readers generally hate school (except when school is better than home), can't wait until they are sixteen so they can drop out, and don't trust adults—parents or teachers.

STRUCTURE AND RULES

Your job is to create a classroom climate that raises the level of the student with learning disabilities to that of a human being, a person able to deal with his own strengths and weaknesses realistically, but with pride and dignity. How are you going to start? First, by establishing very few rules. For youngsters who are accustomed to hearing *don't* much more often than *do,* this in itself represents a major environmental change! No more hollering; no long dittoed list of rules to be followed; no more threats. Keep it simple. We recommend two rules based on common sense: *Rule 1.* Bring a writing implement (don't say *pen* because then you'll have to waste too much time trying to enforce that!), and *Rule 2.* Don't interrupt when someone else is speaking. Two rules—that's all—but they are easily enforced because the students can accept that they are both reasonable.

Rules, of course, are most effective when the students have helped to write them. Depending on how clever you are at leading the class into doing what you want done, you may wish to have the students brainstorm a list of rules that you will write on the board. Generally, they will call out rules they have had in the past or rules that they accept as fair. Basically you want a class that is prepared to work (hence the need for a writing implement) and a room that is reasonably quiet and attentive. If you are clever, you can group most of the suggestions given to you by the students into the two categories you want. Anything to do with being prepared to work becomes Rule 1. Anything to do with courtesy, not talking during class, or disruptive behavior can become Rule 2.

Two rules are not difficult to enforce as long as you are consistent and as long as you enforce them in a positive way. For example, offer to keep a box in your drawer for students who think they may forget to bring pen or pencil. They may store their writing implements for your class in the box, and they will then never violate Rule 1.

Rule 2 takes a little more patience. No one, including you, may talk while someone else is speaking. Your silence while you wait for them to quiet down will be much more effective than yelling. It also shows that because you respect them enough to listen when they are speaking, you expect them to listen when you are talking. Treat one another with positive regard and simple courtesy, one human being to another.

Speaking of rules, be sure to avoid setting up a nitpicking array of rules such as last name first, assignments handed in at beginning of period only, and "If you talk once, you owe me fifteen minutes, twice, thirty minutes." Enforcing this kind of system becomes such a horrendous task that no learning takes place at all. You become more like a lion tamer than a teacher.

POSITIVE GRADING

After you have established your two rules, you are ready to move on in more positive ways. For example, always grade in an affirmative way. If a student misses two questions out of ten, write +8 instead of −2. You want to build on what the student knows, not what he doesn't know. There is nothing in the rulebooks that says every assignment has to have a possible 100 earned points. For example, if you give a quiz with twelve questions and a student misses three, you record +9/12 at the top of his paper. If he wants to convert that to a 100-based score, all he has to do is divide the possible into the actually earned points, thereby getting a math lesson as well. Such a grading system allows you much flexibility. You can convert your grades into whatever the local school district requires, but at the same time you keep it manageable and positive. At the end of a marking period, let's say you have a possible 312 earned points. One student earned 206, and 206/312 = 66. A 66 may not be considered a good grade in any school, but 206 earned points may represent a great deal of hard work to your student. His +206 out of 312 reflects effort, and it does not conjure up the image of a total failure. After all, he earned quite a bit! Even when you have a student who misses eight out of ten, it still sounds better to him if you say, "You got two right," instead of "You got eight wrong!"

In addition, our report cards have a separate column for effort. You can always soften the blow of a 66 with a high effort mark as long as the effort mark truly reflects the student's dedication. When you consider giving a grade for effort, keep a few things in mind. Effort grades can be given to boost sagging morale. They can also serve as motivation for improvement of a specific area of concern. Some years, you may have a class especially weak in skills. This class needs rewards all along the torturous route. When skills are particularly bad, however, be certain to spell out your effort goals clearly and limit your expectations. With one class you might just wish to improve attendance. If the class has averaged two days' absence out of every five, and you wish to reward the class as a whole if it makes an effort to improve its attendance, be sure the class knows what you want. Then reward them if that goal is achieved.

If your experience indicates that a particular unit you are teaching is unusually difficult, you may wish to cushion the impact of poorer grades by establishing an effort mark. This decision is done clearly to bolster sagging morale. Be certain, however, that you establish some goal as the criteria for earning the effort grade, for example, five out of the six assignments turned in on time. Even if the work is not of superior quality, it is possible for students to turn it in punctually. By doing this, you are following the basic rule of effort grading: Only give effort grades if they have been earned.

SEATING ARRANGEMENTS

When trying to develop affective concerns, be alert to the role of seating arrangements. The back-row junior high distractor becomes the senior high recluse. He has learned how to avoid drawing attention to himself. He is no longer climbing on the light fixtures; now he has become a nonperson, so quiet and hidden in the back row that you won't notice him. His very silence tells you a lot about him.

Then there is the student who is the follower. He sits next to a friend who is slightly more skilled than he is. If the teacher will not allow outright collusion, he plans a more subtle form of borrowing information—the furtive glance, or the pair may idly chatter while you are giving directions and then not be able to complete the assigned task. So seating arrangements can be distracting, as well as isolating.

You can, however, use seating in a positive way to improve a student's self-concept. If you are confident and feel sure of yourself in most discipline situations, then we suggest that you let the students choose their own seats. Let them know that you will only make changes if their behavior indicates changes are necessary. This places the burden of staying where they choose on them. If you need more structure and more time to get to know the chemistry of your class, assign the students to seats alphabetically. Tell them that after three weeks they may move to seats of their choice. This gives you time to learn their names, and it prevents them from developing the habit of chatting with their closest friends. We've generally found that by the time three weeks are up, and they are allowed their choice of seats, they will stay where they are.

By changing your teaching styles and shifting the students into pairs, teams, and groups according to topics, interests, skills, and social preferences, you can use seating to enhance self-image. Strong working with weak tends to improve both students. Outgoing working with shy tends to calm down the noisy one while encouraging the shy one to participate since it is only a group of two! Grouping allows the youngsters who don't know the answers to conceal their ignorance. For example, if you want the class to brainstrom a number of ways that the Soviet Union and the United States are similar, break the class into groups of four or five. Give them five minutes to come up with a list of ways in which the two nations are alike. Then ask, "Is there a group that has five or more items?" This way you are rewarding any group that has thought of at least five items, but you are not being punitive to the individual students in the groups who have not come up with five. Choose one group and list its items on the board. Then throw it open to other groups and ask, "Does any group have an item that this group didn't have?" This is yet another face-saving technique. One group may not have as many items as the first group, but it may have an item that the first group did not have. Grouping also allows the slower student who can't make any contribution a place of safety within a group. Being part of a less-than-perfect group is much better than being *the* stupid kid who didn't know the answer.

Assigning two students to work together sharing a dictionary, alternating vocabulary words, questioning one another in review for a test, or even copying outright does have advantages, for you as well as for the students. A tedious task is more fun if you work at it with a friend. Why do we teachers have to develop so many hang-ups over the idea of "cheating?" Why not make it acceptable for students to work together in some assignments? Just because they are laughing and having fun doesn't mean that learning isn't taking place. We don't mean to imply that all learning can be fun, but we do feel that occasionally adding a little variety to an otherwise arduous task does have its merits. Give a pair of students a list of vocabulary words to look up and use correctly in sentences. Suggest that they make their task easier by alternating words. Joe can take the odd words, and Tom can take the even words. When they have found all the definitions, have them switch and write the words in sentences, Tom taking the odd words, and Joe taking the even ones. This is a simple trick that can help to make a boring but necessary assignment more fun.

This kind of pairing can also lead to peer counseling. You can assign two students to work together with a deliberate purpose in mind. For example, if you know that Mary is upset and nervous about an approaching hospitalization, assign her to work with Helen, who you know had a good experience in the hospital last year. Our best dropout counselors have always been the students who dropped out, couldn't get jobs, didn't make it on their own, and returned to school. They "know the score" and are far more believable than any teacher or guidance counselor. When you have a student with a specific problem and know of another student who might be able to help, always be sure to ask the second student if he minds if you refer another pupil to him. This serves to remind the student that you value him and his thoughts, and shows that you will not violate his privacy without his permission. Such teacher-student respect is essential if you wish to enhance a student's self-image.

BUILDING SUCCESS INTO CURRICULUM

The single most important ingredient in enhancing student self-concept is the guarantee of success. Since you will be writing most of the study guides and other instructional materials, you can build that success into the curricular material itself. The criteria to keep in mind when your aim is to help your students succeed are:

1. Design curriculum on student *strengths* while keeping limitations in mind.
2. Design curriculum to meet student *needs*.
3. Design curriculum to meet student *interests*.

When you keep student strengths in mind, you can adjust instruction to individual differences. For example, with a class of students deficient in basic skills, start the year with oral instruction and move to the written work. This way, they have a chance to succeed initially because they have no written work for you to criticize. At the same time, sequence the material so that you move from the easier worksheets to the more difficult ones. Another way to help insure success is to number lines of print or paragraphs on your worksheets and then refer to those numbers in your questions or statements.

Extending the time for an assignment also enables you to cope with individual differences. Some youngsters just cannot complete an assignment in the given period and need encouragement to finish it at home. Even that task can be worded in a positive way: "You've made such a good start here, why don't you take it along with you so that you can wrap it up in peace and quiet?"

Avoiding unnecessary criticism also contributes to good self-image. For example, you don't have to hear *everything* that is said in the room. You can ignore insignificant comments and wisecracks made to a buddy. Your ego isn't on the line. You can afford to lose some small battles . . . better that than the whole war! When a student mutters to his neighbor that he thinks the worksheet is dumb, let it pass; deal only with major interruptions. For another example of unnecessary criticism, suppose that you are stressing the writing of complete sentences. You can emphasize the differences between fragments and complete statements, and avoid criticizing style or choice of words. If a student yells, "Hey, Teach!" don't draw attention to the fact that addressing you in such a manner is not very courteous. Put things in priority. The student is trying to get your attention. That usually means that he is attempting to work on the assignment and needs your help. Worry about his etiquette some other time. After you have gained his confidence and trust, you can suggest the substitution of *Mr. Smith* or *Ms. Jones* for *Teach*. After all, *Teach* may well be an affectionate term rather than a derogatory label.

Still another suggestion for building success into your curriculum is the idea of rewarding good behavior rather than punishing bad behavior. Emphasizing the positive can change attitudes about schoolwork. Give extra points for using correct punctuation. These points will go a long way toward making students feel good about themselves. Instead of taking off points for misspelled words, reward pupils with five extra points if they can write today's journal entry without any spelling errors. Allow your students an extra point every time they use a new vocabulary word. Bonus assignments and opportunities to gain extra rewards stimulate motivation. For a spectacular achievement, why not sell them time out of your class? "Because your book report was so well done, I'm awarding you a free period in the media center to listen to any records you want." Once you have built a good relationship with the class, set up a bank with extra-point coupons good for various rewards. Depending on the number of points the student earns, he can obtain a coupon worth an extra period in the weight lifting room, or a coupon entitling him to be student aide for a day to the school nurse, or a coupon worth a ten-minute head start for lunch. Some of the coupons should be for small rewards obtainable with a small number of points. That way, students who get few extra points can feel they've won something, and they can decide whether to cash in a small amount of points or save up points for a big reward. It doesn't matter what the payment is as long as the rewards are consistent, fair, and truly earned.

When you do create an opportunity for a student to shine, be careful to avoid artificial ploys or contrived situations. There are many instances, however, when you can use students' talents because you really need them. For example, in an English lesson on heroes, call on your motorcycle expert to contribute his knowledge of Evel Knievel. One member of the class may be particularly knowledgeable on the subject of rock music. His expertise can be a natural in a unit on poetry. Have you a student who is employed, so that he can bring in samples of application blanks and share with classmates his experiences in interviewing? Do you have a student from the Far East or a student whose father or uncle served in the Far East? He could bring oriental objects to class for the unit on Japan, China, or Indochina. Ask the student who is good with mechanical things to help you with the audiovisual equipment. Take advantage of the knowledge that some of your students have on cars, motors, and cycles to educate yourself. They can give you ideas before you make a major car purchase or tell you where to get the best body work done on a dented fender. If you're looking for a baby-sitter or for someone to mow your lawn, consider hiring a student who needs some "stroking," some noticing, some money! The subtle comments— "New sweater?", "Who was the cute date I saw you with at the movies Friday night?", "I miss having you in homeroom this year"—all contribute to the student's feeling that you notice him, you know he is alive, he counts. When you build opportunities for success into your classroom, you are becoming a specialist in achievement because your students will thrive and succeed.

THOSE SOLID BARRIERS

Despite all your efforts to improve your students' self-concepts, you must accept the fact that there are some barriers you cannot break down, because some teen-agers find it hard to admit they have difficulties, let alone accept help. This is occasionally compounded by the student's fear of his helper. Sometimes you may even be faced with the student who wants sympathy and support rather than help, because accepting help implies a commitment to change on his part. In a way, this type of student feels *safer* without skills.

Our best efforts are often stymied because we get caught in *telling* rather than *listening*. We also tend to increase pressure when the student resists. Our only advice when dealing with pupils who have developed an "I-can't-succeed-I-never-have" attitude is to remain consistent in your praise when it is merited and firm in your correction when it is needed. Try to place no conditions of worth on your students. Accept them as you find them and help them to build their own self-images rather than force them to emulate yours.

7 Vocabulary

What do you do after you have diagnosed your students, learned their strengths and weaknesses, and chosen most of the curricular material? The rest of part 2 will show you how to develop the kinds of materials we have been discussing.

Depending on the type of unit you are teaching, you may have various published materials to present. Even the best publishing houses, however, rarely provide adequate vocabulary material, so you will probably have to use your own. There are three steps to keep in mind as you develop this material: selecting, preteaching, and reinforcing.

Before your students can comprehend the reading material, they have to understand the words; therefore, *selecting* the important vocabulary words should be your first priority. *Preteach* these key words for the basic understanding of the unit. There may not be very many of these words, but they will be the core vocabulary necessary for comprehending the theme or main idea. For example, an entire biology unit can be built around one vocabulary word: *photosynthesis*. There is no need for a long list of words when real familiarity with one key concept word will help students comprehend the entire unit. Finally, various *reinforcement* exercises can be used to help the students really learn the words. We have found that simply having students look up a word in the dictionary, write the word in a sentence, and then take a quiz on the meaning does not help them remember the word in other contexts. Reinforcement exercises are valuable because they make the students use the word in many ways. This can help them remember the word for more than one week after the end of the unit.

SELECTING VOCABULARY

Let's assume that you want to teach a novel to your class. How do you select the vocabulary? The book is 212 pages long, and there are many words from which to choose.

First, don't choose all the thirteen-letter words just because they are there. There is probably no way you will be able to have the students learn all the words in the book, and if you try, you'll spend most of your time on vocabulary, instead of on the meaning of the book. As the next best approach, skim through the novel and choose those words that you feel your students may see in other subjects or that may help them in their daily lives. Vocabulary word power builders are also important. Words needed for a basic understanding of the theme, plot, or characters of the book should be added to the list. If your reading selection is short, keep the list of vocabulary words to a minimum. Don't overwhelm the students with a list of twenty words for a two-page short story. They will not be able to move past that gigantic list to concentrate on the meaning of the story.

For example, the word *negotiate* is important for understanding the plot of the play *A Raisin in the Sun*,[1] but this word was selected for other reasons as well. If any of the students listen to the news, even half-heartedly, they are sure to have run across the word many times, and because of its importance and frequency of use, it should be included in the vocabulary for this play.

If the book you are teaching is short or only moderately long, you can skim each page for the appropriate vocabulary words; however, if the book is very long, or if there are many words that the students may not know, you can skim every two or three pages. You may miss a few important words, but in the long run, you will find as many words as the students can handle.

PRETEACHING VOCABULARY

After you have previewed the book and have chosen the vocabulary words you wish to teach, you are ready to begin. Give the students a list of all the vocabulary words for the book, so they know what is expected of them. This kind of list works best if you structure it in the format shown in figure 13. It forces the students to use the dictionary. You may find that even seniors have only a vague idea of what various parts of speech mean. For example, they might use the word *inadequate* in the same manner as *inadequacies*. Therefore, a quick review of the parts of

[1]Lorraine Hansberry (New York: Signet Classics, 1958).

speech may be helpful when you are preteaching the vocabulary for the unit.

It is important that you have the students write the words in sentences. Then you can see if they truly understand the meaning of the part of speech. So many times the sentences our students produce have no relation to the vocabulary words that were assigned. We go over these words, parts of speech, and sentences with the students so they can hear how a well-constructed sentence sounds. Although we can't claim to have had a great deal of success with this method, at least the students have a chance to hear proper usage.

A word of caution about dictionaries: Try to find the easier ones that have been published more recently. Some of the dictionaries you may have in your room were probably published in 1912. The explanations in these older books can be obscure and difficult for the students to understand. We recommend *Webster's Intermediate Dictionary*.[2] The print is larger than that of the average dictionary. The part of speech is printed very clearly, and the most commonly used definition is listed first. The language of the definitions is easy to understand, and the students feel confident when they look up the word. This dictionary even includes a sentence in which the word is used in context.

After you have given the list of words to the students, choose the few words that are necessary to the understanding of the book. Stress these words in the context of the book before they begin reading so the words will be familiar when the students come upon them.

One method of stressing key concept words is to use vocabulary wheels. In *Lisa, Bright and Dark*[3] for example, *schizophrenia* is a major concept. By presenting the vocabulary wheel shown in figure 11, the teacher has the opportunity to introduce and discuss several words associated with mental illness and to have the students brainstorm additional terms. Through their reading of the novel and through further discussion, the students can help develop a more elaborate vocabulary wheel that provides many more associations for the original idea (see figure 12). Remember, the more frequent the contact, the more likely the retention.

Another example of preteaching using just one word is the following from a social studies unit on the British Isles. Write the word *island* on the board. To that word add *insular, isolated, alone,* and *independent*. After defining these words, ask the class to provide five situations in their own lives in which they have felt like "islands." From there you can move to the obvious question, "Why did you feel alone?" Allow time for classroom discussion, and then hand out four different worksheets, each describing a different island country. Divide the class into four groups, each taking one of these nations. Given the geography, economics, culture, and natural resources of their respective countries,

---

[2]Springfield, Mass.: G. & C. Merriam, 1972.
[3]John Neufeld (New York: S. G. Phillips, 1969).

Figure 11. Basic Vocabulary Wheel

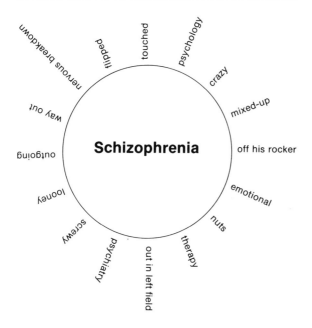

Figure 12. Advanced Vocabulary Wheel

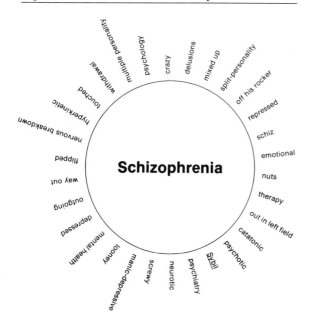

the four groups must respond to a problem. What do they need from one another? What do they have on their island that they can trade to obtain their goals? How can they retain their integrity while achieving national aims? Why is it so difficult to be an island? All of this should precede a reading assignment on the current problems facing Great Britain. In walking your students through such an exercise built around the key vocabulary word *island*, you are providing the general principles against which they will read the selection. The textbook assignment, then, becomes far more meaningful to the students when they have had advance preparations.

As you teach the words on the vocabulary list, stress any words that have common parts like prefixes or suffixes. In other words, pay attention to the structure of words. This is often a good way for students to remember related words and parts of speech. For example, if one of the words is *defiance*, mention related words like *defiant* and *defy*. A word like *misogynist* can be discussed on several levels. By separating the word into its parts, you can talk about the root *gyn* and the meaning *woman*. This can be widened to include other examples, like *gynecologist*, that have the same root. Following a discussion of the root, you can go on to prefixes and discuss *miso*. A quick look in a dictionary by you or one of the students will yield many other words that begin with this prefix and that can be used as examples. Then you can proceed to suffixes with an emphasis on *ist*. Explain that this means *one who is or does*, and then relate the meaning to *misogynist* (*one who hates women*) and *gynecologist* (*one who treats women*). With this method, the students will learn the word on the list and several other related words. Because they have talked about the words and used them in sentences, they will remember them longer. Always stress words the students can use later, or in other classes, or in daily life. If you can have a choice of words to select for the vocabulary list, always choose the word power builders, vocabulary on which you can build other related words with prefixes and suffixes.

Figure 13 shows the vocabulary list for *Black Like Me*.[4] This type of list would normally be given to the students before they begin reading the unit. Several points should be noted here. Numbering the spaces in each column is helpful to the student who has trouble tracking from left to right. He can see the word *flashback* in line 4, but if the sentence blank weren't numbered, he might write his answer in line 5. Lines between words also help the students separate the words. Don't be afraid to leave white space between words, even if this means you use more paper than you are supposed to! And turning the paper lengthwise leaves more room on the right side for writing sentences. Many of the students who have reading problems also have motor problems and cannot write in a tiny, confined space.

[4]John H. Griffin, 2nd ed. (Boston: Houghton Mifflin, 1977).

Figure 13. Vocabulary Sheet

BLACK LIKE ME   *Name:* _____

Find each word below in the dictionary. Write the part of speech and definition for each word. Then use the word in a sentence in the space provided.

Word	Part of Speech	Definition	Sentence
1. scenario			
2. pigmentation			
3. discrimination			
4. flashback			
5. desegregate			
6. mulatto			
7. dignity			
8. controversial			
9. antagonism			

The vocabulary list from *Man Without a Face*[5] (figure 14) is similar to the list in figure 13 with one exception. Next to each word in the first column is the page in the book on which the word can be found. This is helpful for the students and the teacher when discussing the word. Seeing the word used in context may enable a student to understand the meaning of the word on his own. The student feels a sense of accomplishment because he didn't have to rely on the dictionary. This also

[5]Isabelle Holland (New York: Bantam Books, 1972).

Figure 14. Vocabulary Sheet with Page Numbers

MAN WITHOUT A FACE   *Name:* _____

There are twelve words below. For each, write in the proper space what part of speech it is, your definition for it, and a sentence that contains the word.

Word	Part of Speech	Definition	Sentence
1. mania (72)			
2. demented (72)			
3. remote (85)			
4. miffed (85)			
5. putrid (95)			
6. tactless (97)			
7. inevitable (102)			
8. fracas (113)			
9. fallible (113)			
10. debased (118)			
11. inhospitable (127)			
12. judicious (138)			

teaches the skill of using the context for defining a word when a dictionary is not available.

We usually go over the vocabulary lists in class or have the students read the sentences they have written. Then we grade their sentences and provide the necessary corrections. Sometimes, however, it is beneficial to the students to see actual sentences with the vocabulary words used properly. Such a sheet is shown in figure 15. We then have the students

Figure 15. Vocabulary Words Correctly Used in Sentences

BLACK LIKE ME

1. The <u>scenario</u> of the play was very short because the play had only one act.
2. Because of the <u>flashbacks</u> she had, Valerie knew she had been in London before.
3. Because the <u>lighting</u> <u>technique</u> of the movie was poor, you couldn't see the faces of the actors.
4. After listening to the <u>dialogue</u> between the two people, I decided they were having a lovers' quarrel.
5. The <u>editing</u> of a movie is done at the end and is one of the most important parts in making a movie.
6. The <u>tone</u> of the film was dramatic, serious, and moving.
7. The <u>moral</u> of "Little Red Riding Hood" is never talk to strangers.
8. Many people in the South are <u>"white</u> <u>liberals"</u> and are happy to see blacks get more rights and better jobs.
9. The <u>"white</u> <u>intellectuals"</u> think they can use education to insult blacks.
10. John Griffin made the <u>transformation</u> to being black by darkening the <u>pigmentation</u> of his skin.
11. The <u>Deep South</u> has most of the problems concerning.
12. Anyone who can't get his rights has <u>second-class</u> <u>citizenship.</u>
13. There are laws now that forbid <u>discrimination</u> against anyone because of race or religion.
14. Many schools in the country have been ordered to <u>desegregate</u>, so they bus black students to all-white schools across town.
15. Sammy Davis, Jr., married May Britt, and their children are <u>mulatto.</u>
16. John Griffin was <u>"passing"</u> when he changed from white to black.
17. Street bums who don't have jobs and who drink all the time probably don't have much <u>dignity.</u>
18. Whether or not to legalize marijuana is a <u>controversial</u> issue in America today.
19. My sister showed <u>antagonism</u> toward me when she slammed my foot in the door.

compare our sentences with their own, and have them explain the differences in the usage of the words, the parts of speech, and the complexity of the sentences. Usually, our sentences have more contextual clues to help the students define and retain the words. Students' sentences generally are simple and often use the words incorrectly.

Another part of preteaching vocabulary words is to have the stu-

Figure 16. Syllabication Worksheet

Name: _____

Fill in the word or phrase from the following list that fits the definition and has the right number of letters and syllables.

body of speech	posture
body language	communication
extemporaneous	introduction
impromptu	conclusion

1. A way of speaking with your body: _ _ _ / _

   _ _ _ / _ _ _ _ _

2. A way of standing while speaking: _ _ _ / _ _ _ _ _

3. Transmitting verbal or written messages:

   _ _ _ / _ _ / _ _ / _ _ / _ _ _ _

4. Speaking on the spur of the moment without notes:

   _ _ / _ _ _ _ / _ _ / _ _ / _ _ / _ _ _

5. The beginning of a speech: _ _ / _ _ _ _ / _ _ _ _ / _ _ _ _ _

6. The main part of a speech: _ _ _ / _ _ _ _ _ _ _ _ _ _ _

7. The end of a speech: _ _ _ / _ _ _ _ / _ _ _ _ _

8. A kind of speech made with little preparation:

   _ _ / _ _ _ _ _ _ / _ _

dents divide them into syllables. They have been doing this since elementary school, but many of them still don't have the skill. To vary the task, we use a worksheet (figure 16) that gives a clue or part of the definition of the word, and a blank space for each letter in the answer, with slashes to show the syllabic divisions. In this way, the slower students have many clues—the definition, the number of syllables, and the number of letters in the word. Essentially, this task is one of matching. In the process, the student is thinking about the words and dividing them into syllables.

For the more advanced students, this exercise can be modified by providing the definition and a line for each syllable instead of for each letter:

A way of speaking with your body: _____ / __ _____ / _____

Yet another way to help the students develop syllabication skills is to use a syllable matching exercise (figure 17). The definitions are given on the right. Each word or phrase is three syllables long. The students must track from left to right through the chart to match the syllables that will form a word that fits the definition. This type of exercise teaches the students which groups of letters commonly combine to form syllables.

REINFORCEMENT WORKSHEETS

So far we have been talking about preteaching techniques. Next we will deal with reinforcement techniques. As the students are working on the content of a unit, they should be working simultaneously with the vocabulary words. If they study vocabulary words on the first day of a unit and then don't see them again until the day of review or the final test, we guarantee that they will forget them. Our reinforcement worksheets were developed to help the students use the words in many different situations, so they would have to think about the words. Of course, not all of these worksheets need be used in every unit. Maybe three or four could be chosen at a time. Remember, too much reinforcement is as bad as too little. The experienced, sensitive teacher can intuitively feel the saturation point of the students. There is a fine line between having too few worksheets and having so many that the students "turn off" at the idea of being passed another sheet of paper!

Parts of Speech

One way of combining skills in the English class is to develop vocabulary exercises that involve grammar skills. English teachers have

Figure 17. Worksheet for Syllable Matching Exercise

Name: _____

Choose one syllable from each of columns A, B, and C to make a word that fits the meaning given on the right. Write your answers in the space provided.

Meanings

A	B	C
im	clu	gy
eu	i	tact
eye	con	tion
con	flec	sion
per	lo	tu
re	promp	sion
ev	sua	dence
a	part	ment

1. Speech honoring the dead:

   _____

2. Coaxing someone to do something or to sell something: _____

3. Speech given on the spur of the moment with a few notes or with little time to think: _____

4. Reviewing or thinking over a topic:

   _____

5. Facts to prove your point:

   _____

6. Summary of a speech: _____

7. Looking at the whole audience:

   _____

always stressed the importance of knowing the parts of speech, and they usually feel this will help the students to write better. Even if this doesn't always work, exercises developed around this concept are valuable because they give the students some practice with the dictionary. Select words from your vocabulary list that have related forms in other parts of speech. Provide a verb, for example, and have the students supply the related noun and adjective. For the worksheet in figure 18, we chose verb, noun, adjective, and adverb. If it is the first time the students have seen this type of reinforcement sheet, we suggest that you provide an example by filling in all the forms for the first word. This assignment also has the advantage of being supportive, because the task

Figure 18. Worksheet Combining Vocabulary Reinforcement with Parts of Speech

A RAISIN IN THE SUN   *Name:* _____

Complete the chart below, placing the correct form of a vocabulary word in the appropriate part of speech column. Where there is no form of a word for a given part of speech, the word NONE has been written.

Verb	Noun	Adjective	Adverb
1. agitate	1. _____	1. _____	1. _____
2. _____	2. _____	2. emasculating	2. _____
3. _____	3. _____	3. _____	3. defiantly
4. _____	4. graft	4. NONE	4. NONE

is partially completed, has some success built in, and does not appear insurmountable.

A variation on the fill-in-the-blank format can be used to combine practice in parts of speech and using vocabulary words in sentences. In this exercise, the student is given a sentence with a word missing and a vocabulary word in different forms (see figure 19). The student must decide which word sounds best in the sentence and which part of speech works best in the sentence. This exercise also provides an example of the word used correctly in context.

Reasoning

Getting the students to think about how the vocabulary words are used in context is another way of reinforcing them. Have the pupils determine the logic of the words. We use a worksheet containing sentences in which vocabulary words are used illogically, and we ask the students to rewrite the sentences so they are logical. (See figure 20.)

You can take your students through this exercise step by step if they are unfamiliar with the pattern. First, give them completed examples, so they know what to do. After they have gone through these, let them do some on their own. Finally, you can ask the students to write their own illogical sentences and correct them. This step-by-step processing is

Figure 19. Worksheet Combining Parts of Speech and Use of Vocabulary Words in Sentences

---

LISA, BRIGHT AND DARK   *Name:* _____

Fill in the correct form of the vocabulary word to complete the sentence.

1. I like to (basking, bask) _____ in the sun.

2. We knew she had (palsy, palsied) _____ by the way she walked.

3. The teacher (censorship, censored, censoring) _____ his paper.

4. The (psychiatrist, psyche, psychedelic) _____ helped by listening to my story sympathetically.

5. There was a (rex, rule, regal, regally) _____.

6. She walked (rex, rule, regal, regally) _____.

7. His whisper was almost (inaudibility, inaudible, inaudibly)

    _____.

8. He was a (staunching, staunch) _____ supporter of the team.

9. He made a (realist, realistic, realistically) _____ decision.

10. He showed (indecision, indecisive, indecisively) _____ when he was unable to make up his mind.

---

essential; don't move immediately to the more advanced level of performance.

   Ask your students questions that use the vocabulary words to check their understanding of the meanings. For example:

   How might you *divert* a teacher's attention?
   List some things that are *vast*.
   A psychic often has *premonitions*. What is a psychic?
   If a man on the street *implores* you for a dime, what is he doing?
   Why would you feel *leery* if a loaded gun were pointed in your
        direction?

Figure 20. Vocabulary Worksheet Stressing Reasoning Skills

TWELVE ANGRY MEN   *Name:* _____

Each of the vocabulary words below is used in a sentence that is not logical. Rewrite the sentence so that the underlined word is used logically.

EXAMPLE: The parts were so complex that the toy was simple to put together.

CORRECTION: The parts were so complex that the toy was difficult to put together.

_____

1. Our unanimous decision was reached by a four-to-four tie vote.

   _____

   _____

2. We had a monopoly on the shoe repair business because there were four other shops in town.

   _____

   _____

3. Our rapport was so good that we fought all the time.

   _____

   _____

4. The proposition gives us no choice.

   _____

   _____

5. The hung jury found him guilty by a vote of 12–0.

   _____

   _____

6. The acquittal meant that he had to serve five years in jail.

   _____

   _____

7. He intimidated me so much that I loved to sit near him.

   _____

   _____

List some things that *bewilder* you.
What are some things that make your mother *shudder?*
What is one way to *stifle* a person?
When might you feel *rueful?*

As with anything, the more practice you've had, the better you are. The above questions can serve as the basis for much class discussion. They also provide more opportunities for student contact with the vocabulary words.

Synonyms and Antonyms

Synonyms and antonyms can also help to reinforce vocabulary. There are several variations we have found successful. The most common is to give one list of vocabulary words and a second list of either synonyms or antonyms. Then the student must do the matching. Some examples of this format are shown in figures 21 and 22.

We have also had good results with the format of listing the vocabulary words in the middle of the worksheet, with space on the left for a synonym and on the right for an antonym. An example is given in figure 23.

Once you have given your students enough of these worksheets so that they are familiar with more than the dictionary definitions of the words, you can go on to some more involved reinforcement exercises. Instead of simply using the dictionary meanings to complete the exercises, the students will now have to use more interpretive and applied levels of thinking.

Categorizing

Several kinds of categorizing skills can be developed, from easy to more difficult levels. One of the easiest for the students to understand is shown in figure 24. Provide a list of vocabulary words. Under the list of words, head several columns with the names of the various categories. The students must write the vocabulary words in the proper columns. Note that the exercise in figure 24 can also be used to review parts of speech.

As the students advance in their ability to categorize you can offer worksheets giving groups of four words chosen so that one of the words does not belong in the group. (See figure 25.) Some of the words in these groups may not be actual vocabulary words, but they should be related to the group of words in some way and should be words that the students know without the aid of a dictionary. (This helps build confidence.) The students must select the word in each group that does not belong. Be open minded, because some student may see a different

(continued on page 92)

VOCABULARY **89**

Figure 21. Vocabulary Worksheet Using Antonyms

Name: _____

Each of the vocabulary words in the list below is the <u>antonym</u> of one of the words or pairs of words in the numbered list. Write each antonym on the correct line.

impinge	undulate	subversive
ruse	affirmative	pestilence
vindicate	concede	retaliation
deplete	evade	dissonance
pinion	strenuous	facet
rakish	terse	plaintive
traitor	potential	

1. fact, reality *ruse*
2. humble *rakish*
3. deny, refuse *concede*
4. confront, prove *evade*
5. impossibility *potential*
6. accuse *vindicate*
7. honest, open *subversive*
8. hold firm, steady *undulate*
9. let alone, ignore *impinge*
10. easy *strenuous*
11. wordy, rambling *terse*
12. accept *retaliation*
13. health, sanitation *pestilence*
14. negative *affirmative*
15. whole *facet*
16. patriot *traitor*
17. enlarge *deplete*
18. consonance *dissonance*
19. arm *pinion*
20. happy, cheerful *plaintive*

Figure 22. Vocabulary Worksheet Using Synonyms and Associations

THE PIGMAN *Name:* _____

Some of the words in the following list are synonyms or words associated with the vocabulary words at the end of the worksheet. Write each synonym and/or words you associate with the vocabulary word on the line next to the vocabulary word. The first one is done for you. Words may be used more than once.

(continued)

Figure 22. *(continued)*

gestapo _police, hostility, enforcement, secret_

subliminally _____

avocation _____

thrombosis _____

depress _____

philanthropy _____

patron _____

disdain _____

antagonistic _____

perpetual _____

ingrate _____

interrogate _____

mundane _____

transformation _____

infantile _____

hovel _____

incongruous _____

edit _____

proficiency _____

police	gift	expert	house
continual	protector	unsuitable	inconsistent
babyish	mortal	hut	constant
revise	childish	free time	disagreeable
skilled	able	unaware	development
contempt	enforcement	lump	ordinary
conflict	coagulation	earthly	mismatched
hostility	subconsciously	hobby	test
restrain	secret	unpleasant	inquire
clot	scorn	examine	discord
hobby	arrogance	worldly	supporter
publish	permanent	change	hold back
variation			

Figure 23. Vocabulary Worksheet Using Synonyms and Antonyms

A RAISIN IN THE SUN   *Name:* _____

The vocabulary words are listed in the center column. Provide one synonym and one antonym for each vocabulary word.

Synonym	Vocabulary	Antonym
_____	idealist	_____
_____	desperation	_____
_____	outmoded	_____
_____	deplore	_____
_____	negotiate	_____

Figure 24. Vocabulary Worksheet Using Simple Categorization

Name: _____

Write each of the following vocabulary words in the correct column below.

proficiency   ingrate   patron
edited   perpetual   compensation
incongruous   avocation   syndrome
hovel   gestapo   philanthropy
infantile   nocturnal   repress
transformation   antagonistic thrombosis
mundane   disdain   subliminally
interrogate   maternal

Noun	Verb	Adjective	Adverb

Figure 25. Vocabulary Worksheet Stressing Criteria for Categories

Name: _____

One of the words in each group below does <u>not</u> belong in the group. <u>Circle</u> the word that does not belong. In the space below each group, write your own title for that group of words.

local	communication	propaganda
state	(plagiarism)	crusade
national	editorial	(editor)
(crusade)	message	opinion
_____	_____	_____

(foreign)	UPI	political
editor	(plagiarism)	editorial
copywriter	syndicated	(feature)
reporter	AP	opinion
_____	_____	_____

relationship among the words than you did. The beauty of this kind of exercise is that there is no set right answer, and the students feel less threatened.

This categorizing worksheet reinforces vocabulary words several ways. First, the students need to know the meanings of the words before they can tackle the exercise. Second, they must determine the relationship among the words. Third, they must generalize a topic for the three remaining words. We have found that these exercises generate quite a bit of class discussion if the class is allowed time to think about the words. Because students may see different relationships among the words, they have to find a way to defend their choices. This helps the students to develop logic and discussion skills.

As the students progress in their ability to handle more difficult categorizing worksheets, you can have them try to write groups of related words on their own. For example, in the worksheet in figure 26, we begin with several traditional categorizing examples in part A. Then in part B we provide the general category and numbered spaces for four words. The students must go to the general list of vocabulary words and choose some words to fit the group, taking care to have one word that is *not* a member. When we discuss the exercise later, each student has to defend his or her choice of words.

In part C we give the students one of the words in the group. They have to decide if they can find two other vocabulary words that belong with the word given or if the word given is the one that will not belong. This categorizing can also be used as a means of review prior to testing. If some of the vocabulary words pertain to a certain character, you can provide a group similar to the second one in part B of figure 26. Here, the students are forced to think about the character as well as about how some of the vocabulary words relate to that character. In the process, they may also be thinking about some of the events of the story.

Analogies

Perhaps the most difficult type of vocabulary reinforcement exercise for students to understand is the analogy. Unless they have been exposed to analogies before, they may have no idea what they are. Scholastic Book Services publishes several good books that have analogy exercises. Make certain that your students understand all the symbols in the analogy before you provide some simple exercises for practice such as:

Hot : cold   : :   up : _____
              down
              basement
              attic
              high

These analogies help the students to see the relationships between words and to review the meanings of words. It is possible to arrange the analogies on the worksheet so that they are clearer for the students. (We have already mentioned that for the slower reader, the more white space around the words, the better.) The following example is not very clear:

usurp : abdicate   : :   antagonistic :   a) sure
                                          b) pessimistic
                                          c) helpful
                                          d) angry

Figure 26. Vocabulary Worksheet Stressing Criteria for Categories (Advanced)

OF MICE AND MEN

Name: _____

Part A. One of the words in each group below does <u>not</u> belong in the group. Circle the word that does not belong. In the space below each group, write your own title for that group of words.

malicious	persuasive	inevitable
ferociously	insistent	(love)
(reassuring)	(understanding)	death
irritable	relentless	solemnly

_____   _____   _____
_____

Part B. In the following two groups, the title for the groups has been provided. Create your own category by writing three words that have something to do with the title and one word that does not belong.

1. _____   1. _____
2. _____   2. _____
3. _____   3. _____
4. _____   4. _____
Characteristics of Lennie   stereotype

Part C. Again, you are asked to create your own category. This time one word of the group has been provided. Provide the remaining three words, plus the title for the group. Be sure to circle the word that does not belong.

1. ___staccato___   1. ___concealing___
2. _____   2. _____
3. _____   3. _____
4. _____   4. _____
_____   _____

Figure 27 illustrates a much better way of setting up your analogy questions. The students should always have ample time to complete the worksheet, and there should be time for discussion afterwards. There are always questions and disagreements, and the healthy classroom is one in which the students feel encouraged to think and express their own opinions without threat of reprimand from the teacher.

Another advantage to using analogies is that you are providing valuable practice for your students with a type of question often used on entrance examinations for the military service, as well as on job placement and college entrance exams.

Figure 27. Vocabulary Worksheet for Analogies

OF MICE AND MEN   *Name:* _____

For each of the analogies below, choose the word that best completes the thought and write the letter of that word on the blank line.

_____ 1. rigid : flexible : : casual :   1. _C_
        a. concentrating
        b. informal
        c. formal

_____ 2. plaintively : sadly : : skeptically :   2. _a_
        a. doubtfully
        b. happily
        c. tragically
        d. lovingly

_____ 3. pantomime : charades : : maneuvers :   3. _b_
        a. homework
        b. battle
        c. family

_____ 4. flattered : praised : : confidential :   4. _C_
        a. concentrating
        b. casual
        c. with trust
        d. without charm

Vocabulary Power Through Word Parts

Another useful kind of reinforcement worksheet is the prefix, root, and suffix worksheet. Obviously, one of your goals in teaching vocabulary is to enable your students to recognize words in other contexts and to relate one word to another. This task becomes easier if the students can recognize words that have the same roots, prefixes, or suffixes. A reinforcement worksheet that helps students examine the vocabulary words in light of their parts is called a word power builder since so many other words can be formed from the parts. The examples range from the elementary to the more complex. We show only a few of the many kinds of possibilities in this area. Figure 28 simply asks the students to fill in the correct vocabulary word. A follow-up discussion of the worksheet could emphasize the role that the prefix plays in each word's definition. Figure 29 illustrates a slightly higher level of thinking about prefixes. The students are asked to match a prefix with a root to form a vocabulary word. This is a valuable exercise for students who do not understand the importance of the parts of words. In figure 30 the students must apply more of their knowledge about prefixes. Not only must they use a dictionary, but they must also choose the most applicable vocabulary words for the exercise. If they choose vocabulary words that don't have many root derivatives, they will have difficulty. This worksheet also asks them to find the meaning of the root, which may require some investigative dictionary skills.

Figures 31 and 32 deal with combining roots with prefixes and suffixes. The student must take apart the word and then reassemble a new word. This is a higher-level activity. Many students have a difficult time visualizing anything other than what is on the printed page. This forces them to try some new combinations and experiment with new words.

In Figure 33, the directions for the worksheet are probably the most formidable aspect of the task. Once the students understand exactly what is expected, they will most likely go ahead and do very well. This exercise provides practice with meanings, roots, suffixes, and prefixes, and gives the students practice in taking words apart and putting them back together again.

REVIEW WORKSHEETS

All of the examples in the last part of this chapter can be used as a means of review. Some of the sheets also incorporate other skills, such as following directions. Whenever possible we try to combine skills in our worksheets so that students can practice following directions or finding the main idea at the same time that they are reviewing vocabulary words or the important ideas of the story.

(continued on page 102)

Figure 28. Vocabulary Worksheet Stressing Words with Prefixes

Name: _____

Below is a list of vocabulary words followed by twenty numbered definitions. Choose the word that best fits each definition, and write the word on the blank line next to the definition.

preview	perform	permit
remove	appraise	replant
transform	translate	foreman
perfume	unjust	deport
transfuse	import	improve
appoint	forehead	transmit
prolong	refuse	

1. To take away: *remove*
2. Something that smells sweet: *perfume*
3. To name officially: *appoint*
4. To act; to do: *perform*
5. To turn into one's own or another language: *translate*
6. The part of the face above the eyes: *forehead*
7. To allow: *permit*
8. The chief man: *foreman*
9. To make better: *improve*
10. To decline to accept: *refuse*
11. To send out either by radio waves or over a wire: *transmit*
12. To send a person out of the country: *deport*
13. To plant again: *replant*
14. To bring from a foreign country: *import*
15. Without fairness: *unjust*
16. To set a value on: *appraise*
17. To lengthen in time: *prolong*
18. To transfer blood into the vein of a man or animal: *transfuse*
19. To change the form of: *transform*
20. To see beforehand: *preview*

Figure 29. Vocabulary Worksheet on Prefixes and Roots

Name: _____

Below are some prefixes and root words. You can make at least thirty-nine words by combining a prefix and a root word, in that order. You may use the dictionary. For example, you could combine <u>ap</u> and <u>point</u> to make <u>appoint</u>. You may not change the spelling of the prefix or the root to make a word. When you finish finding the thirty-nine words, see if you can fit twenty of the words with the definitions on the next page.*

Prefixes

ap	per
be	pre
de	pro
fore	re
im	trans
in	un

Roots

form	little	point
fume	long	port
fuse	man	praise
head	mit	prove
just	move	view
late	plant	

1. appoint
2. appraise
3. approve
4. behead
5. belittle
6. belong
7. deform
8. defuse
9. deport
10. forehead
11. foreman
12. implant
13. import
14. improve
15. inform
16. infuse
17. perform
18. perfume
19. permit
20. preview
21. prolong
22. reform
23. refuse
24. relate
25. reman
26. remit
27. remove
28. replant
29. report
30. reprove
31. review
32. transform
33. transfuse
34. translate
35. transmit
36. transplant
37. transport
38. unjust
39. unman

*This worksheet, not reproduced here, would consist of the twenty numbered definitions in Figure 28 without the preceding list of words.

Figure 30. Vocabulary Worksheet Stressing Root Derivatives

HEY, DUMMY   *Name:* _____

Choose five words from the vocabulary words. Write as many words as you can find that are built from the same root word as the one you have chosen. You may use the dictionary. <u>Monotony</u> is used as an example. Find the meaning of the root you choose.

1. monotony	2. _____	3. _____	4. _____	5. _____
monogram	_____	_____	_____	_____
monologue	_____	_____	_____	_____
monoplane	_____	_____	_____	_____
monopoly	_____	_____	_____	_____
monosyllable	_____	_____	_____	_____
monotheism	_____	_____	_____	_____
monotone	_____	_____	_____	_____
monarchy	_____	_____	_____	_____
monastery	_____	_____	_____	_____
monk	_____	_____	_____	_____
monotonous	_____	_____	_____	_____
mono = one	_____ =	_____ =	_____ =	_____ =

Figure 31. Vocabulary Worksheet on Combining Prefixes and Roots

Name: _____

Below are twelve words. Each word has two syllables. First, divide the words into syllables. Then see how many new words you can make by matching the beginning syllable of one word (the prefix) with the ending syllable of another word (the root). For example, <u>subject</u> is divided into <u>sub</u> and <u>ject</u>. <u>Admit</u> is divided into <u>ad</u> and <u>mit</u>. By combining <u>sub</u> with <u>mit</u>, you can make the word <u>submit</u>.

subject	invent	refuse	admit
produce	contest	absent	define
digest	elate	exhale	verdict

(continued)

Figure 31. (*continued*)

1.	abject	15.	induce
2.	advent	16.	inhale
3.	confine	17.	inject
4.	confuse	18.	profuse
5.	conject	19.	project
6.	consent	20.	protest
7.	convent	21.	reduce
8.	deduce	22.	refine
9.	defuse	23.	reject
10.	deject	24.	relate
11.	detest	25.	remit
12.	dilate	26.	resent
13.	eject	27.	submit
14.	indict		

Figure 32. Vocabulary Worksheet on Roots and Suffixes

Name: _____

Below are some root words and suffixes. See how many words you can make by combining a root and suffix in that order. You may use a dictionary.

Roots				Suffixes		
depart	change	edit		ion	ure	ous
month	danger	impress		dom	ance	ive
laud	cost	boy		ment	ern	ly
mission	recover	appear		ary	ish	iss
hand	object	arrange		y	able	ful

1. _____		12. _____	
2. _____		13. _____	
3. _____		14. _____	
4. _____		15. _____	
5. _____		16. _____	
6. _____		17. _____	
7. _____		18. _____	
8. _____		19. _____	
9. _____		20. _____	
10. _____		21. _____	
11. _____		22. _____	

Figure 33. Vocabulary Worksheet on Combining Prefixes, Roots, and Suffixes

Name: _____

THE BOY WHO COULD MAKE HIMSELF DISAPPEAR

Below are listed prefixes, suffixes, and root words and their meanings. You are to use these word parts to "assemble" words from your vocabulary list. To assemble each word, place each word part and its meaning in the correct column, and the meaning of the assembled word in its column. Some word parts may be used more than once. One has been done for you. Not every word you make must have all three parts.

Prefixes	Roots	Suffixes
sub-, under	side, settle	-ic, like
pre-, before	thrall, press, trap	-ate, cause to
in-, in, at, not	litho, stone	-ity, condition of
en-, make, cause to	tense, stretch	-ive, tending to
per-, through	cept, understand, feel	-ous, full of
mono-, one	dolent, feel pain	
	histrio, actor	
	sarcas, speak bitterly	
	contempt, despise	
	deris, ridicule	
	tens, aim	
	humili, humble	

Prefix and Meaning	Root and Meaning	Suffix and Meaning	Assembled Word and Meaning
mono-, one	litho, stone	-ic, like	monolithic, like one stone (solid)

The worksheet in figure 34 combines following directions with reviewing vocabulary words. Some of the words in each group of three are from the vocabulary list. Some are not; however, they all relate to one another. The student may also follow the directions and find the letters that spell the general heading. Even though they are scrambled, most students don't have too much trouble finding the heading once they have all the letters. One word of caution for this type of worksheet: This *will not* work if the teacher has made some mistakes in the numbering. Double-check to make sure the students won't run into any incorrect letters that could alter the final answer.

Figure 35 provides a way to change the boredom of simply reviewing words and definitions into the challenge of solving the magic square. Math- and science-oriented students especially like this kind of puzzle. The magic number can be changed so that if you use this idea more than once a year, the students are not able to transfer the answers from one puzzle to another. Be sure to give an example to reinforce the directions for those students who may have difficulty.

Figure 36 is a worksheet that combines the skill of following directions with a review of the facts and vocabulary words of a story. The students are forced to be accurate. If they're not, they probably won't come out with the correct message at the end. Granted, once they get down toward the bottom of the sheet, they may be able to decipher the message, but most students will go on to the end just for the satisfaction and curiosity of doing so.

Many students hate unscrambling words. Some find it nearly impossible to do; however, a short worksheet in unscrambling like the one in figure 37 can be beneficial. The students are forced to think about the definitions and to try to form syllables that work. They may also become aware of a prefix or suffix that was unclear before.

If you feel very creative while you are making up your vocabulary review worksheets, you might try composing a short story or poem containing blank lines in which the students must write missing vocabulary words. (See figure 38.) Keep the story to a manageable length so the students don't lose the plot line. If possible, put the list of vocabulary words to be used in the story on a separate sheet of paper so the students don't have to keep flipping back to the first page to find the words.

Figure 39 shows a worksheet that combines vocabulary review and spelling practice. It also is a task that you should tackle only if you have a great deal of time. Once again, try to put the clues on a separate sheet of paper so the students can refer back and forth more easily.

Crossword puzzles are always popular. They take some time to construct, but you'll find that the more puzzles you do, the easier they will be to organize. A sample puzzle appears in figure 40.

The puzzle in figure 41 is a variation of the crossword puzzle. You can use your ingenuity and apply these ideas to your subject matter. In this example, we were studying *A Raisin in the Sun*. Although many students were oblivious to the significance of the form of this worksheet (note the drawing of the raisin inside the sun!), the variety in form was a welcome change from the usual study guide format.

Careful selection of words, preteaching of troublesome or especially important words, reinforcement worksheets during the unit, and review sessions that combine vocabulary skills can help students learn and retain vocabulary words. There is no guarantee, of course, but we have had more success with this method than with the traditional method. Try it and judge for yourself!

Figure 34. Worksheet Combining Vocabulary Review with Following Directions

LILIES OF THE FIELD   *Name:* _____

Under each blank below, you will find several words listed. You are to identify the category to which these words belong and write its name on the blank provided. To help identify the category, you may find all of the letters in the word by following these simple directions. There are single numbers (15, for example) and double numbers (4–3, for example) under each set of words. To the left of each single or double number is a blank. A single number refers to a letter of the alphabet (15, for example, refers to the letter O); a double number refers to a letter in the list of words (4–3, for example, refers to the fourth letter in the third word from the left). You are to find each letter so identified, then unscramble all the letters to spell the name of the category you are seeking.

1. _____

      incomprehensible   fruitless   desolate

____ 23   ____ 7–1   ____ 6–3

2. _____

      shrewd   aggressiveness   prominent

____ 1–3   ____ 12   ____ 9–3   ____ 3   ____ 1–2

____ 3–3   ____ 8–2   ____ 5–3   ____ 8–2   ____ 6–3

3. _____

      sustain   excavation   culture

____ 6–3   ____ 6–1   ____ 3–1   ____ 2–1   ____ 10–2

Figure 35. Vocabulary Worksheet with Magic Square Puzzle

OF MICE AND MEN   *Name:* _____

Match each of the vocabulary words in the column on the left with the correct definition in the column on the right. After you have written the correct numbers on the lines next to the definitions, place the number that is next to each definition in the box with the correct letter in the puzzle below. (Not all the definitions have a box.) When you are finished, all the numbers in the boxes will add up to the same number whether you add across each row or down each column. That number is the magic number.

1. tules   _____ a. stiff, stern; like a board

2. visible   _____ b. hold back; stop

3. skeptically   _____ c. seriously; with respect

4. rigid   _____ d. persistently; demanding notice

5. flattered   _____ e. skillful movements

6. impressed   _____ f. feeling certain of success

7. confidently   _____ g. hateful; vicious

8. pantomime   _____ h. can't be avoided or prevented

9. restrain   _____ i. convincing; making someone believe something

10. maneuvers   _____ j. boring

11. apprehension   _____ k. copy; communicate without words

12. reassuring   _____ l. complimented

13. malicious   _____ m. motion with parts of the body

14. insistently   _____ n. restoring confidence

15. persuasive   _____ o. influenced deeply

16. staccato   _____ p. dread; fear of the future

17. inevitable   _____ q. weeds by a river

18. gesture   _____ r. can be seen

19. monotonous   _____ s. doubtfully

20. solemnly   _____ t. short, sharp movements or sounds

Figure 35. (*continued*)

a 4	b 9	c 20	d 14
e 10	f 7	g 13	h 17
i 15	j 19	k 8	l 5
m 18	n 12	o 6	p 11

The magic number is __47__ .

Figure 36. Worksheet Combining Practice in Following Directions with Review of Vocabulary and Facts

HEY, DUMMY Name: _____

Follow each instruction carefully and write your answers on the blank lines. When you reach the end of the worksheet, you will find a message. You may use your book if you wish.

1. Write the title of the book by Kin Platt. _Hey Dummy_

2. Write the title as one word with no capital letters. _heydummy_

3. If there were three children in Neil's family, cross out the h. If there were two children in Neil's family, change the d to g. _heygummy_

4. The setting of this book is California. If this is true, change the m's to n's. If this is false, cross out the m's. _heygunny_

5. If Desdemona suffers from schizophrenia, cross out a y. If Desdemona suffers from autism, change the first vowel to o. _hoygunny_

6. Alan calls a football a throwkick. If this is true, add two t's on the end. If this is false, cross out the h. _hoygunnytt_

7. If Mr. Alvarado is a Puerto Rican and lives in the ghetto, add an s at the beginning. If Mr. Alvarado is a Chicano and lives in the barrio, change the first y to c. _hocgunnytt_

8. Alan has never been in trouble much. If this is true, cross out all the vowels. If this is false, switch the h and c around. _cohgunnytt_

9. If Neil's parents hate him, change the h to an n. If they hate Susie, change the o to x. _congunnytt_

10. If Neil is fourteen and Alan is twelve, add an l after the second vowel. If Alan is thirteen and Neil is twelve, add an r after the third vowel. _congunnyrtt_

Figure 36. (*continued*)

11. Does <u>inter</u> mean <u>between or among</u>? If so, cross out the third <u>n</u>. If not, add a <u>b</u> to the beginning. *Congunytt*

12. Neil's mother works in a bakery. If this is true, cross out the <u>o</u>. If this is false, add two <u>a</u>'s at the beginning. *aacongunytt*

13. Is this book written from the personal point of view? If so, change the <u>y</u> to <u>ol</u>. If not, change the <u>a</u> to <u>u</u>. *aacongunoltt*

14. The root of <u>humanity</u> is <u>human</u>. If this is true, add <u>si</u> after the second <u>t</u>. If this is false, cross out the <u>r</u>. *aacongunolrttsi*

15. If Mr. Alvarado disappoints Neil when he comes for help, place one of the <u>t</u>'s <u>before</u> the <u>u</u>. If Mr. Alvarado is always helpful to Neil, cross out a <u>t</u>. *aacongtunoltsi*

16. Alan is shot by a policeman. If this is true, add an <u>ra</u> after the <u>u</u>. If this is false, do nothing. *aacongratulnoltsi*

17. If Neil's last words in the book are "Aaaah!" switch the second <u>t</u> and second <u>n</u> around. If his last words are "Please listen, Dummy," don't do anything. *aacongratultornsi*

18. Does <u>mani</u> mean <u>many</u>? If so, add an <u>l</u> to the end. If it means <u>hand</u>, place the <u>i</u> after the second <u>t</u>. *aacongratultiorns*

19. Was it a mistake for Neil to tie Alan's feet together? If so, drop the first <u>a</u> and place the second <u>a</u> between the <u>l</u> and the <u>t</u>. If not, cross out an <u>a</u>. *Congratulatiorns*

20. Neil is completely alienated at the end of the book. If this is true, drop the second <u>r</u>. If this is false, start over again with instruction no. 1. *Congratulations*

Figure 37. Worksheet with Scrambled Vocabulary Words

MAN WITHOUT A FACE   Name: _____

Below are eighteen scrambled vocabulary words. Unscramble the words and write each unscrambled word and its number on the line next to the correct definition.

1. aniam	7. difmfe	13. dtpiur
2. leertnav	8. luml	14. ltseacts
3. pirroyti	9. yspmndueo	15. blllafie
4. crsait	10. siteloh	16. vnibeelait
5. bihinti	11. mdsena	17. sujicdiou
6. ssperre	12. mertoe	18. craafs

inhibit   a. stop, slow the growth of something

pseudonym   b. false name

relevant   c. to the point; important to what is going on

remote   d. distant; far off

mull   e. think over

fracas   f. noisy fight

inevitable   g. can't be avoided

hostile, miffed h. angry; mean

judicious   i. wise; showing sound judgment

priority   j. order of importance

repress   k. cut down; stop

fallible   l. able to make mistakes

amends   m. payment for injury or loss

putrid   n. rotten; foul-smelling

tactless   o. not saying the right thing

Figure 38. Vocabulary Worksheet Using Story with Missing Words

MAN WITHOUT A FACE   *Name:* _____

Fit the vocabulary words in the list below into the story that follows.

Oedipus complex	repressed	remote
manipulate	reactionary	miffed
relevant	racist	putrid
amends	hostile	tactless
priority	inequity	inevitable
inhibited	deduction	fracas
speculate	turmoil	fallible
mulled	equivalent	debased
alternative	manias	inhospitable
pseudonym	demented	judicious

THE CHIPMUNK AND THE WORM

Once upon a time, Charles Chipmunk was returning home after a long trip. Many problems had _____*inhibited*_____ his journey. Charles was resting by a stream, and he _____*mulled*_____ over the things that had happened to him. Charles had left home because his psychiatrist had been concerned about Charles's _____*Oedipus Complex*_____, his deep attachment to his mother. The cure was to go on a vacation to a _____*remote*_____ place, far from everyone. Charles's _____*alternative*_____ had been to go to a mental hospital for _____*demented*_____ chipmunks. When he thought about having to go to a mental hospital to live with other chipmunks, moles, and gophers that had _____*manias*_____ and did weird things, he decided to take the trip. A trip seemed to be the most _____*judicious*_____ way to forget about his mother.

He had only traveled two miles from the hole of his birth when he met a raccoon going in his direction. The raccoon was filthy because he had just been in a _____*fracas*_____ with a dog and a cat. The

(continued)

Figure 38. *(continued)*

raccoon seemed _____*hostile*_____ and angry, so Charles tried to make conversation.

"Gee, you sure smell _____*putrid*_____!" exclaimed Charles in his usual _____*tactless*_____ manner.

The raccoon was _____*miffed*_____ at Charles's comment and said, "You wouldn't smell too good either if you had just defended your garbage can against the enemy. Besides, I never have anything to do with the lower animals like dogs, cats, and chipmunks. Get out of my way, you moron."

The raccoon pushed Charles into a large mud puddle as he waddled by. Not being much of a swimmer, Charles sputtered and splashed his way to the edge of the road. The raccoon had _____*debased*_____ Charles, so he felt very small. He began to _____*speculate*_____ about the rest of his trip and and wondered if he should run home to his mother; however, the thought of the mental hospital changed his mind.

So Charles made the _____*deduction*_____ that he should continue on his trip. Later that afternoon as he rested, scraping the mud from between his toenails, he spied a very worried-looking worm. Because he was somewhat of a _____*racist*_____, and he didn't have much to do with worms, Charles almost didn't speak. The worm looked so miserable that Charles _____*repressed*_____ a desire to step on him and said instead,

"My, my, a wiggly worm. What are you doing on this road? Aren't there enough puddles?"

"Oh, sir, please don't hurt me. I was on my way to grandmother's when a large raccoon stepped on me and tore my tail off. Now, I'm only half instead of whole."

Being a _____*reactionary*_____ and wishing for the old days when worms had no right to be on the road, Charles granted, "Well, it was probably your own fault. Raccoons are _____*fallible*_____, and he just didn't see you. You should act like worms did fifty years ago when there was _____*inequity*_____, and worms weren't allowed anywhere but mud puddles. Be thankful you are a half and not dead instead."

Without trying to make _____*amends*_____ for hurting the worm's feelings, Charles scampered away.

Figure 38. (*continued*)

Charles's top _priority_ had been to reach safely his family's summer tree, where he could be alone and think. Four days and nights later, he recognized the familiar bark, and he snuggled into the nest of acorns. After two months of meditation, he felt he had changed his attitude toward his mother so he decided to return home.

Now, as he sat by the stream daydreaming of the past several months, he was suddenly jolted by a terrible _turmoil_ . Birds were screeching, fish were chattering, and trees were roaring. It was _inevitable_ that Charles would jump up and dart around looking for the problem. A few hundred yards ahead of him, Charles saw a mass of marching worms. They were led by the half wiggly worm Charles had insulted earlier. Each worm was _equivalent_ in size to a loaf of bread. Charles was terrified. He raced to a nearby tree, but it shut its branches and was quite _inhospitable_ . Charles then tried to _manipulate_ some rocks and nuts to throw as weapons, but he was all paws.

The worms advanced, and Charles was concerned. The half wiggly worm in front shouted, "You were terrible to me. You didn't say one _relevant_ thing to help me out of my misery. You deserve to die!"

Charles thought of the hole of his birth, his brothers and sisters, his last acorn meal, and especially his mother, whom he still loved passionately. As he drew his breath in to speak in his defense, one of the larger worms swallowed him up.

MORAL: Don't try to run away from problems. You may meet worse problems before you solve the first ones.

or

Don't treat people like worms, or you may get swallowed up by your own prejudice.

THE END

Figure 39. Puzzle Worksheet for Vocabulary Review

Name:

There are eighty-three words hidden in the puzzle below. Some of them are vocabulary words from the public-speaking unit. Use the clues on the following pages to find them. The words are spelled from left to right in rows 1–15 and from top to bottom in columns 16–29. Write each word you find on the line next to its clue.

	16	17	18	19	20	21	22	23	24	25	26	27	28	29
1	R	I	P	O	S	T	U	R	E	V	I	E	W	S
2	E	R	I	R	S	E	C	O	N	D	U	C	T	U
3	P	A	N	T	I	M	C	W	D	A	R	H	O	E
4	E	X	T	E	M	P	O	R	A	N	E	O	U	S
5	A	E	R	L	P	E	M	O	M	E	F	C	R	Y
6	T	C	O	L	L	R	M	M	E	U	L	O	G	Y
7	B	O	D	Y	I	S	U	A	T	P	E	Y	E	S
8	O	N	U	O	C	U	N	N	J	O	C	E	L	L
9	D	C	C	U	I	A	I	C	O	N	T	A	C	T
10	Y	L	T	T	T	S	C	E	H	D	I	R	H	R
11	E	U	I	H	Y	I	A	T	N	E	N	T	U	Y
12	A	D	O	N	T	O	T	H	E	R	G	I	R	L
13	R	E	N	T	O	N	I	P	U	B	L	I	C	O
14	L	J	I	M	P	R	O	M	P	T	U	M	H	O
15	Y	E	V	I	D	E	N	C	E	A	B	O	U	T

Figure 39. (*continued*)

CLUES AND ANSWERS

Row 1.   a word meaning to steal _____ *rip* _____

        carriage or bearing _____ *posture* _____

        preparing for a test _____ *review* _____

        opinions _____ *views* _____

Row 2.   what comes after first _____ *second* _____

        behavior _____ *conduct* _____

        a tube or pipe _____ *duct* _____

Row 3.   a type of suit _____ *pant* _____

        a small bug _____ *ant* _____

        boy in our class _____ *Tim* _____

        garden tool _____ *hoe* _____

Row 4.   a speech made without notes _____ *extemporaneous* _____

        past tense of run _____ *ran* _____

Row 5.   nickname for mother _____ *mom* _____

        opposite of smile _____ *cry* _____

Row 6.   speech made at a funeral _____ *eulogy* _____

Row 7.   a type of language _____ *body* _____

        important contact during speech _____ *eyes* _____

Row 8.   small room in prison _____ *cell* _____

Row 9.   relationship or touching _____ *contact* _____

        saying things in a nice way _____ *tact* _____

Row 10. no words

Row 11. no words

Row 12. antonym for do _____ *don't* _____

Row 13. fee paid to live in apartment _____ *rent* _____

        2000 pounds _____ *ton* _____

        antonym for private _____ *public* _____

        nickname for a bar _____ *pub* _____

(*continued*)

Figure 39. (*continued*)

Row 14. character in <u>Tuned Out</u> _____ *Jim*
   unplanned speech _____ *impromtu*
   a nuisance _____ *imp*
   synonym for junior dance _____ *prom*
Row 15. supporting facts _____ *evidence*
   approximately _____ *about*
   antonym for in _____ *out*
Col. 16. boy in our class _____ *Arly*
   say something over again _____ *repeat*
   type of moss _____ *peat*
   antonym for fast _____ *eat*
   type of language _____ *body*
   annually _____ *yearly*
   365 days _____ *year*
   needed to hear _____ *ear*
Col. 17. initials for Irish rebels _____ *IRA*
   to end speech _____ *conclude*
Col. 18. two cups _____ *pint*
   beginning of speech _____ *introduction*
   small pipe or tube _____ *duct*
Col. 19. antonym for keep secret _____ *tell*
   antonym for in _____ *out*
   antonym for old age _____ *youth*
Col. 20. uncomplicatedness _____ *simple*
   antonym for country _____ *city*
   antonym for bottom _____ *top*
Col. 21. display of anger _____ *temper*
   convincing _____ *persuasion*
Col. 22. exchanging ideas _____ *communication*
   feline _____ *cat*

Figure 39. (*continued*)

Col. 23. move a boat _____ *row* _____

story about love _____ *romance* _____

synonym for male _____ *man* _____

Col. 24. synonym for finale _____ *end* _____

synonym for female _____ *dame* _____

past tense for meet _____ *met* _____

character in *Black Like Me* _____ *John* _____

Col. 25. a person from Denmark _____ *Dane* _____

antonym for under _____ *on* _____

synonym for think _____ *ponder* _____

small body of water _____ *pond* _____

Col. 26. thinking back _____ *reflecting* _____

type of metal _____ *tin* _____

sound associated with drowning _____ *glub* _____

Col. 27. repeated sound _____ *echo* _____

shy in a flirting way _____ *coy* _____

slang for yes _____ *yea* _____

365 days _____ *year* _____

needed for hearing _____ *ear* _____

painting, sculpture, etc. _____ *art* _____

Col. 28. a trip to Europe _____ *tour* _____

antonym for their _____ *our* _____

place of worship _____ *church* _____

Col. 29. girl's name _____ *Sue* _____

takes to court _____ *sue* _____

to put out effort _____ *try* _____

stolen items _____ *loot* _____

Figure 40. Vocabulary Crossword Puzzle

Name: _____

ACROSS

1. unsure; uncertain
3. split personality
5. sunbathe
7. kingly; royal
9. what you do in a race
10. realizing something after it has occurred
11. doctor trained in dealing with mental illness
12. inability to move; paralysis

DOWN

2. not able to be heard
3. loyal; trustworthy
4. person who tells it like it is
6. it opens doors
8. eliminating offensive parts of a movie
9. see 4 down

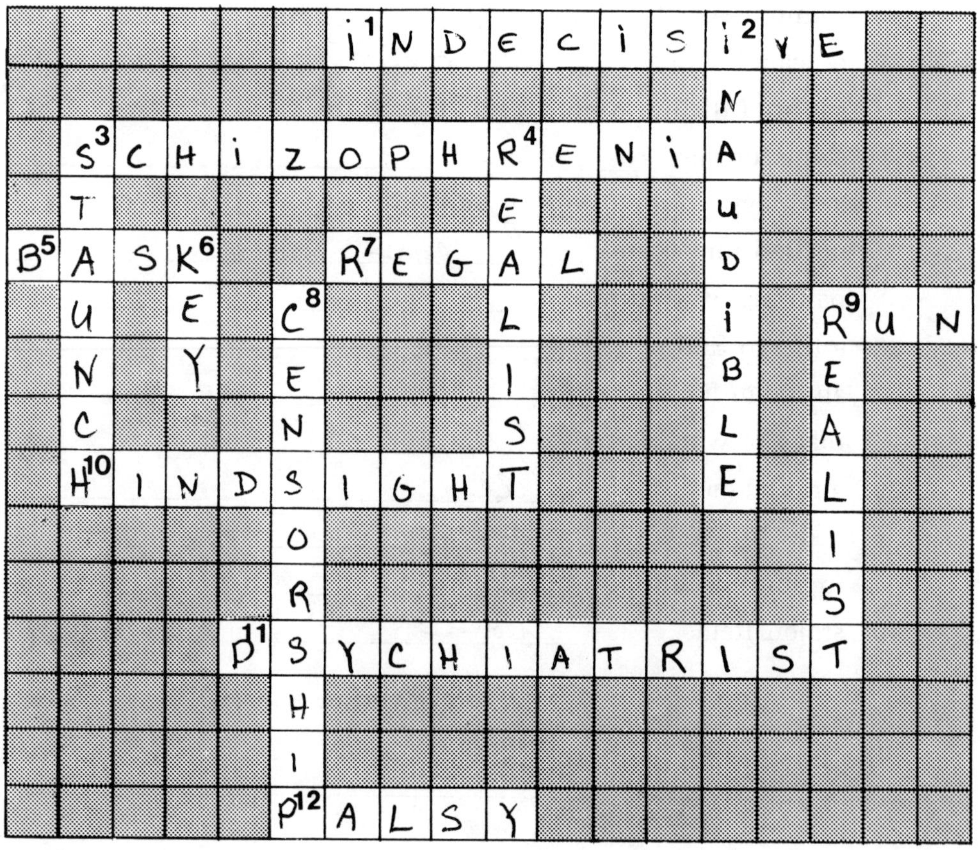

Figure 41. Vocabulary Reinforcement Puzzle

A RAISIN IN THE SUN   Name: _____

Below is a "raisin in the sun" made up of your vocabulary words. Use the clues below to help you identify the words in the circles. Write each word on the line next to its definition.

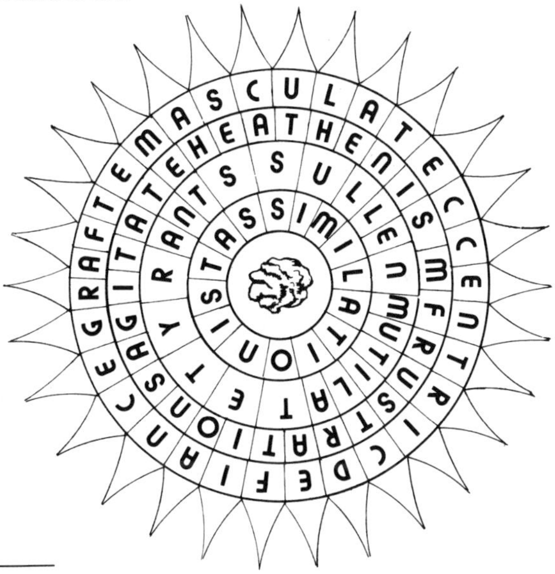

Circle 1 (outer circle)

odd _____

opposite of cooperation _____

illegal money _____

remove manhood _____

Circle 2

irritate _____

un-Christian _____

problems _____

Circle 3

destroy _____

cruel dictator _____

sour mood _____

Circle 4

definition _____

word _____

_____

8 Comprehension

After acquiring vocabulary, the single most important skill that students develop is comprehension. First they must be able to decode and understand the words they read, but then they must be able to comprehend the complete sentence, paragraph, or story. What is the author's message? Why did the main character commit that act of violence? What are the larger implications of the literature when applied to life? In this chapter, we will first explain the components of the skill of comprehension. Then we will show how you can use the different levels of comprehension to help your students' skills grow, and how you can develop study guides that will foster these comprehension skills.

Basically, the skill of comprehension can be divided into three levels. When we develop study guides and worksheets, we keep in mind these three levels, as described by Harold Herber in his book *Reading in the Content Areas*.[1] Herber defines the levels as follows:

> The *literal* level of comprehension applied to a content textbook produces knowledge of what the author said.
>
> The *interpretive* level of comprehension is applied to what the author said in order to derive meaning from his statement. The reader looks for relationships among statements within the material he has read.
>
> The *applied* level of comprehension takes the product of the literal (what the author said) and the interpretive (what the author meant by what he said) and applies it in some pragmatic or theoretical exercise. [Pp. 62–63]

Finally, Herber puts these definitions together into what he terms a "working definition" of the levels: One takes in information (literal), determines what it means (interpretive), and makes use of the ideas that have been developed (applied).

[1]Englewood Cliffs, N.J.: Prentice-Hall, 1970.

All this sounds fantastically impressive, but what does it actually mean for your students? First, most students should be able to answer the straight factual questions concerning the literature. True, a few of the students may not be able to go beyond this point, but the majority of the class should function at the literal level of comprehension. At the beginning of the year, one half to three quarters of the class will probably also be able to handle some questions at the interpretive level. Remember, this level is a little more difficult because the answer is not written in black and white in the book. The students will have to think about what the author meant by what he said. Traditionally, the poorer readers have not been called upon to answer questions other than those on the literal level. This does not mean they *cannot* answer interpretive-level questions, but they may need extra instruction to feel confident in answering this type of question.

Finally, most of the students will have difficulty with the applied-level questions. Because these questions generally ask opinions of the students, and students are unaccustomed to giving their own opinions, you may notice a reluctance on their part to answer the applied-level questions honestly. We have been asked: "But, this isn't a question. How can we answer it?" "What is the right answer to this question? There isn't just one answer." "Will you take off if we put our own ideas down?" With practice and reassurance the students soon see that most applied-level questions aren't asking for a definite answer. They become more comfortable stating their own opinions with the knowledge that you will not grade *what* they say but, rather, *how* they say it.

The traditional method of teaching is to have students read material and then give quizzes to test it. We initiated the use of a study guide to help the slower students through the reading. By going over the questions on the study guide before doing the reading, the students know what to look for and what the teacher thinks is important. As you introduce study guides in the beginning of the year, you may have to spend time with individual students explaining the questions and the kinds of answers that are expected. Most catch on fairly quickly to the format of the study guides, and after several months you will see a marked improvement in the ability of the class to use study guides independently. This frees you to spend more time helping students individually.

What are study guides? How do you compose them? How do you incorporate the three levels of comprehension into study guides? What kinds of reading skills fall under the various levels? What is the most efficient method of structuring a study guide in order to place the fewest obstacles in the path of the students? How do you guide students in answering the questions? In the remainder of the chapter, we will discuss the kinds of questions that you will find under each level of comprehension, and will illustrate with actual questions from our study guides.

READING COMPREHENSION SKILLS

Several basic reading skills make up the literal, interpretive, and applied levels of comprehension. In order of difficulty, they are: finding the main idea, noticing details, sequencing, determining cause and effect, comparing and contrasting, making inferences, drawing conclusions, and making judgments. (The last six skills involve discerning organizational patterns.) Consciously or unconsciously, most English teachers stress the three levels of comprehension and these basic reading skills in their daily curriculum. Let's examine these skills and see how each functions at the different levels of comprehension.

Finding the Main Idea

Possibly the most common question asked by English teachers on tests and in discussions is, ''What is the main idea?'' We seem to feel that if students glean nothing else from literature they should understand the author's main idea. Finding the main idea, therefore, is the most basic comprehension skill that students acquire.

Earlier in this chapter we discussed the three levels of comprehension—literal, interpretive, and applied. When writing study guides in all the areas of comprehension skills, keep in mind these three levels. Depending on the ability of the students, questions can usually be written on all levels of comprehension. For example, let's look at a poem and accompanying study guides that deal with the main idea at the literal, interpretive, and applied levels.

DON'T BE FOOLED BY ME

Don't be fooled by me.
Don't be fooled by the face I wear,
For I wear a thousand masks, masks that I'm afraid to take off
    and none of these are me.
Pretending is an art that's second nature to me, but don't be
    fooled, for God's sake don't be fooled.
I give the impression that I'm secure,
    that all is sunny and unruffled with me,
    within as well as without,
    that confidence is my name and coolness my game;
    that the water's calm, and I'm in command,
    and that I need no one.
But don't believe me, Please.

My surface may be smooth, but my surface is my mask,
Beneath this lies no complacence,
Beneath dwells the real me in confusion, in fear, and aloneness,
    but I hide this, I don't want anybody to know it,

I panic at the thought of my weakness and fear of being exposed,
That's why I frantically create a mask to hide behind,
   a nonchalant, sophisticated facade,
   to help me pretend, to shield me from the glance that knows.
But such a glance is precisely my salvation, My only salvation
   and I know it.
That is, if it's followed by acceptance, if it's followed by love.
It's the only thing that will assure me of what I can't assure
   myself—that I am worth something.

But I don't tell you this. I don't dare. I'm afraid to.
I'm afraid your glance will not be followed by acceptance and love.
I'm afraid that deep-down I'm nothing, that I'm no good.
So I play my game, my desperate game,
   with a facade of assurance without, and a trembling child within.
And so begins the parade of masks. And my life becomes a front.

I idly chatter to you in the suave tones of surface talk.
I tell you everything that is really nothing,
   and nothing of what's everything,
   of what's crying within me!
So when I'm going through my routine, do not be fooled by what
   I'm saying.
Please listen carefully and try to hear what I'm not saying.
What I'd like to be able to say,
What for survival I need to say, but what I can't say.

I dislike hiding. Honestly!
I dislike the superficial game I'm playing, the phony game.
I'd really like to be genuine and spontaneous, and me,
   but you've got to help me. You've got to hold out your hand,
   even when that's the last thing I seem to want.
Only you can wipe away from my eyes the blank state of breathing
   death.
Only you can call me into aliveness.
Each time you're kind, and gentle, and encouraging,
   each time you try to understand because you really care,
   my heart begins to grow wings, very small wings, very feeble
   wings, but wings.
With your sensitivity and sympathy, and your power of understanding
   you can breathe life into me. I want you to know that.

I want you to know how important you are to me,
   how you can be the creator of the person that is me if you
   choose to.
Please choose to. You alone can break down the wall behind
   which I tremble.
You alone can remove my mask.
You alone can release me from my shadow-world of panic and
   uncertainty, from my lonely person. Do not pass me by.

Please . . . do not pass me by.
It will not be easy for you.
A long conviction of worthlessness builds strong walls.
The nearer you approach me, the blinder I strike back,
I fight against the very thing I cry out for,
    but I am told that love is stronger than walls, and in this
    lies my hope.
Please try to beat down those walls with firm hands,
    but with gentle hands—for a child is very sensitive,
Who am I, you may wonder. I am someone you know very well,
For I am every man you meet and I am every woman you meet.

—Anonymous

If you are working with a group of students whose skills are very basic, you might develop a study guide on the literal level, much like the following:

From a Study Guide for "DON'T BE FOOLED BY ME"

Answer the following questions about this poem by circling the letter of the correct answer. Always draw your support from the poem itself. If you do not feel the correct answer is included in the choices, you may use the blank space to make up an answer you feel is more correct. Your teacher will assign you to work with several other people discussing this guide. When you have finished this study guide, break up into your groups. Discuss the answers you chose with your group. Do you all agree? What answers are different? Try to come up with one answer per question from your group. When you have resolved your differences, make a list of the situations in which you feel people "wear masks."

1. The author wears masks because
    a. he doesn't like his face.
    b. he wants to hide his real self.
    c. he thinks we won't like him.
    d. _____

2. "Pretending is an art that's second nature to me" means
    a. I don't have to think about pretending. I just do it.
    b. pretending takes skill.
    c. I have to practice at pretending.
    d. _____

3. The author believes
    a. he needs no one.
    b. he is confident.

        c. he needs help.

        d. _____

4. The author is afraid that if we see his real self
    a. we will think less of him.
    b. we will like him too much.
    c. we won't want to play the game.
    d. _____

5. We talk in "surface talk" because   a. we don't know how to talk any other way.
        b. we're afraid we'll cry.
        c. we're afraid to say what we really mean.
        d. _____

    Several of the questions here deal with the main ideas of the poem as literally expressed by poet. The students are asked to complete statements using actual knowledge of the poem. Questions 3 and 4, in particular, deal with the main ideas. Note that space is provided for an alternative response if a student is not happy with the ones that are given. This gives the students practice in thinking up their own ideas and having the confidence to share them. So often, students at the literal level of comprehension skills are used to regurgitating facts that the teacher has provided. At first, these students will probably lack the confidence to express their opinions. However, if encouraged by you, they will eventually begin to write their own thoughts.

    Many of your students may be able to read a story or poem and find the main idea with little problem. They may be ready for the second level of comprehension, the interpretive level.

    In the following example, the students are asked to interpret what they have read in the poem. Several statements that present main ideas are excerpted from the poem. The students are asked to match the main ideas with everyday expressions. You are hoping that they will begin to sense the relationships among statements on the study guide and in the poem. Because this involves more opinion and thought, they must be able to defend their choices. Allowing more than one choice for an answer also gives the students a chance to develop more confidence in their opinions.

From a Study Guide for "DON'T BE FOOLED BY ME"

Match the statements from the poem in column A with the real-life situations in column B. You may have more than one number to match the situations. Be prepared to <u>defend your choices</u>.

Column A	*Column B*
1. Don't be fooled by the face I wear.	___ a. Who me? I don't need you to get me a date. I can get one on my own.
2. Pretending is an art.	
3. I give the impression that I'm secure.	_____ b. You didn't call on me and I had my hand up.
4. . . . a nonchalant, sophisticated, facade	_____ c. Then I go, "Well, why didn't you just ask me?" and he goes, "How did I know you'd say yes?" and I go, "Well, next time, try."
5. I idly chatter with you.	
6. Each time you try to understand . . . my heart begins to grow wings.	
7. Please . . . do not pass me by.	_____ d. You mean you might be able to help me find a job?
8. I fight against the very thing I cry out for.	_____ e. I figured I'd smile and she'd never know how much she hurt me.
	_____ f. I can read well if I feel like it.
	_____ g. I sauntered down the hall with an air of self-assurance.
	_____ h. Wicked want to help me. You're just nosy.

The next study guide is on the applied level of comprehension. The students must take the main ideas they have been discussing and apply them creatively to real-life situations. This study guide uses the technique of role playing, which usually works well with the lower-ability students. They can move around the room, which allows them to let off a little steam, and most of them can identify with the roles they are asked to play.

From a Study Guide for "DON'T BE FOOLED BY ME"

Imagine becoming a person with a mask on. The new person has different characteristics than the old. Wear the new masks that you have made back into your groups. Choose three or more of the following statements, and respond to these statements as the personality of your mask would.

1. Parents are reasonable. Just wait until you become one.
2. School is a waste of time. You don't ever learn anything you can use.
3. I wish I didn't have to grow up.
4. I can't wait until I'm eighteen.
5. Money is not important to me.
6. I never get away with anything. I always get caught.
7. I get kicks out of conning the teacher.

As these examples show, you can construct study guide questions that deal with the main idea on the three basic levels of comprehension. This is not to suggest that a study guide for the main idea on the interpretive level, for example, must always be in the form given here. In Appendix E, beginning on page 265, we provide complete study guides that include many examples of questions that deal with the main idea on all three levels. However, if finding the idea is the major skill you are emphasizing for a work of literature, the students might benefit more from an entire study guide written on one level.

Noticing Details

After a teacher helps the students see the general idea of a piece of literature, the next step is usually to stress the details that contribute to understanding of the main idea. Obviously, most questions concerning details will be written on the literal level of comprehension. Take another look at the first study guide for *Don't Be Fooled by Me"* earlier in this chapter. This study guide contains questions concerning main idea on the literal level; however, some of the questions also deal with details of the poem. Note especially questions 1 and 5. The answers to these questions can be found quite easily by reading the poem. You can see from this that a study guide composed of questions on the literal level may stress various reading comprehension skills. The complete sample study guide at the end of this chapter contains additional examples.

Here are more examples of detail questions on the literal level of comprehension.

From a Study Guide for HEY, DUMMY, by Kin Platt

CHAPTER 5.   What is Neil discovering about his town as he walks Alan home?

CHAPTER 9.   When Neil finally found Alan, an angry man had Alan by the arm. What was the problem?

From a Study Guide for LILIES OF THE FIELD, by William E. Barrett

CHAPTER 1. List six adjectives that describe Homer Smith.

_____ _____ _____

_____ _____ _____

CHAPTER 2. Why is Homer in such a good mood as he heads toward the car? (p. 32)
Why is it necessary for Homer and Mother Marthe to use their Bibles?

These examples of literal-level questions involving details bring to mind several things about writing such questions on a study guide. First of all, because of their shallow nature, literal-level questions should not be the primary emphasis of a study guide. Unless you have a special purpose, a study guide should normally contain questions covering many kinds of reading skills on all three levels of comprehension.

In addition, the format of the question is important, especially for poor readers or students who are not familiar with study guides. Several of the examples above are simply questions asking for knowledge of some details from the reading. However, even here, you can decide how much help to give. You may just ask a question and expect the students to remember where in the chapter to find the answer, or you may ask a question and give a page reference in parentheses. This helps the slower students who may have difficulty remembering where to locate information.

The study guide question for chapter 1 of *Lilies of the Field* above is a detail question, with a reinforcing format. The students know immediately that they are being asked for six answers, and they are given a space in which to write each one. This kind of detail question is excellent for the slower students, who need lots of structure and direction. A study guide for a whole book can contain questions in several different formats on all three levels of comprehension.

READING COMPREHENSION SKILLS: DISCERNING ORGANIZATIONAL PATTERNS

Most authors follow some sort of organizational pattern when they write. These patterns may be quite evident, or they may be more subtle. Organization may also be taught on all three levels of comprehension.

Sequencing

Sequencing is a literal-level skill that students must master if they are going to have any elementary knowledge of the organization of the material they are reading. After reading a selection, they should be able to recall what happened first, second, and third. This is sequencing. Below is an example of a simple literal-level sequencing exercise. Most students have no difficulty handling this kind of literal-level exercise.

From a Study Guide for OF MICE AND MEN, by John Steinbeck

Number the following events in the order in which they happened:

_____ Lennie kills Curley's wife.
_____ You discover what kind of person Curley's wife is.
_____ You first hear of George and Lennie's plans to buy a ranch.
_____ George shoots Lennie.
_____ Lennie kills the puppy.

Study guides themselves can promote the skill of sequencing if the questions are written to follow the reading selection through from beginning to end. Many of us tend to take this sequencing skill for granted, but some students do have difficulty with this literal-level skill. If they can't remember the order in which things happened in the book, they will also have difficulty with other reading skills and organizational patterns such as cause and effect, and comparison and contrast. Development of the sequencing skill is an effective method of training the memories and expanding the thinking skills of the students, too. It takes more effort to think back over the reading to remember the order of events than it does to answer multiple-choice questions.

Another method of structuring sequencing exercises may provide some variety for the students. This is a little more difficult for the students to grasp, but once they understand the directions, most of them do fairly well.

From a Study Guide for LISA, BRIGHT AND DARK, by John Neufeld

Column B contains a list of events that happened in the novel. Some of the events are missing and are shown only by a letter. The missing events are listed in column A. Place the number of each event in column A on the line next to the appropriate letter in column B. When you are finished, column A should fit into column B and all the events should be in the right order.

Column A	Column B
1. Lisa attacks Elizabeth.	*a.* _____ Lisa shows signs of her illness at her and Brian's anniversary party.
2. For the first time, M.N. hears Lisa plead with her parents for help.	
3. Betsy tries to talk to Mr. Bernstein about Lisa.	*b.* _____ Lisa goes to Florida for a rest.
4. Brian breaks up with Lisa.	*c.* _____ Betsy and M.N. try to talk with Lisa but Lisa wants Elizabeth there too.
5. Elizabeth tries to explain the nature of mental illness to Betsy and M.N.	
	d. _____ Mr. Fickett and Mr. Milne try to talk to Mr. Schilling about Lisa.
	e. _____ Lisa walks through the glass in front of Mr. Goodman.

Although the above sequencing exercise should be classed under the literal level of comprehension, its format raises the difficulty above the literal to the interpretive level. First of all, the directions are more difficult to follow. One of the skills students should cultivate is following directions. In this example, they must read the directions and interpret the problem based on what they are told to do. For many students, this is a difficult task. They have trouble following the simplest directions, and the ones in this problem are more complicated than usual. Once students understand the directions, either on their own or with help from you, they should be able to proceed with the sequencing.

The next study guide example presents the same material at a more purely literal level of comprehension, with a much simpler format.

From a Study Guide for LISA, BRIGHT AND DARK

Five events from the story are listed below. Write each event on the appropriate line below to complete the plot line in sequence.

Events

Lisa attacks Elizabeth.
For the first time, M.N. hears Lisa plead with her parents for help.
Betsy tries to talk to Mr. Bernstein about Lisa.
Brian breaks up with Lisa.
Elizabeth tries to explain the nature of mental illness to Betsy and
  M.N.

Plot Line

1. _____

2. Lisa shows signs of her illness at her and Brian's anniversary
   party.

3. _____

4. Lisa goes to Florida for a rest.

5. _____

6. Betsy and M.N. try to talk with Lisa, but Lisa wants Elizabeth
   there, too.

7. _____

8. Mr. Fickett and Mr. Milne try to talk to Mr. Schilling about
   Lisa.

9. _____

10. Lisa walks through the glass in front of Mr. Goodman.

Students must be able to sense some kind of organization to a piece
of literature in order to develop logical reading skills. They must learn
that there is a plan to the writing of most authors. Observing that most
writers pattern their works logically helps students organize their own
thinking. By mastering the more elemental skill of sequencing, students
are training their thinking for the more complex and difficult skill of
sensing cause and effect as an organizational pattern to writing.

Determining Cause and Effect

The next reading comprehension skill in order of difficulty is determining cause and effect. Students need to understand that the details of
a story or poem are organized in various ways to enable the reader to
follow the author's intention. Cause and effect is one of the most frequently used organizational patterns in literature as well as in textbooks
in such content areas as social studies.

On study guides, students should be asked questions that stress the cause-and-effect pattern. These questions can be formulated on all three levels of comprehension. You might choose to begin by assigning a reading that has an obvious cause-and effect pattern and then constructing a study guide that explores this pattern specifically. Students tend to have a vague idea about why things happen in a story, but they usually are not able to verbalize the relationships among the facts in the story unless the pattern is identified for them. They may have an idea that "if A occurs, B will happen next," but they are not able to explain what has happened or why.

The following set of examples show how questions dealing with cause and effect can be written on the literal, interpretive, and applied levels of comprehension. The reading material, a newspaper editorial, is followed by excerpts from three study guides, one at each level of comprehension. After the students have had this practice with a short nonfiction piece, they should be better able to answer questions stressing this organizational pattern in fiction.

JOB MARKET[2]

by Dr. Edward T. Green, Superintendent, Oneida City Schools

Several weeks ago, we used Career Education as the main topic of this column. In recent months we have visited a number of college and university campuses and talked with several hundred young people seeking employment following their graduation in June.

As has been reported before, the job market for college graduates seems not to be very bright. Statistics are usually behind chronologically and, so, we will quote from figures dealing with the start of the 1970's. In the fall of 1971 the overall national unemployment rate stood at 5.4 per cent and, at the same time, 7.4 per cent of those who had graduated from college in 1970 and 1971 were out of work.

There are many factors at work. As our economy changes and as new demands for trained persons emerge, the picture changes. As an example, the predictions are that the economy will certainly grow in the 1970's. With this growth comes the need for trained persons—including professionals. An estimate given by the Labor Department indicates that of the 9.8 million new graduates seeking jobs in the 1970s, approximately 9.6 million will find them. However, the search and final decision will be much more demanding than ever before. Those persons who find exactly the job they are seeking will, indeed, be extremely fortunate.

It is dangerous to make long range predictions as to the future job market. We must always face the cycle which governs, to a high degree, entry and placement in the professions. When there is an oversupply of people, there are not enough employment opportunities and, thus, en-

[2]Oneida (N.Y.) Dispatch, March 31, 1973. Used by permission.

trants into the preparatory programs for the professions diminish. As a result, a shortage of persons exists. Under the law of supply and demand, as the supply decreases, salaries go up in order to meet competition. As salaries increase, more persons enter into the field thereby building to an oversupply of people. Such cycles tend to run through four- or five-year periods.

One source indicates that markets for engineers and accountants tend to follow the same sort of cycle as found for lawyers and holders of master's degrees in business administration. We suspect that futher research will add other professions to this list.

The Bureau of Labor Statistics has predicted that employment in most professions will grow more slowly this decade than last. Among the exceptions to this are jobs in health care, accounting, and programming where the growth will tend to be much greater.

We saw a quotation which we share with our readers at this point. It states that the right training at the right time—not just a college degree—is the best guarantee of success in the tightening professional job market in the 1970s. No one can guarantee that right training will be provided in all cases. What is very important is that much more careful attention be paid to the matter of careers by all persons involved.

Students should first be given a study guide that stresses the *literal* understanding of the passage:

From a Study Guide for a Newspaper Editorial

The author of an editorial uses the opportunity to speak out on an issue or problem with which he is concerned. In a first reading of an editorial, it is helpful if you can recognize the problem, the effects of this problem on society, its causes, and the author's solution. Find problem, cause, effect, and solution in this editorial and write each one in the proper space below. Keep in mind that an editorial reflects the opinion of its writer only.

Problem _____

Cause _____

Effect _____

Solution _____

Once the students have mastered the literal-level study guide, they can go on to a study guide written on the interpretive level. The following study guide is for the second level of comprehension.

From a Study Guide for a Newspaper Editorial

Going back to the editorial for a second reading, look more carefully for the details that contribute to the cause-and-effect pattern. In column A is a list of possible causes. Match them with the effects in column B by writing the number of the cause from column A on the blank line in front of its effect in column B.

Column A—Causes	Column B—Effects
1. visit to college campuses	_____ fewer employment opportunities
2. search for jobs will be much more demanding	_____ mistake in future estimate due to rapid change in economy
3. oversupply of people	_____ recognition of tight job market
4. growth of economy	_____ those who find jobs of their first choice will be very fortunate
5. making long-range job market predictions	_____ need for trained professionals
6. right training at the right time	_____ success in a tightening professional job market
7. salaries increase	_____ oversupply of people
8. fewer entrants into preparatory programs	_____ more people enter professions
9. more people at entry level of professions	_____ starting salaries increase

An applied-level study guide is given as an example below. In this type of study guide there is more than one possible answer for each question. After the students have completed the study guide, you can have them discuss and defend their choices in a class discussion or in small groups. Remember, though, that many students feel threatened by this kind of study guide because it requires more of the students' own opinions and thinking. Too many students are only used to answering literal-level questions. Applied-level guides can be given when the students feel secure with the study guide format and with their own opinions.

From a Study Guide for a Newspaper Editorial

Below is a list of several causes with which you dealt in the preceding exercise. Taking the possible effects a step beyond the text of Dr. Green's editorial, see if you can match the causes with the effects expressed in the statements below. You may have more than one cause for an effect, and you may use a cause more than once.

<u>Causes</u>

a. growth of the economy
b. search for jobs will be much more demanding
c. oversupply of people
d. fewer entrants into preparatory programs
e. salaries increase
f. more people enter professions
g. right training at the right time

<u>Effects</u>

_____ 1. Oneida High School has one opening in the special education department and one opening in the reading department.

_____ 2. Ross Pharmacy has a graduate engineer working as a stock clerk.

_____ 3. The line outside the employment office at Oneida Limited is very long.

_____ 4. Starting salaries in Long Island Schools are $8,800.

_____ 5. After Smith-Lee closed, Mr. Jones had to move to Ardsley, New York, since that was the only place he could find employment in his field.

_____ 6. Oneonta College and Cortland College had fewer applicants for their teacher preparatory programs this year than last year.

_____ 7. The new Oneida City Hospital has openings for lab technicians and a great need for more physicians.

_____ 8. Within two minutes of the announcement on the public address system, the guidance office had 28 applicants for the job opening at Grant's.

_____ 9. Because there are so few graduate ceramics engineers, Hubbard Industries offers new college graduates $30,000.

The preceding examples, which concentrated on cause and effect, are helpful for students who are just beginning to understand this organizational pattern. Cause-and-effect questions can also be included in study guides covering many comprehension skills. These questions obviously cannot delve into the detail of the longer study guides, but the main principle is there. Following are some examples of literal- and interpretive-level questions from study guides for novels read in high school English classes.

From a Study Guide for LISA, BRIGHT AND DARK

CHAPTER 7. Mr. Bernstein tries to avoid the problem. Can you find any explanation for this?

CHAPTER 8. Why could Lisa's home life make her paranoid?

CHAPTER 11. What is the danger you see in the girls' plan to help Lisa?

From a Study Guide for HEY, DUMMY

CHAPTER 14. What circumstances in this chapter help Neil to see that Mr. Alvarado was right?

CHAPTER 15. What are Mr. Alvarado's reasons for not getting involved?

From a Study Guide for THE BRIDGES AT TOKO-RI, by James Michener

SEA. How do the weather and condition of the sea affect the carriers?

LAND. 1. Explain why the admiral decides to tell Nancy about Brubaker's crash and about the bridges at Toko-ri.

2. Explain the different reactions of the captain of the Savo and Admiral Tarrant to the brawl caused by Mike as the Savo and Essex crews are boarding.

   Captain of Savo:

   Admiral Tarrant:

Comparing and Contrasting

Another organizational pattern that is predominant in literature and social studies is comparison and contrast. For example, two characters are described comparatively. The settings of two houses are different. The reasons two people make a decision are similar. In many cases, this pattern is quite obvious. On the literal level, many students have little difficulty picking out and understanding examples of comparison and contrast once the pattern has been brought to their attention, so this is the main task of a study guide. Then they may see how this form of organization helps in the logical development of the book.

Although most questions on comparison and contrast are written on the literal and applied levels, there are some instances when interpretative-level questions would best uncover the shades of meaning in the book. Literal and applied questions are not that difficult to formulate, but the interpretive-level questions are more "slippery." They require more skill in question writing by the teacher and more thinking by the students. Let's look at examples from study guides that have actually been used in the classroom with some success. First, we'll examine some questions on the literal level.

From a Study Guide for HEY, DUMMY, by Kin Platt

CHAPTER 5. The author uses a phrase to describe Dummy: "He was like a bee buzzing from flower to flower sipping the nectar." Why does the author use this phrase and how does it relate to Alan?

CHAPTER 12. How is the game of "tease" in this chapter different from the game earlier in the book?

From a Study Guide for LISA, BRIGHT AND DARK, by John Neufeld

CHAPTER 4. Divide Lisa's appearance and behavior into two columns:

Good Days   *Bad Days*

CHAPTER 9. What is schizophrenia? How does it differ from paranoia?

In all these examples, the students must make a direct comparison between characters, events, or words in the book. What qualities do a bee and Alan have in common? The students must think of the various attributes of a bee, do the same thing for Alan, and then see where these attributes are similar or different. They must remember a game of "tease" from the beginning of the book and decide how it is the same as or different from the one later in the book. The students must see that there is a connection between the two games. The author is trying to say something by describing the two games differently and by having Neil react differently to them. *Lisa, Bright and Dark* is a book full of contrasts, as the title itself indicates. The answers to these sample questions should be obvious. Lisa definitely looks and acts differently depending on her mood from day to day. Since much of the book concerns mental illness, the students need to understand the specific differences between the terms *schizophrenia* and *paranoia*. Students often use the words interchangeably, and they don't really understand what they mean. They need to see the contrasts between the words to have a full appreciation of the character of Lisa.

Here are sample questions on the interpretive level from actual study guides. Remember the purpose of interpretive-level questions—to determine what the author *means* by what he has said.

From a Study Guide for LISA, BRIGHT AND DARK

CHAPTER 6.   How did the kids know that Lisa's trip to Florida had not helped?

From a Study Guide for THE BRIDGES AT TOKO-RI, by James Michener

SEA.   Why is the admiral angered when Brubaker suggests that he, Tarrant, does not understand war?

LAND.   Explain the significance of the carrier pilot's version of the Twenty-third Psalm.

SKY.   What significance does the Korean peasant family hold for Brubaker?

The question about Lisa's trip to Florida is attempting to help the students see that the author was making a comparison of Lisa's condition before and after the trip. To interpret the book properly, the students must distinguish what the author meant by the implied comparison of Lisa before and after the trip.

For each of the questions from *The Bridges at Toko-ri*, there is an implied comparison. The students again are asked to interpret what the author meant by the comparison. In the question from "Sea," Brubaker and Admiral Tarrant are comparing each other's understanding of war. While the comparison isn't spelled out in detail in the narrative, by reading Tarrant's discussion of war, the student can interpret what Brubaker and the author think about the ravages of war. Under the section "Land," the comparison is between the original version of the Twenty-third Psalm and the pilot's version.

Twenty-third Psalm	Pilot's Version[3]
The Lord is my Shepherd; I shall not want.	The Beer Barrel is my shepherd; I shall not crash.
He maketh me to lie down in green pastures; he leadeth me beside the still waters.	He maketh me to land on flat runways: he bringeth me in off the rough waters.

[3]James Michener, *The Bridges at Toko-ri* (New York: Fawcett Crest, 1953).

He restoreth my soul: he leadeth me in the paths of righteousness for his name's sake.

Yea, though I walk through the valley of the shadow of death, I will fear no evil; for thou art with me; thy rod and thy staff they comfort me.

Thou preparest a table before me in the presence of mine enemies: thou anointest my head with oil; my cup runneth over.

Surely goodness and mercy shall follow me all the days of my life; and I will dwell in the house of the Lord forever.

He restoreth my confidence.

Yea, though I come stalling into the groove at sixty knots, I shall fear no evil: for he is with me; his arm and his paddle, they comfort me,

He prepareth a deck before me in the presence of mine enemies. He attacheth my hook to the wire; my deck space runneth over.

The students must first make a literal comparison between the two before they can go to the next level of comprehension and interpret the significance of the contrast. In the pilot's version, God is replaced by Beer Barrel. The feeling of the pilots for Beer Barrel is similar to the feeling that many have for the Lord. He can give security and make the men feel safe. They don't have any fear if Beer Barrel is there to flag them in when they land their planes on the carrier. This is the literal understanding of the pilot's version of the psalm, along with the obvious fact that many of the phrases in the two are the same, and only key words have been changed.

On the interpretive level, the students are asked to compare the *significance* of the two versions. What does the author mean by making a comparison between God and Beer Barrel? One answer to this question might be: Just as many people can take the knocks that life hands them because they know God is with them, so can the fliers take the tensions of a war because they know they will be able to land safely under Beer Barel's professional direction. The students are going one step beyond the obvious literal comparisons of the two versions and are discovering the meaning behind the Pilot's Version.

In the last question the students are asked about the implied contrast between Brubaker's own family and the Korean family he meets. They must first make a literal comparison to see the similarities between the two and then take the exercise one notch higher and determine the *significance* of this comparison. The students must decide why the author has Brubaker meet the Korean family at this time. Because we have had a good deal of information about Brubaker's own family, the impulse is strong to compare the two. We see that the appearance of the

Korean family at the end of the novel is a foreshadowing of events to come, that Brubaker is having one last chance to think about his family before he dies. Another comparison is implied on a symbolic level—that of peace and war. Here Brubaker's plane has been shot down behind enemy lines, and he is waiting to be found. The Korean family, oblivious to the hostilities of war, ignores him. In each case, the student must interpret what the author means by the words he uses and the comparisons he develops.

Comparison and contrast questions can be written on the applied level of comprehension. In this type of question the students are asked to take the information that they have read in the book and compare it with situations from their own experience. Would they act differently or similarly? Below are some sample questions taken from study guides.

From a Study Guide for HEY, DUMMY

CHAPTER   1.   What traits would a foreigner and Dummy have in common?
CHAPTER   9.   How might your family react if you brought a moron home?
CHAPTER 11.   Why is Mr. Alvarado pleased with Neil? Does the word *involvement* have any meaning in your life?

From a Study Guide for LISA, BRIGHT AND DARK

CHAPTER 11.   Would you respond the same as or differently than M.N. did if your close friend lit into you as Lisa did to M.N.? Why?
CHAPTER 21.   Does Betsy's insight in recognizing that Mr. Bernstein has problems surprise you? Do you know adults who you think could profit from psychiatric help?

For the questions from *Hey, Dummy,* the students are asked to remember a person who was new to this country and compare his reactions to Dummy's. They must draw on their own experiences or reading and must try to determine any similarities. For the second question each pupil must remember the reaction of Neil's family to his involvement with Alan and then compare that response to what his or her own family's reaction might be in a similar situation. In the question for chapter 11, the students should understand why Mr. Alvarado was pleased with Neil's involvement with Alan and then decide if similar involvement is important in their own lives.

The questions from *Lisa, Bright and Dark* are similar. For each, the pupils must have an understanding of the event from the book and then make comparisons to similar situations in their own lives. Would their reactions be the same or different? Can they compare Mr. Bernstein to any other adults?

Sequencing, cause and effect, and comparison and contrast are the basic organizational patterns in fiction. Your study guides will probably contain a majority of questions about comparison and contrast or cause and effect.

Making Inferences, Drawing Conclusions, and Making Judgments

The last three skill areas we will discuss are on a higher plane and only apply to the interpretive and applied levels of comprehension. The three areas of making inferences, drawing conclusions, and making judgments are often interrelated. For the purposes of our discussion, we will treat making inferences and drawing conclusions as one topic and making judgments as a separate topic.

Let's first define the terms, since many times the three are confused with one another. The dictionary definition of *infer* is "conclude from evidence." From this definition, we can see how closely related the skills of making inferences and drawing conclusions are. Actually, when making an inference, we are seeking the meaning behind the words of the author. We are making a deduction about what is on the written page based on the facts; that is, we are drawing a conclusion.

The other reading skill to be discussed in this chapter is making judgments. When we make a judgment about a person's character or actions, or about the appropriateness of a political tenet, we are deciding about the "rightness" or "wrongness" of the situation. What is effective or ineffective? What is moral or immoral?

Now that we have defined the three skills, we can examine some study guide questions on making inferences and drawing conclusions. The first questions are on the interpretive level of comprehension.

From a Study Guide for THE MAN WITHOUT A FACE, by Isabel Holland

CHAPTER	2.	What are two things about McLeod's house and his pet that tell you about McLeod the man?
CHAPTER	3.	How do you know McLeod may have taught before?
CHAPTER	6.	Why do you think McLeod reacted the way he did when Chuck reached out and touched his arm?
CHAPTER	20.	What might be a reason for Chuck's fainting in church?

From a Study Guide for HEY, DUMMY, by Kin Platt

CHAPTER 6. Can you explain why Neil feels self-conscious with Alan?

CHAPTER 8. Can you tell in this chapter how Susie feels about her brother's sticking up for Alan?

The first thing to notice about these questions is that the pupils must have read the chapter in order to have a working knowledge about its details. For example, to answer the first question for *The Man Without a Face*, the students must know two things about McLeod's house and his pet. Then, they must take that information one step further and draw a conclusion from it. They infer something about McLeod the man from characteristics of his house and pet. The whole question involves drawing a conclusion. In the next question, based on several things McLeod does (his manner of speaking like a teacher, catching the fake composition, and realizing that the wording in the composition didn't sound like a student's), the students can infer that McLeod was a teacher before. They are taking *facts* in the book and drawing a conclusion from them.

The questions for *Hey, Dummy* are similar. By noting descriptions of Neil's behavior when he is around Alan (impatient, anxious to leave), we can see that he is self-conscious. What has Alan done to make Neil feel this way? The students must infer from Neil's and Alan's actions why Neil is self-conscious.

Similarly, Susie, Neil's sister, is concerned about and supportive of Neil for befriending Alan. In order to reach this conclusion, a reader must know some facts from the chapter. Susie makes Neil lemonade; she asks concerned questions; and she kisses his cheek. The students take these facts and infer from them. Anyone who acts like this is probably approving or showing support; therefore, the students can conclude that Susie feels good about her brother's sticking up for Alan.

Applied-level questions about making inferences and drawing conclusions can be written in various ways. Here are some examples from actual study guides.

From a Study Guide for LISA, BRIGHT AND DARK

CHAPTER 5. How can the kind of family a person is raised in determine that person's personality, hang-ups, and fears?

From a Study Guide for HEY, DUMMY

CHAPTER 5. In your experience, you have probably played a game like "Grab Your Hat," or "Grab His Lunch Bag." Why do we do it, and how do we pick our victim?

CHAPTER 14. How can you explain that people will do things in a mob that they wouldn't do if they were alone?

CHAPTER 19. There are several unsolved details in this story. Tell what you think may have happened:
    Who hurt the girl in the park?
    Why was there such a change in Mr. Alvarado?
    What response do the Comstocks have to Neil's difficulty?
    How does Neil learn to live with his crisis?

What factors in the above questions signal that they are on the applied level of comprehension? For most of them, the students are asked to take experiences in their own lives and apply them to events in the literature. They must understand what has happened in the story in order to apply that to their own lives and to give their opinions.

For the question for *Lisa, Bright and Dark*, the pupils must have a working knowledge of the kind of family that Lisa had. They need to see what that family did to raise Lisa to become the girl she was. Perhaps the students can best answer the question by looking into their own lives to analyze what determined personality, hang-ups, and fears.

In the book *Hey, Dummy*, the boys tease Alan by grabbing his hat and running with it, while Alan stands in the street wondering what is happening. The first question here asks the students to remember when they played a game similar to this and to remember their motives and feelings while playing it. In this manner, the pupils may come to a fuller realization of the consequences of their actions. They will be able to transfer their feelings while playing the game to the feelings of Alan in the novel.

The questions for chapter 19 of *Hey, Dummy* are particularly effective. At the end of most novels, details of the plot are left unresolved. One way to get students to use applied-level thinking is to ask them to predict what might have happened after the end of the novel. In order to do this the students need to have basic knowledge of the book. They must understand the character of Mr. Alvarado and must see how his personality changes during the course of the novel. Based on their knowledge of the personality change and on the facts in the story that caused the change, they can make a prediction.

For all of these prediction questions, students must exhibit an understanding of the plot and character development and then extend that knowledge to cover a future situation in which the people in the novel would continue to act in character. These are the more difficult questions, and they are also the questions that make the students think the most. Those students who haven't read the novel carefully or who haven't thought a great deal about the larger consequences of the characters' actions will have a difficult time trying to predict what will happen after the conclusion of the novel. These are good questions to save for last to help the students tie up loose ends and see the novel as a whole.

The final reading comprehension skill that we will discuss is making judgments. Previously, we defined making judgments as deciding about the "rightness" or "wrongness" of a situation. Most judgment questions on study guides are written on the applied level, since we make judgments based on our experiences and knowledge. Only occasionally will you have the opportunity to use an interpretive-level question. One such question does appear as the last question in the sample study guide for *The Man Without a Face* at the end of this chapter: Is this book a tragedy or a comedy? The students must make a judgment, or a decision, based on their knowledge of the book. First, they must understand the characteristics of a tragedy or comedy. Then, they must think of the entire novel and decide which elements fit it best, those of comedy or those of tragedy. They are making a judgment; however, this judgment is on the interpretive level because they are taking facts about the novel and interpreting them as tragedy or comedy. There is an element of opinion here, but, on the whole, there is a more correct answer that can be substantiated by facts from the book. This puts the questions on the interpretive level.

The questions that follow are judgment questions on the applied level.

From a Study Guide for HEY, DUMMY

CHAPTER 7.   Would you rather not talk at all or talk and sound like a moron?

From a Study Guide for LISA, BRIGHT AND DARK

CHAPTER   1.   Why do you think people find it hard to admit that they need psychiatric help?

CHAPTER 15.   What is your reaction to the statement: "The teachers and guidance counselor wanted to help but were afraid of Lisa's parents"?

CHAPTER 21. Does Betsy's insight in recognizing that Mr. Bernstein has problems surprise you? Do you know adults who you think could profit from psychiatric help?[4]

These questions are asking the students to make a judgment about a situation. How would you feel if you were a moron? With your knowledge of people, why would you feel it is difficult for the average person to ask for psychiatric help? How much influence do parents have in a child's life? Can you recognize when an adult is having mental problems and needs help? Based on their understanding of their environment and of people, the students judge the reaction they would predict or the feelings they would have in the given situation. They are applying facts and experiences they have had outside the realm of school and of books. In forming their opinions they are making a judgment.

Constructing questions on the applied level for the skill of making judgments is not difficult. You simply take a situation for which you think the students may have had some outside experience and ask their opinion about it. The situation you choose, of course, should be relevant to the events and action in the novel.

WRITING A STUDY GUIDE

Perhaps you have never written a study guide. What exactly is a study guide? A study guide can serve several purposes. First, it provides an outline for the students to follow while reading the book. Second, it tells the students what points in the story are important and what they should read more carefully. Third, it provides a guide that the students and the teacher can follow for discussion and review purposes.

Here are several points to keep in mind when writing a study guide.

1. *Do not* make the study guide excessively long. Do not overwhelm the students with a ten-page guide for a 200-page book.
2. *Do not* ask questions about every little detail in the book.
3. *Do not* make the students hunt for an answer. The purpose of the study guide is to help them comprehend the material, not to send them on a scavenger hunt.
4. *Do* ask, on the average, about five questions per chapter. This will force you to ask only about the pertinent material.

[4]Note that this question also occurs in the *Lisa, Bright and Dark* study guide that presents comparison and contrast questions. This double use of questions is often beneficial, for it helps pupils think in different ways.

5. *Do* leave enough space for the answer, so the students don't have to squeeze their writing and possibly get a wrong answer because you can't read it.

6. *Do* occasionally give the page number on which an answer can be found. This gives an extra boost to the slower students and helps them focus their reading.

7. *Do* vary your questions so that they include all levels of comprehension. The majority of the students can handle material above the literal level of comprehension. A study guide that is replete with questions asking only for literal details is not truly measuring the students' ability to comprehend.

We use a helpful *FIVE* acronym in structuring our study guides. For every chapter we try to have questions that cover the following points:

Fact

Inference

Vocabulary

Experience

A *factual* question asks about a literal detail that is particularly important to that chapter. Perhaps there are two or three important details in a chapter that you want the students to remember. Be flexible, but remember not to depend solely on this type of question for the entire guide.

An *inference* question is often written at the interpretive level of comprehension. The students are asked to take information they have from the chapter and expand their knowledge of the character and the situation based on that information. They must infer, or "read between the lines."

Although for most novels you will undoubtedly have a vocabulary list that stresses the most important words, there are usually words that can be emphasized in the study guide in *vocabulary* questions. The words chosen for these questions should be important for the comprehension of the chapter and should not be words that are on the main vocabulary list. Do not make a student do work twice. Words can also be chosen to stress word parts, decoding techniques, and connections or transitions with other words in the guide.

The fourth kind of question on the study guide should incorporate the students' *experience* in some way. Most of these questions will be on the applied level of comprehension. The students are given an event or quote from the chapter and are asked to respond to the question as they might in a real-life situation.

If this basic formula is followed, all levels of comprehension will be covered, though this, of course, depends on the length and content of each chapter. In general, we have found that most chapters do have material that falls into these four categories.

A SAMPLE STUDY GUIDE

Let us now analyze a study guide in detail. We have had good success with a study guide we wrote for *The Man Without a Face*, by Isabel Holland.[5] This has been a favorite book of adolescents for several years, and although the reading level is about ninth grade, the content is somewhat more sophisticated. In order to understand the themes, the students need detailed guided reading and discussion. We have labeled each question on the study guide as to comprehension level, type (factual, inferential, vocabulary, or experiential), and reading skills emphasized. If necessary, special notes about individual questions have been added.

A Study Guide for THE MAN WITHOUT A FACE, by Isabel Holland

CHAPTER 1

1. Why does Chuck want to be a pilot when he grows up?
   Comprehension level: literal
   Question type: factual
   Reading skill: details
2. What is Chuck's relationship with his family? How does this influence his second attempt to get into St. Matthews?
   Comprehension level: literal
   Question type: factual
   Reading skill: details
3. How many stepfathers did Chuck have? What effect did his stepfathers have on Chuck?
   Part 1:
   Comprehension level: literal
   Question type: factual
   Reading skill: sequencing
   Part 2:
   Comprehension level: interpretive
   Question type: inferential
   Reading skill: cause and effect

[5]Isabel Holland, *The Man Without a Face* (New York: Bantam, 1972).

4. Did the fact that he had no brothers make a difference in Chuck's personality?

   This question could be answered in two ways, depending on whether a student has brothers or not. If the student has brothers, he would answer the question based on the information in the chapter:

   Comprehension level: interpretive
   Question type: inferential
   Reading skill: making inferences

   If the student had no brothers, he might depend more on his own experiences:

   Comprehension level: applied
   Question type: experiential
   Reading skill: making judgments

5. The boys *speculate* about the appearance of Justin McLeod. What does *speculate* mean? (p. 16)

   Comprehension level: literal
   Question type: vocabulary
   Reading skill: details

CHAPTER 2

1. Why is the phrase "I don't think it's his parasites that bug her" considered a pun? (p. 19)

   This question could be considered on two levels depending on the skills of the student:

   If the student didn't know the meaning of the word *pun*, he would first have to look it up.

   Comprehension level: literal
   Question type: vocabulary
   Reading skill: details

   Then the student would have to look at the entire question and apply the definition to the statement from the book.

   Comprehension level: interpretive
   Question type: inferential
   Reading skill: drawing conclusions

2. What is the main difference between Gloria and Meg?

   Comprehension level: literal
   Question type: factual
   Reading skill: comparison and contrast

3. What action does Chuck take that shows he is really serious about getting into St. Matthew's?

   Comprehension level: interpretive
   Question type: factual
   Reading skills: details, cause and effect

4. McLeod writes under a *pseudonym*. What is this?
   Comprehension level: literal
   Question type: vocabulary
   Reading skill: details
5. What are two things about McLeod's house and his pet that tell you about McLeod the man?
   Comprehension level: interpretive
   Question type: inferential
   Reading skill: drawing conclusions
6. Describe Justin McLeod's appearance.
   Comprehension level: literal
   Question type: factual
   Reading skill: details
7. What does Chuck mean when he says "With my usual luck, I have found another Hitler"? (p. 29)
   Comprehension level: interpretive
   Question types: inferential, experiential (based on the student's knowledge of Hitler)
   Reading skill: drawing conclusions

CHAPTER 3

1. What attitude does McLeod have toward tutoring Chuck?
   Comprehension level: literal
   Question type: factual
   Reading skill: details
2. How do you know McLeod may have taught before?
   Comprehension level: interpretive
   Question types: inferential, experiential (based on the student's knowledge of teachers)
   Reading skill: drawing conclusions
3. What does *racist* mean? What does the following sentence mean: "Grammar is a racist device for repressing the language of the people"? (p. 42)
   Part 1:
   Comprehension level: literal
   Question type: vocabulary
   Reading skill: details
   Part 2:
   Comprehension level: interpretive
   Question type: factual
   Reading skill: cause and effect

CHAPTER 4

1. How does Chuck get around telling his friends where he is going during the days?

Comprehension level: literal
Question type: factual
Reading skill: details

2. Why does Meg like "Barry Rumble Seat"?
Comprehension level: interpretive
Question type: inferential
Reading skill: drawing conclusions

3. Why does Meg come to talk to Chuck just before dawn?
Comprehension level: literal
Question type: factual
Reading skill: details

4. What might McLeod and his horse, Richard, have in common? (p. 56)
Comprehension level: interpretive
Question type: inferential
Reading skill: comparison and contrast

5. Chuck found it *disconcerting* that he was beginning to like McLeod. What does *disconcerting* mean? Why did this bother Chuck? (p. 61)
   Part 1:
   Comprehension level: literal
   Question type: vocabulary
   Reading skill: details
   Part 2:
   Comprehension level: interpretive
   Question type: inferential
   Reading skill: drawing conclusions

CHAPTER 5

1. The school psychologists gave Chuck *Rorschach tests.* What is a *Rorschach test?*
Comprehension level: literal
Question type: factual
Reading skill: details

2. Why does Gloria ask Meg questions about where Chuck is studying?
Comprehension level: interpretive
Question type: inferential
Reading skill: details

3. Why does Gloria have so much against Chuck? What is a *vendetta?*
Comprehension level: interpretive
Question type: factual
Reading skill: cause and effect

4. How does Chuck feel about his natural father? How does Gloria feel about Chuck's natural father?
   Comprehension level: interpretive
   Question types: factual, interefential
   Reading skills: comparison and contrast, drawing conclusions

CHAPTER 6

1. Why did Chuck want to stay at McLeod's house to study after they were finished tutoring?
   Comprehension level: literal
   Question type: factual
   Reading skill: details
2. Who is Terrence Blake?
   Comprehension level: literal
   Question type: factual
   Reading skill: details
3. Chuck says what he wants most is to be free from being crowded. What does he mean? (p. 81)
   Comprehension level: interpretive
   Question type: inferential
   Reading skill: drawing conclusions
4. What is tragic about the cause of McLeod's disfigured face?
   Comprehension level: interpretive
   Question type: inferential
   Reading skill: drawing conclusions
5. Why do you think McLeod reacted the way he did when Chuck reached out and touched his arm?
   Comprehension level: interpretive
   Question type: inferential
   Reading skill: making judgments

CHAPTER 7

1. How does Chuck react to McLeod's apparent rejection?
   Comprehension level: literal
   Question type: factual
   Reading skill: details
2. What does Chuck seem to be allergic to?
   Comprehension level: interpretive
   Question type: factual
   Reading skill: drawing conclusions
3. Why does Chuck feel guilty about the afternoon he spent with his friends?
   Comprehension level: interpretive
   Question type: factual
   Reading skill: making inferences

4. Why isn't Chuck too excited about the news of his mother's engagement to Barry?
   Comprehension level: interpretive
   Question type: inferential
   Reading skill: drawing conclusions, comparison and contrast (with Chuck's other stepfathers)

5. Meg says Gloria puts down Chuck and Meg because she (Gloria) has to be Number One. Is there a child in every family who feels he or she has to be Number One? Why?
   Comprehension level: applied
   Question type: experiential
   Reading skill: making judgments

CHAPTER 8

1. When McLeod sees Chuck is hung over, he stops the tutoring. What does this show you about McLeod's personality?
   Comprehension level: interpretive
   Question type: inferential
   Reading skill: drawing conclusions

2. Chuck has a happy, *euphoric* feeling. What does *euphoric* mean? What gives Chuck this feeling? (p. 111)
   Comprehension level: literal
   Question type: vocabulary
   Reading skill: details

3. How is Chuck feeling differently toward McLeod? Why? (p. 113)
   Comprehension level: interpretive
   Question type: inferential
   Reading skills: making inferences, drawing conclusions

CHAPTER 9

1. What events bring Justin and Chuck closer together?
   Comprehension level: literal
   Question type: factual
   Reading skill: details

2. What new things does Chuck learn about Justin?
   Comprehension level: literal
   Question type: factual
   Reading skill: details

CHAPTER 10

1. What might be a reason for Chuck's fainting in church?
   Comprehension level: interpretive
   Question type: inferential
   Reading skill: drawing conclusions

CHAPTER 11

1. Why is this chapter the climax of the book?
       Comprehension level: interpretive
       Question types: factual, vocabulary (the student must know
          the meaning of *climax*), inferential
       Reading skills: drawing conclusions, cause and effect
2. Percy's boot killed Moxie, but Chuck was as much to blame.
    Why?
       Comprehension level: interpretive
       Question type: inferential
       Reading skills: comparison and contrast, drawing conclusions
3. How does Gloria get even with Chuck for embarrassing her?
       Comprehension level: literal
       Question type: factual
       Reading skill: details
4. How is Chuck comforted by Justin? (p. 143)
       Comprehension level: interpretive (This is not a literal ques-
    tion because the description of the climactic encounter between
    Justin and Chuck is not spelled out in the book. The language is
    more indirect, and unless the reader pays close attention, he
    may not understand what is happening.)
       Question type: inferential
       Reading skills: details, cause and effect, drawing conclusions
5. Justin says, "The only thing you can't be free from is the conse-
    quence of what you do." How does this apply to Chuck's ac-
    tions with Moxie and Justin?
       Comprehension levels: literal (the meaning of the statement),
          applied
       Question type: inferential
       Reading skill: making judgments

CHAPTER 12

1. Who is the man without a face?
       Comprehension level: literal
       Question type: factual
       Reading skill: details
2. Why does Justin mention to Chuck that Barry had been an Air
    Force pilot?
       Comprehension level: interpretive
       Question type: inferential
       Reading skills: making inferences (about how Chuck will get
          along with Barry because Chuck himself wants to be a pi-
          lot), comparison and contrast (with the relationships
          Chuck has had with his other stepfathers)

3. What happens to Gloria, Justin, Chuck, and Barry?
    Comprehension level: literal
    Question type: factual
    Reading skill: details
4. Is this book a tragedy or a comedy? (Does it have a happy or a sad ending?)
    Comprehension level: interpretive
    Question type: experiential
    Reading skill: making judgments (If a student dwells on the fact that Justin dies, he may feel that the book is a tragedy. If he sees the reconciliation of Barry and Chuck as the major conclusion of the book, he may think it is a comedy. This is an opinion question which may be supported several ways with facts from the story.)

The skills of comprehension are many and varied. Writing comprehension questions can be quite complicated or quite simple, depending on how you approach the task. At first you may have to think specifically of the levels and kinds of comprehension while writing the questions, but you will soon develop the knack of constructing a study guide. The basic rule you should remember is the *FIVE* (Fact, Inference, Vocabulary, Experience) acronym. If you base your questions on this guideline, you'll find that most of the comprehension skills will be represented.

Before we started using study guides when we taught literature, many of our students floundered and had difficulty grasping the themes and details of the books. They frequently hated reading because they were afraid we would ask them questions about the literature that they would not be able to answer.

Our introduction of comprehension study guides changed all that. Now, the students know from the beginning what they are expected to read and what is important in the book. In addition, giving page references occasionally, boosts their self-images because they can find the answer more easily. We have noticed, also, that students are more apt to contribute to class discussions, because they feel more confident that they may have the right answer.

We would not think of teaching a novel, play, or long poem without the aid of a study guide. In fact, many content area teachers, especially in social studies and science, also use study guides. The students are now complaining that there are too many study guides, but we will continue to use them because the alternative is a return to the confused student who, after reading a novel for two weeks, doesn't know the difference between the theme and the main characters.

Writing 9

After reading and comprehension, writing is usually the weakest area for the poorer students. Because they have never understood grammatical rules, these students are used to being marked off on papers for poor writing and incomplete and run-on sentences. Unfortunately, for the past ten or fifteen years, teachers have tended to teach writing not through formal exercises but by simply having the students write. Somehow, we thought, the "feeling" for writing would develop, and the students would miraculously come to understand complete sentences and proper paragraph structure. Practice does help, of course, but practice by itself is not enough.

Today, writing is being stressed more. With the "back-to-basics" movement and the growth of state competency requirements, parents and school boards are demanding more accountability from teachers as to how Johnny is learning to write. Teachers are more concerned about teaching writing and are looking for ways to improve their students' sagging skills in this area.

There are several methods that can help the slower students improve their writing. The first is journal writing. We make extensive use of journal writing, and our students write for at least five or ten minutes at the beginning of each class period. Because of this extended writing practice, we see a gradual improvement throughout the year and a marked difference in the quality of the writing from September to June. Second, writing can be stressed in all four grades (ninth through twelfth) and can be stressed in social studies and science classes as well. Of course, having writing (and reading) stressed in all content areas is the ideal situation, and we realize that it may not be possible in most schools. The increased emphasis on competency, however, has schools looking for new ways to improve students' skills, and more schools may be willing to experiment with cross-curriculum ideas. Third, we have

153

developed a series of writing skills exercises for all four years of high school English. The exercises include practice in grammar, basic sentence construction, basic paragraph construction, composition writing, report writing, and various types of letter writing. These are the areas tested on the New York State Competency Test for Writing, which every graduating senior in the state must pass beginning in 1982. In this chapter we will look at each of these areas more carefully and show how you can implement these and other exercises in your classroom.

JOURNAL WRITING

By the time students with weak skills enter high school, they have probably given up trying to write well. They long ago despaired of ever understanding any of the complicated grammar rules; besides, the language they hear at home probably isn't the same one the teachers expect them to speak and write. For these students, writing just one paragraph is a horrendous task. When they do write, the teacher corrects so much that it hardly seems worth their effort. On top of that, the teacher never seems to have the time to spend with them individually to explain what they have done wrong, so they just keep making the same mistakes year after year.

When we tell these students who hate to write even one sentence that they will be writing in a journal for at least five or ten minutes every day, they moan and groan. For the first month or two, the students' struggles are obvious. It is an effort on the part of the students to write and on the part of the teacher to be tenacious enough to insist that they do write. We set no limits on how much the students write; we only ask that they write something every day. At first they often have difficulty thinking of a topic, so we do give some suggestions early in the school year. For example, we provide unfinished sentences on the board: "The dream that upset me the most was about . . ." or "The characteristics I am looking for in my wife/husband are. . . ." Sometimes we give a topic that has to do with the piece of literature we are studying: "I think Tuck should have handled Elva Grimes's mother's cruelty by. . . ." By Thanksgiving, however, the students are not as threatened by the idea of the journals and can write for longer periods of time about their own experiences.

We do not grade the journals. We do read the entries on a regular basis and make corrections and comments. This may sound time-consuming, but the amount of actual writing is very small, especially in the first part of the year. When the students gain more confidence in their writing, some may ask to have their entries graded. We only grade journal entries when students request that we do so, and we treat these grades as extra credit. Toward the end of the year, many of the students ask to have most of their entries graded because they know that their writing has improved, and the journal grades actually boost their overall average.

Sometimes we combine journal writing with reading in a week or two of Hooked-on-Books. (See chapter 4 for a complete description of this reading program.) Briefly, the students read any material they wish for the first part of the period. During the last ten minutes of the class, they write in their journals based on what they have read. They may summarize, criticize, or editorialize. This system accomplishes two purposes, especially for the ninth graders who are just being introduced to the idea of writing in journals. They are encouraged to read, another activity they hate, and they are writing. Most of them complain at first, but after they find a good book or magazine to read, they look forward to English class and later even to writing.

Even though journal writing adds to the workload of the teacher, we feel that the benefits to the students make journal writing worthwhile. If the students write faithfully for the entire school year, they will almost certainly see a marked improvement in their writing by June. Our students enjoy comparing their September entries to the May ones. Imagine how the students' writing would improve if they could write every school day for four years!

GRAMMAR

We noticed several years ago that many of the students entering high school did not know how to write. When we began to teach a new ninth-grade class in September, nearly all the students wrote incomplete and run-on sentences. We began with the usual questions: "Does that sentence sound complete? Does it express a complete thought?" Almost invariably the answer we received was yes. Obviously, we needed a different approach. We backed up a step and gave the students the basic rule for a complete sentence: Every sentence must have a subject (noun), a predicate (verb of action or being), and punctuation, and must express a complete thought. This was fine, but we found that most of the students didn't know which word in the sentence was the verb. We even had to explain the concept of a verb's showing action. The students weren't sure what we meant by *action!* It soon became clear that we would have to teach the "bare bones" of grammar before these students would be able to write anything substantial.

Grammar is probably the most ignored section of English curriculum because the students don't like it, don't understand it, and make a teacher's life miserable by complaining and groaning at every attempt to teach it. Because students begin high school on different skill levels, we have devised an individualized grammar program to screen those students who already know the basics of grammar from those who need intense drill in one or more areas of basic sentence structure. The course is divided into five main sections: complete sentences; run-on sentences; verbs; present, past, and future tenses; and has, have, and had usage. Each section consists of an initial diagnostic quiz, three or four packets of practice material, and a second diagnostic quiz. The students take the diagnostic quiz at the beginning of each section. Those who score 80 percent or better simply go on to the diagnostic quiz for the next section. A few students sail through the quizzes and then move on to other parts of the curriculum. The majority of the students, however, do not pass the diagnostic quizzes. They are assigned individualized packets for practice before they try to pass the second diagnostic quiz for each section. Because most of these students are also poor readers, the packets are on tape, as well as in written form, for easier comprehension.

Let us follow Tom, a poor reader and writer, through some of the steps of the individualized grammar. He has taken the first diagnostic quiz on complete sentences (figure 42) and has not passed it. The teacher gives Tom the first packet of practice material on complete and incomplete sentences. The practice material is typed on 3-by-5 index cards (one sentence per card, with the directions printed on the first card in the group). When Tom opens the packet, this is what he reads on the first card and hears on the tape:

> There will be ten sentences in this packet. Write your name on a piece of paper, and number from 1 to 10. If a sentence is complete, write C on your paper. If a sentence is not complete, STOP the tape. Write NC on your paper and rewrite the sentence to make it complete. Start the tape again and continue with the next sentence.

The following sentences are typed, one per card, on the remaining cards in the packet.

1. The team's main weakness
2. Can't be done
3. She will be ready soon
4. Is very friendly
5. Jim is a poor sport
6. A very stupid idea
7. Never tasted anything so good before
8. That book contains humor and suspense
9. Found the door of the room locked
10. I was sick

If Tom scores 90 percent or better on this packet, he may take the second diagnostic quiz (figure 43). If he doesn't, he goes on to the second packet, which contains ten more practice sentences. He continues

Figure 42. First Diagnostic Quiz on Complete Sentences

Name: _____

Below are ten sentences or parts of sentences. Write <u>C</u> in front of each <u>complete</u> sentence. Write <u>NC</u> in front of each sentence that is <u>not</u> <u>complete</u>. Then, on the blank lines at the bottom of the page, rewrite each group of words you marked as <u>not</u> <u>complete</u> (<u>NC</u>) to make it a complete sentence.

_____ 1. Was delivered yesterday.

_____ 2. That building with the red roof.

_____ 3. Without the slightest warning a heavy blow.

_____ 4. And was greeted by the entire family.

_____ 5. The whistle blew a few minutes ago.

_____ 6. If more paper is necessary.

_____ 7. Go home, Tippy!

_____ 8. What causes that noise?

_____ 9. Akron, the place where I was born.

_____ 10. George fell.

_____

_____

_____

_____

_____

_____

_____

_____

_____

_____

Figure 43. Second Diagnostic Quiz on Complete Sentences

Name: _____

Below are ten sentences or parts of sentences. Write C in front of each complete sentence. Write NC in front of each sentence that is not complete. Then, on the blank lines at the bottom of the page, rewrite each group of words you marked as not complete (NC) to make it a complete sentence.

_____ 1. Who painted the picture?

_____ 2. Jim gave the order.

_____ 3. Of course you can go.

_____ 4. Some nails and tacks which are in the jar.

_____ 5. We passed the car three times.

_____ 6. Mother my sister.

_____ 7. Our friends visited us.

_____ 8. Into the room.

_____ 9. Are mine.

_____ 10. The motorcycle was stolen.

_____

_____

_____

_____

_____

_____

_____

_____

_____

_____

with the practice packets until he scores 90 percent or better on one of them; then he takes the second diagnostic quiz. Since there are four packets of ten sentences each, Tom should have enough practice to complete this section successfully before moving on to the next one. Should he fail the second diagnostic quiz, the teacher would then design additional practice and testing material for him individually.

The second through fifth sections of our grammar program follow the same format. There are four packets of ten sentences each for each section. The students take a diagnostic quiz before beginning each section, and after scoring 90 percent or better on the packets, take a second diagnostic quiz to complete the section. By the time the students have worked through the five sections, they have a basic grasp of grammar, or at least they understand when we talk about complete sentences and verbs.

At the end of the unit, the students take a final test (figure 44). Most of the students pass this test, but there are a few who, after weeks of individualized effort and help from us, still do not comprehend the basic rules of grammar. For these students, we schedule extra help after school or ask the reading teacher who is helping in the room during the period to give extra attention to these students.

Management Sheets

Another aspect of this individualized grammar unit is management sheets on which the students record their scores. The students keep their sheets in their student folders in the English room. These management sheets are very simple and can take only a half a sheet of paper (figure 45).

With these sheets, the students know their scores on the quizzes at all times, and they know which packets to use each day. Because students are aware of their progress, they are not surprised when we tell them to work on an extra packet or to stay after school for extra help.

We also have a management sheet for the class so that we can tell at a glance where each student is working and how each student is progressing in relation to the others in the class. We can then give more attention to the slower students while moving the better students to other areas of the curriculum. An example of the teacher's management sheet is shown in figure 46.

WRITING SKILLS AND PRACTICE EXERCISES

Over the last several years, we have developed a series of exercises designed to improve the writing skills of the poorer student. This is a

(continued on page 162)

Figure 44. Final Test on Individualized Grammar Unit

Name: _____

I. Complete and Incomplete Sentences

Write a C next to the number if the item is a complete sentence. Write NC if the item is not complete. On the blank lines below, rewrite the items you marked NC to make them complete sentences.

_____ 1. Up until now.

_____ 2. Joan yelled.

_____ 3. Running up the street, Mary started to fall.

_____ 4. While running up the field, the boy.

_____ 5. The house next door to the broken red barn.

_____ 6. He occasionally slept until 10:00 a.m.

_____

_____

_____

_____

_____

II. Run-on Sentences

Add the proper punctuation to the sentences below so that they will no longer be run-on sentences.

1. Mr. Danova wore a green sweater he also had on green pants.

2. School is necessary in order to earn a living you need an education.

3. Mr. Baker spoke on the loudspeaker about the game it was cancelled.

4. Because he was tired, the boy fell asleep the dog was also sleeping.

5. The Senior Lobby is always crowded it is rarely quiet there.

6. The weather makes a difference in the kind of weekend we have rain can ruin the whole thing.

III. Verbs

Underline the complete verbs in the following sentences.

Figure 44. (*continued*)

1. The machine continued all night.

2. She has called me before.

3. He is driving over to my house tonight.

4. He will have been there at least three times before tonight.

IV. Tenses

On the blank line next to each sentence, write <u>present</u>, <u>past</u>, or <u>future</u> to identify the tense of the verb.

_____ 1. He thought of going over to her house.

_____ 2. He decided to call first.

_____ 3. She is answering the phone while the doorbell rings.

_____ 4. The salesman will bring the new car tomorrow.

_____ 5. I had already brought it to him.

_____ 6. She has had enough attention already.

_____ 7. I will have had it with her.

_____ 8. He has come to my house many times before.

V. Practical

On the long lines below, write a paragraph on the topic "I would like to own . . ." On the shorter lines at the left, write the tenses of the verbs that appear in each line in your paragraph. It will help you if you underline the verbs. When you have finished, be sure to proofread so that you catch any incomplete or run-on sentences.

_____   I would like to own _____

_____ _____

_____ _____

_____ _____

_____ _____

_____ _____

_____ _____

Figure 45. Student's Management Sheet for Grammar Unit

Name: _____

Unit	Diagnostic Quiz 1	Diagnostic Quiz 2	Packets Assigned
Complete Sentences			
Run-on Sentences			
Verbs			
Tenses			
Has, Have, and Had			

cross-grade curriculum, which we have implemented in grades nine, ten, and eleven. The series breaks writing down into several manageable units. It may be used as a complete course in basic writing skills or for occasional help in conjunction with the regular English curriculum. The units correspond to the skills tested by the New York State Writing Competency Test, but they are basic skills that any student in any state should master.

The chart in figure 47 shows the complete breakdown of the units by grade level. You will notice that the longer, more intense exercises are scheduled for the ninth grade. This is because ninth graders need more drill and practice than tenth and eleventh graders. Also, we like to start emphasizing writing as early as possible, so the students have a greater chance for success in their high school careers. There is more material here than can be used, so teachers can shoose which assignments to give and which skills to emphasize during the year. We will discuss the introductory sheets and some of the exercises in each unit in detail.

Figure 46. Individualized Grammar Unit Management Sheet

Student	Complete-Incomplete Sentences					Run-on Sentences					Recognizing Verbs					Verb Tenses					Has, Have, Had					FA
	Q	1	2	3	4	Q	5	6	7	8	Q	9	10	11	12	Q	13	14	15	16	Q	17	18	19	20	Q	

KEY: Q = Quiz
Pretest is recorded at the beginning of each segment.
Posttest is recorded at the conclusion of each segment.
Numbers refer to packets of remedial material.
FA = Final Average

Figure 47. Writing Skills Curriculum Overview

Grade 9	Grade 10	Grade 11
I. Grammar/Sentence Patterns a. Introductory sheet b. Scrambled sentences c. Subject/predicate d. Complete sentences e. Dividing sentences	**I. Paragraphs** a. Structure review b. Practice writing review c. Practice exercises based on novels read during the year	**I. Paragraphs** a. Structure review b. Practice exercises (two per novel read during the year)
II. Paragraphs a. Introductory sheet b. General-Specific c. Topic sentences d. Details e. Practice sheets for novels read during the year	**II. Compositions** a. Introductory/study review sheet b. Practice exercises based on novels	**II. Compositions** a. Structure review sheet b. Composition assignments and practice exercises for selected novels
III. Compositions a. Introductory/study sheet b. Transitions c. Development sheet d. Practice sheets for use with novels during year	**III. Report Writing** a. Review categorizing b. Organizing notes c. Practice report writing based on selected novels	**III. Persuasive Composition** a. Structure review sheet b. Sample composition to write for novels read during year
IV. Persuasive Composition a. Introductory/definition sheet b. Aim for audience c. Practice sheets for novels read during year	**IV. Persuasive Composition** a. Structure review sheet b. Practice compositions for use with novels during the year	**IV. Report Writing** a. Structure review sheet b. Practice organizing, sequencing, and note taking c. Report writing using basic techniques for three novels read in course
V. Report Writing a. Introductory/definition/ categorizing sheet b. Organizing c. Sequencing d. Practice sheets for organizing, categorizing, and sequencing e. Note taking f. Sample report based on novel read during year	**V. Letter Writing** a. Review structure and parts of friendly, business, and social letters b. Practice friendly letters and business letters c. Final test	**V. Letter Writing** a. Structure review sheet b. Practice exercises for friendly, business, and social letters

Figure 47. (*continued*)

Grade 9	Grade 10	Grade 11
VI. Letter Writing a. Outline to fill in based on lecture on kinds and parts of letters b. Form for labeling different parts of letter c. Addressing envelopes d. Writing friendly letters e. Social notes (explanation and practice) f. Business letters (outline to fill in based on lecture) g. Practice exercises h. Final tests		

Basic Sentence Patterns

The ninth grade is the only grade that has a separate unit on sentence patterns and grammar skills. We have found that the students often need to begin with the most basic elements of writing. Figure 48 is an example of the introductory study sheet for the first unit. Each unit begins with a similar sheet giving the background details for the unit and explaining the various parts of the topic. For this unit, the introduction defines the terms *subject, predicate,* and *complete thought,* which are the three basic parts of a complete sentence. For the next few worksheets, the students practice with sentences, unscrambling to gain a sense of order, dividing sentences into two major parts (subject and predicate), recognizing complete sentences, combining two sentences to form a complex sentence, and punctuating a paragraph to indicate the number of complete sentences it contains. By the time the students have completed these worksheets, they should have enough of a grasp of sentence structure to be able to move on to the next basic writing unit, the paragraph. As with anything else we teach, if a student is in obvious need of remedial help, we are available after school or individually during the class period.

During the tenth and eleventh grades, we assume that the skill of recognizing complete and incomplete sentences is partially rooted. We realize that most students must be reminded constantly to write complete sentences, but at least by the tenth and eleventh grades the stu-

Figure 48. Introductory Sheet for Sentence Structure Unit (Grade 9)

Name: _____

We use sentences all the time, but we have more experience in speaking sentences than in writing them because we talk more than we write. We may not always write well-constructed sentences. It is important for us to practice writing good sentences because the sentence is the main way by which we tell others our complete thoughts. If our words aren't in order or don't make sense, we are not able to communicate our ideas and thoughts very well to others.

This year we will stress four main ingredients of good sentence writing. All sentences:

   a. have a <u>subject</u>.
   b. have a <u>predicate</u> (<u>verb</u>).
   c. convey a <u>complete</u> <u>thought</u>.
   d. have punctuation.

Look at the following examples.

Subject *(Noun or Pronoun)*	*Predicate* *(Verb)*
You	will read <u>The Skating Rink</u> this year.
Tuck Faraday	is the main character.
He	has a speech defect.
His mother	is dead.

Note these points:

1. The <u>subject</u> of a sentence is a noun or pronoun and all the words related to it.
2. The <u>predicate</u> of a sentence is the verb and all the words related to it.
3. Usually the subject appears first in the sentence and the predicate follows.
4. All sentences express a <u>complete</u> <u>thought</u>.
5. All sentences end with a mark of punctuation (period, question mark, or exclamation point).

dents have heard the lecture on sentence patterns so much that they have a working knowledge of the skill. Of course, when necessary, we do review sentence patterns during the sophomore, junior, and senior years, for an entire class or an individual pupil.

Paragraphs

We next direct the students to paragraphing. The unit on paragraphing is essential to good writing, and we spend a great deal of time on this skill in the ninth and tenth grades. Again, the ninth-grade level puts the major emphasis on background and structure. The students may have heard about writing compositions in junior high, but the poorer students may not have understood it at all, and the others may have forgotten the material over the summer.

Since we try to coordinate the teaching of writing throughout high school, we try to be consistent as to which rules we expect the students to learn. It is helpful for the students and the teachers to have some continuity from class to class and grade to grade. For this reason, all of the teachers in the program expect the students to write in complete sentences and to have at least four sentences in every paragraph.

From the beginning of ninth grade, we teach paragraph writing according to the introductory sheet in figure 49. Every paragraph has a topic sentence, two detail sentences, and a concluding sentence. If the writer has more to say, there may be more detail sentences of course; but we have found that the slower students, especially, adhere to the four-sentence rule fairly religiously.

The ninth graders spend more time than the other students on paragraph procedure. After reading the initial introductory sheet, they complete several exercises dealing with aspects of basic paragraph writing; namely, moving from general topics to specific details, writing topic sentences, organizing facts for the detail or body of the paragraph, and writing concluding sentences.

The first worksheets of the paragraph unit should be taught together; however, after that the teachers have a choice because the remaining worksheets provide practice in writing based on the novels read during the year. For example, the ninth grade reads *West Side Story; Rumble Fish,* by S. E. Hinton;[1] *Patch of Blue,* by Elizabeth Kata;[2] *The Skating Rink,* by Mildred Lee;[3] and several short stories and poems. For each of these selections, we have devised two exercises that, using the content of the literature, give the students practice in paragraph writing. In this way, teachers can teach the technique of good paragraph

[1]New York: Dell, 1975.
[2]New York: Popular Library, 1961.
[3]New York: Dell, 1969.

Figure 49. Introductory Sheet for Paragraph Unit (Grade 9)

Name: _____

When we want to write about something for more than a few sentences, we usually organize the sentences into the form of a paragraph. Almost everything we read is organized into paragraphs: reports, stories, newspaper articles, and essays. Paragraphs are the basic building blocks of most written literature. Because one paragraph emphasizes one main idea, we can follow and understand what we read more easily. Paragraphs are very important in writing. All paragraphs have several things in common:

1. The <u>topic</u> sentence is a general statement (usually the first sentence) that tells the reader what the paragraph is about.
2. The <u>body</u> of the paragraph contains several sentences that give details about the general topic.
3. The last sentence wraps up or <u>summarizes</u> what the paragraph has been saying. Sometimes this sentence will be a bridge tying together two paragraphs. (This is called a <u>transition</u>.)

Read the following paragraph. Notice the different parts.

topic { Most experts think barbiturate addiction is harder to cure than narcotic dependency. A

body { user must take bigger and bigger doses to feel an effect. If he stops taking the drug all at once, he may suffer cramps, nausea, convulsions, and, in some cases, sudden death. Withdrawal— stopping the use of the drug—should take place in a hospital, over a period of many weeks. It

conclusion { takes several months for the body to return to normal.*

Most paragraphs that you write should have at least <u>four</u> sentences:
     one topic sentence
     two detail sentences
     one concluding or summary sentence

---

*William Goodykoontz, *Drugs: Insights and Illusions* (New York: Scholastic Magazines, 1971), p. 14.

writing in conjunction with the novels that the students are reading. We vary the format of these worksheets so that the students aren't simply writing a paragraph for every book. The formats also reinforce some of the major points of building a good paragraph. Figures 50, 51, 52, and 53 are examples of exercises that we use for *West Side Story* and *Rumble Fish*.

Figure 54 illustrates the kind of introductory structure review sheet we give the students in the tenth grade as a way of reviewing the material that they studied in more depth in the ninth grade. For comparison, look at figure 55 and see the difference in the review sheet for the eleventh grade. This is the shortest review sheet because these students have studied paragraph structure for two years and most of them should have the technique well in hand. Of course, seasoned teachers know this isn't always the case, but at least the eleventh graders recall more quickly after having learned about paragraphs during the two previous years.

Compositions

Next in the writing skills curriculum is the composition. As before, the most extensive instructions and examples are found in the ninth-grade curriculum. Figure 56 is our introductory sheet for the ninth grade. It contains a section on the importance of composition writing and a diagram showing the parts of a composition. We also compare the structure of the paragraph with the structure of the composition. The slower readers may find this comparison complicated and may require some additional worksheets from you.

Figure 57 shows our worksheet on the use of transitions. We like to introduce the idea of transitions in the composition unit. Because the composition is longer than the paragraph, it needs more organization and should have bridges between the paragraphs. Many students write one paragraph after another and don't understand that the paragraphs should be connected in some manner. The purpose of the transitions worksheet is to make the students familiar with the use of transitions and to give them some practice in using transitions.

Finally, we give a sample composition. (See figure 58. This sample composition is fairly complex. Both the theme and the difficulty of the composition you select should be appropriate for your students.) We arranged this worksheet in the order that the students might follow if they were going through the process of writing a composition. Some of the skills taught here, narrowing a topic, arranging details in order, and sequencing, are skills that the students will use in writing reports later in the writing unit. We conclude this worksheet with an actual composi-

(continued on page 180)

Figure 50. Worksheet for Paragraph Unit (Grade 9)

WEST SIDE STORY   *Name:* _____

Choose one of the following topic sentences and write a short paragraph of at least four sentences. Remember to include supporting detail sentences and the concluding sentence.

1. The Sharks and the Jets are rival street gangs in New York City.
2. All the members of the gangs have nicknames that tell us something about the people.
3. Falling in love doesn't depend on the nationalities of the two people involved.
4. Maria is a young girl who is trying to grow up in a difficult time and place.
5. Tony is more mature than other characters in the play.

Figure 51. Worksheet for Paragraph Unit (Grade 9)

WEST SIDE STORY   *Name:* _____

Read the following paragraph. Then rewrite the paragraph, taking out the sentences that do not have anything to do with main idea.

In the play *West Side Story*, the adults do not have a major role. The majority of the characters are young people who live on the streets of New York City. Consuelo is Pepe's girl. In fact, we see that the adults don't seem to want to have much to do with the young people. Tony is almost an adult. Perhaps the reason the adults avoid contact with the youths is that they feel threatened by them. The adults don't understand the kids' way of life or their values. The Sharks and the Jets are fighting for territory all the time. This is a play that illustrates what little influence adults have with inner-city youth.

Figure 52. Worksheet for Paragraph Unit (Grade 9)

RUMBLE FISH   *Name:* _____

Below are several sentences taken from a paragraph in the story. They are not in the right order for a good paragraph, however. Put these sentences in the right order and write a good paragraph.

1. He couldn't do much about it except hate the kids, though.
2. The high schoolers used to go there, but when the younger kids moved in, they moved out.
3. Benny's was the hangout for the junior high kids.
4. Benny was pretty mad about it.
5. If a place gets marked as a hangout, that's it.
6. Junior high kids don't have as much money to spend.

Figure 53. Worksheet for Paragraph Unit (Grade 9)

RUMBLE FISH   *Name:* _____

Choose one of the following statements from the story and write a paragraph explaining it in your own words. Remember all the points of good paragraph writing:

1. topic sentence (main idea)
2. detail sentences (supporting ideas)
3. concluding sentence (summary)
4. indent the first line and write complete sentences

1. "Progressive country, integrated mugging," Steve muttered. (p. 79)
2. Blind terror in a fight can easily pass for courage. (p. 85)
3. You get crazy enough in a fight without being doped up. (p. 24)
4. Even the most primitive societies have an innate respect for the insane. (p. 85)
5. If you were the toughest, you were the leader. (p. 98)

Figure 54. Structure Review Sheet for Paragraph Unit (Grade 10)

Name: _____

The paragraph is the main structure for organizing writing in the English language. If we want to write so that the reader can follow logically, we must write good paragraphs. Each paragraph develops one main idea. Paragraphs contain:

1. a <u>topic</u> sentence, or general statement (usually the first sentence), that tells the reader what the paragraph will be about.
2. the <u>body</u>, or middle, of the paragraph, which contains several sentences that give details about the general topic.
3. a <u>concluding</u> sentence that wraps up or summarizes what the paragraph has been saying. Sometimes this sentence will be a bridge tying together two paragraphs. (This is called a <u>transition</u>.)

Most paragraphs that you write should have at least <u>four</u> sentences:
one topic sentence
two (or more) detailed sentences
one concluding sentence

Read the following paragraph and notice the different parts:

topic

    Margot is very sweet and would like me to trust her, but still, I can't tell her everything.

body

She's darling, she's good and pretty, but she lacks the nonchalance for conducting deep discussion; she takes me so seriously, much too seriously, and then thinks about her queer little sister for a long time afterwards, looks searchingly at me, at every word I say, and keeps on thinking: "Is this just a joke or does she really

conclusion

mean it?" I think that's because we are together the whole day long, and that if I trusted someone completely, then I shouldn't want them hanging around me all the time.*

Anne Frank: The Diary of a Young Girl, trans. B. M. Mooyaart (New York: Pocket Books, 1953), p. 155.

Figure 55. Structure Review Sheet for Paragraph Unit (Grade 11)

Name: _____

The paragraph is the main structure for organizing writing in the English language. If we want to write so that the reader can follow logically, we must write good paragraphs. Each paragraph develops one main idea. Paragraphs contain:

1. a topic sentence, or general statement (usually the first sentence), that tells the reader what the paragraph will be about
2. a body, or middle, of the paragraph, which contains several sentences that give details about the general topic
3. a concluding sentence that wraps up or summarizes what the paragraph has been saying. Sometimes this sentence will be a bridge tying together two paragraphs. (This is called a transition.)

Most paragraphs that you write should have at least four sentences:
one topic sentence
two (or more) detail sentences
one concluding sentence

Read the following paragraph and notice the different parts:

topic { Darry didn't deserve to work like an old man when he was only twenty. He had been a

body { real popular guy in school; he was captain of the football team and he had been voted Boy of the Year. But we just didn't have the money for him to go to college, even with the athletic scholarship he won. And now he didn't have time between jobs to even think about college.

conclusion { So he never went anywhere and never did anything any more, except work out at gyms and go skiing with some old friends of his sometimes.*

---

*S. E. Hinton, *The Outsiders* (New York: Dell, 1967), p. 14.

Figure 56. Introductory Sheet for Composition Unit (Grade 9)

Name: _____

We have been studying about how to write a good paragraph. Now, we will take our study of writing one step further and discuss the composition. A composition is a series of related paragraphs grouped together under one title.

Why is it important to learn to write good compositions? To answer this question, let's talk about communicating. One of our main jobs in life is to try to make others understand how we feel and what we are saying. We can do this more easily if we put our thoughts in some logical order, and in language that is common to most people. For example, if we understood the language below, the following conversation between a waiter and a customer would be easy to read:

"FUNEX?" (Have you any eggs?)
"SVFX." (Yes we have eggs.)
"FUNEM?" (Have you any ham?)
"SVFM." (Yes we have ham.)
"OK, LFMNX." (Okay, I'll have ham and eggs.)

Sometimes experimenting with new languages and codes can be fun. But when we are writing compositions to communicate our thoughts and feelings, it is best to stick to language and structure that the readers will understand.

When we write compositions, the structure, or order, is important. Let's use the following group of short sentences as an example:

Jack owned a car. He wanted to repair it. He wanted to save money. He took a course. It was for auto mechanics. He completed the course successfully. He was able to repair his car.

Some readers might put these sentences in one order to say one thing:

After Jack successfully completed the auto mechanics course, he was able to repair his own car and, as a result, save money.

But, other readers might put the sentences in a different order to say something different:

Jack successfully completed the auto mechanics course because he wanted to save money by repairing his own car.

Figure 56. (*continued*)

You can see how important structure is if the reader is going to understand what is written. Therefore, you, as the writer, need to know the basic structures of written literature so you can make your ideas known. When your teachers ask you to write a composition, they expect your paper to be in an accepted format so that they can follow what you are saying.

Like a paragraph, a composition has three basic parts:

	Introduction	Body	Conclusion
Paragraph	topic sentence (first sentence)	detail sentences (middle sentences)	Summary sentence (last sentence)
Composition	first paragraph	middle paragraph(s)	last paragraph

FORMAT OF A COMPOSITION

Introduction
> first paragraph: Make general statements about the topic. Point ahead to some details to be discussed.

(transition phrase or sentence)

Body
> middle paragraph(s): Discuss details that back up the general topic and make your point. (If you have many details that need to be organized, you may need more than one middle paragraph.)

(transition phrase or sentence)

Conclusion
> last paragraph: Conclude your discussion. Summarize what you have said in the body (without repeating word by word).

Figure 57. Worksheet on Transitions for Composition Unit (Grade 9)

Name: _____

We want the person who is reading our writing to be able to follow our thoughts. In order to help the reader we use bridges, or links, called transitions to carry him from one thought to the next. These transitions can be a word, a phrase, or an entire sentence. A transitional word or phrase is followed by a comma in a sentence.

Word and phrase transitions

Here are some common transitional words and phrases:

as a result	furthermore	nevertheless
besides	in addition	namely
finally	in other words	second
first	likewise	therefore
for example	moreover	yet

Examples:

The principal and the parents met to discuss discipline of the student; <u>however</u>, they accomplished nothing.

They decided, <u>as a result</u>, to suspend the student from school.

Exercise 1

Add a transition word or phrase to combine the two sentences to make one sentence.

1. Three months ago John Smith announced his candidacy for the Senate. _____ Last week he decided not to run.
2. Bears in national parks overturn waste cans, trying to get food. _____ They tear up picnic baskets and food storage sacks.
3. The speeding car hit a power pole. _____ At least 4,000 homes had no electricity until the damage was repaired.

Exercise 2

Add commas (,) or semicolons (;) to set off the transitions from the sentences.

Figure 57. (*continued*)

1. Finally Tom realized that Joan would not return.
2. The Webers bought a new house in addition they purchased a second car.
3. Mike therefore admitted the error.
4. Jane's father insisted that she continue to live at home nevertheless she rented an apartment anyway.

Sentence transitions

Parts of a sentence or whole sentences may be used as transitions within a paragraph and between paragraphs. Sometimes the first sentence in a paragraph will mention a fact that was discussed in the previous paragraph as a means of connecting the two paragraphs. Read the following paragraph and notice the transitions in CAPITAL LETTERS:

> WHEN THE GRAVE IS FINISHED, the wasp returns to the tarantula to complete her ghastly enterprise. FIRST, she feels it all over once more with her antennae. THEN, her behavior becomes more aggressive. She bends her abdomen, protruding her sting, and searches for the soft membrane at the point where the spider's legs join its body—the only spot where she can penetrate the horny skeleton. FROM TIME TO TIME, as the exasperated spider slowly shifts ground, the wasp turns on her back and slides along with the aid of her wings, trying to get under the tarantula for a shot at the vital spot. DURING ALL THIS MANEUVERING, which can last for several minutes, the tarantula makes no move to save itself. FINALLY, the wasp corners it against some obstruction and grasps one of its legs in her powerful jaws. NOW AT LAST the harassed spider tries a desperate but vain defense. The two contestants roll over and over on the ground. It is a terrifying sight and the outcome is always the same. The wasp FINALLY manages to thrust her sting into the soft spot and hold it there for a few seconds while she pumps in the poison. ALMOST IMMEDIATELY, the tarantula falls paralyzed on its back. Its legs stop twitching; its heart stops beating. YET, it is not dead, as is shown by the fact that if taken from the wasp it can be restored to some sensitivity by being kept in a moist chamber for several months.
>
> AFTER PARALYZING THE TARANTULA, the wasp cleans herself. . . .*

---

*Alexander Petrunkevitch, "The Spider and the Wasp," in *Writing with a Thesis*, ed. David Skwire (New York: Holt, Rinehart and Winston, 1979), p. 62.

Figure 58. Worksheet for Composition Unit (Grade 9)

Now we will follow the writing of a composition from beginning to end—from selection of a general topic to the finished composition. These are steps you might follow when asked to write a composition on any topic.

1. Choose a general topic.
   chipmunks

2. Narrow the topic to something you can write about in a few paragraphs.
   Chipmunks are cute.
   Some chipmunks hoard nuts.
   Chipmunks have enemies like shrikes. (This is the selected topic.)
   Chipmunks take good care of their families.

3. List some details about the topic you have chosen. They don't have to be in any order yet.
   escapes death at a banquet   hoards nuts in piles
   male and female chipmunks   shrike wants to catch
   killed taking walk by Stoop,   chipmunk
      shrike's brother   gets husband up early, gets
   male is helpless   exercise
   female returns   can't get into door—too
   female leaves   clogged with dirty laundry
   cleans house   shrike killed by hitting head
   arranges nuts in designs   on a tree branch

4. Arrange the details in some order, using an outline or other method.
   a. male and female chipmunk
      arranges nuts
      hoards nuts
      female leaves
      male is helpless
      escapes death at banquet
   b. shrike wants to catch chipmunk
      can't get into door—too clogged with dirty laundry
      killed hitting head on tree branch
   c. female returns
      cleans house
      gets husband up early, gets exercise
      killed taking walk by Stoop, shrike's brother

This composition will be three paragraphs based on a, b, and c above.

Figure 58. (*continued*)

THE SHRIKE AND THE CHIPMUNK*

Introductory Paragraph

topic sentence {
Once <u>upon a time</u>† there were two chipmunks, a male and female. The male chipmunk thought that arranging nuts in artistic patterns was more fun than just piling them up to see how many you could pile up. The female was all for piling up as many as you could. She told her husband that if he gave up making designs with the nuts there would be room in their large cave for a great many more and he would soon become the wealthiest chipmunk in the woods. <u>But</u>† he would not let her interfere with his designs, so she flew into a rage and left him. "The shrike will get you," she said, "because you are helpless and cannot look after yourself." <u>To be sure</u>, the female chipmunk had not been gone three nights before the male had to dress for a banquet and could not find his studs or shirt or suspenders. <u>So</u> he couldn't go to the banquet, but that

concluding sentence {
was just as well, because all the chipmunks who did go were attacked and killed by a weasel.

Body Paragraph

topic sentence {
<u>The next day</u> the shrike began hanging around outside the chipmunk's cave, waiting to catch him. The shrike couldn't get in because the doorway was clogged up with soiled laundry and dirty dishes. "He will come out for a walk after breakfast and I will get him then," thought the shrike. <u>But</u> the chipmunk slept all day and did not get up and have breakfast until after dark. <u>Then</u> he came out for a breath of air before beginning work on a new design. The shrike swooped down to snatch up the chipmunk, but could not see very well on ac-

concluding sentence {
count of the dark, <u>so</u> he batted his head against an alder branch and was killed.

Concluding Paragraphs

topic sentence {
<u>A few days later</u> the female chipmunk returned and saw the awful mess the house was in. She went to the bed and shook her husband. "What would you do without me?" she demanded. "Just go on living, I guess," he said. "You wouldn't last five days," she told him. She swept the house and washed the soiled laundry. <u>Then</u> she noticed her lazy husband.

"You can't be healthy if you lie in bed all day and never get any exercise," she told him. <u>So</u> she took him for a walk in

concluding sentence {
the bright sunlight and they were both caught and killed by the shrike's brother, a shrike named Stoop.

MORAL: Early to rise and early to bed makes a male healthy and wealthy and dead.

---

†Underlined words = transition words.

*James Thurber, "The Shrike and the Chipmunk," Copr. © 1940 James Thurber. Copr. © 1968 Helen Thurber. From *Fables for Our Time*, published in the United States by Harper & Row and in England by Hamish Hamilton Ltd. Used by permission.

tion that we analyze for all the elements that we have emphasized: introduction, middle paragraphs, concluding paragraph, topic sentences, and transitions. Although the teaching of compositions could be quite an involved task, we try to keep the instruction to a minimum because the slower students need to have things simplified. Even though you can probably think of at least another two weeks' worth of material to cover, try to give your class the basics only.

The tenth and eleventh grade classes each have review sheets that describe the basics of composition writing. In all of these grades, the teacher has several options that will give the class practice in writing compositions. Usually, each assignment accompanies a reading selection. For example, in ninth grade after completing *The Skating Rink*, by Mildred Lee, the students are asked to write a composition on one of the following topics:

1. Describe the major character in the book and explain why the story revolved around him or her.
2. Which of the following parts of a novel do you think was most important to this book: plot, characterization, setting, theme?
3. We all have met others who have a physical problem or an emotional handicap. After reading this book, has your attitude toward the physically or emotionally handicapped person changed? How would you act towards such a person now?

The students then write a three-paragraph composition based on the guidelines given in the introductory material. Since the guidelines are consistent from grade level to grade level, the basic format is reinforced every year. By the time the students take the basic competency test in the eleventh grade, they are well prepared. Of course, the success of this system depends on the teachers. All the teachers involved in teaching the slower students must understand the sequence of writing materials and be willing to spend the class time working on these skills with the students.

Persuasive Compositions

Probably the most advanced type of composition to teach is the persuasive composition. Actually, many teachers of ninth graders may not get to the persuasive composition, especially if their students are quite slow readers. As you can see from figure 59 the persuasive composition is a bit more complicated than the simple three-paragraph composition. With the persuasive composition, the student must write four paragraphs and each paragraph has a specific purpose. The first one is the introductory paragraph that states the purpose, the second states the

Figure 59. Worksheet for Persuasive Composition Unit (Grade 9)

This year, we have studied paragraphs, and three-paragraph compositions. The next step in writing is the four-paragraph persuasive composition. What is the difference between the three-paragraph composition and the four-paragraph persuasive composition?

	Three-Paragraph Composition	Four-Paragraph Persuasive Composition
Purpose	to entertain; to show knowledge of a book	to persuade someone to think like you do about a topic
Format	par. 1: introduction par. 2: body (details) par. 3: conclusion	par. 1: introduction/state your position par. 2: first reason for your opinion, and facts par. 3: second reason for your opinion, and facts par. 4: conclusion
Audience	usually the teacher who wants to see if you understand the literature	could be anyone you want to convince

Several of the steps in writing the three-paragraph composition still
apply to the persuasive composition:

1. Decide on a general topic.
2. Narrow the general topic down to two or three possibilities for the
   composition.
3. List two reasons for your position on the topic.
4. List details and facts to back up your two reasons. Have at least two
   facts for each reason.
5. Write your lists and reasons in a composition.
6. Make sure each paragraph of the composition has a topic sentence,
   body sentences, and a concluding sentence.

first reason for the student's opinion on the issue, the third paragraph states the second reason for the student's opinion, and the fourth paragraph concludes and reiterates the position. This is quite sophisticated for ninth graders, especially slower ninth graders. In addition to being aware of the specific purpose of each paragraph, they must also be aware of their audience. They must understand who is going to be reading the composition. Whom are they trying to persuade? Figure 60 illustrates a worksheet that teaches the students about writing for a certain audience. So much in a persuasive composition depends on how the writer approaches the audience. This is a difficult concept to explain to students, and they may need more than a little practice with it if they are to delve into persuasive composition.

Finally, we take the pupil step by step through the preparation and writing of a persuasive composition. The best way to write these worksheets is to put yourself in the place of the students. Try to remember when you didn't know anything about writing. How can you simplify writing down to a few basic steps? Always keep things simple. We teachers have a constant battle with the problem of accumulated knowledge. Because we learn more and know more every year, we expect our students to know more too. Every bit of knowledge seems ultimately important to us. This is not so, and we should condense our knowledge to a few small kernels in the interest of helping the slower learners acquire the basics. In figure 61 you will see how we condensed the problem of writing the persuasive composition to ten steps.

The tenth and eleventh grade curricula also include the persuasive composition, but in a review form that covers only the main ideas. If the ninth-grade teacher has not had time to initiate work on persuasive compositions, then the tenth-grade teacher will wish to start with the introductory-level material instead of the prescribed review. Each grade level offers the teachers opportunities to include persuasive composition assignments during and after the novels that the class studies. This method of combining writing with reading does several things. The students practice their writing all during the year, and they see some reason for writing. The process of writing often prepares them for a test or helps in review by pulling together the main ideas or characters. While organizing their ideas in preparation for writing, the pupils are essentially reviewing for a test. Writing for review also aids the slower students who cannot "think on their feet" and who feel more secure when given a definite topic. Many students hate writing, especially when teachers say, "Today you are going to write a composition on anything you want." The teachers may think that they are doing the students a favor by leaving the topic up to them; however, most times the slower students can't think of any topics that they feel would be worthwhile. When reading, literature, and writing are intertwined, the students see a reason for writing and may not be as repelled by the task.

(continued on page 186)

Figure 60. Worksheet for Persuasive Composition Unit (Grade 9)

Name: _____

Whom are you trying to persuade?

One of the important things to remember in writing a persuasive composition is the person you are trying to convince. For example, if you were trying to gain permission from an adult to allow you to hitchhike alone across the country, you would use different arguments depending on whether you were talking to your older sister or your grandmother. When you are writing a persuasive composition, it is important to keep in mind the kind of person you are trying to convince.

Argument: I have to drive the car to school today.

    Reason for mother: I can save you a trip to the store and pick up the groceries on the way home.

    Reason for teacher: I can drive part of the class to the museum since we can't get a bus for the field trip.

Argument: I want to go to college (get a job) in another state.

    Reason for father: You have done a good job of raising me and I am independent and can take care of myself.

    Reason for friend: Living on my own will give me freedoms I don't have at home.

Argument: I shouldn't be punished for wrecking the car.

    Reason for policeman: I hit the tree because I swerved to avoid hitting the six-year-old on the bike.

    Reason for father: I am so shook up that I have learned my lesson; besides, if you could see the car, you would be thankful that I'm alive.

Argument: I should be able to stay out until midnight on weekends.

    Reason for friend: Nothing starts happening until 11:00.

    Reason for mother: _____

                            _____

(continued)

Figure 60. (*continued*)

Argument: There should be no homework assigned on weekends.

Reason for teacher: _____

_____

Reason for sister: _____

_____

_____

Figure 61. Worksheet for Persuasive Composition Unit (Grade 9)

Let's take a topic and follow it through to see how a persuasive composition would be organized and written.

1. Choose a general topic.
   teen-agers and parents

2. Narrow the topic to several possibilities for argument.
   a. parents are easier on boys than girls
   b. rules for taking the car
   c. rules for dating
   d. girls dating older boys (This is the selected topic.)

3. Write a sentence that states what you plan to argue in your composition.
   A ninth-grade girl should be allowed to attend the Senior Dinner Dance with a senior boy, and she should not have to be in by 11:00.

4. Think about whom you are trying to persuade in your composition.
   You are pretending to talk to the parents of the ninth-grade girl, to convince them that she should go to the Senior Dinner Dance.

5. List two reasons for your opinions.
   a. The senior has spent the money for the tickets already.
   b. It is unfair to the boy that he will not be able to attend his senior dance.

Figure 61. (*continued*)

6. List facts and details to back up your reasons in step 5.
   a. spent money already
      1. had to buy the tickets
      2. bought new clothes and fixed up his car
   b. unfair not to attend dance
      1. the final social affair for his class
      2. would get depressed if he sat home

7. Write the first paragraph of the composition. Do the following things in this paragraph:
   a. Have a topic sentence, and a concluding sentence.
   b. Introduce your subject, give your opinion, and identify your audience.
   c. Explain what your composition will be about.

8. Write the second paragraph of the composition. Do the following things:
   a. Write a topic sentence stating your <u>first</u> <u>reason</u>, or argument, why the girl should attend the dance.
   b. Write <u>two</u> <u>detail</u> <u>sentences</u> backing up this argument.
   c. Write a concluding sentence for the paragraph.

9. Write the third paragraph of the composition. Do the following things:
   a. Write a topic sentence stating your <u>second</u> <u>reason</u>, or argument, why the girl should attend the dance.
   b. Write <u>two</u> <u>detail</u> <u>sentences</u> backing up this argument.
   c. Write a concluding sentence for the paragraph.

10. Write the fourth paragraph of the composition. Do the following things:
    a. Write a topic sentence repeating what your purpose was in writing the composition.
    b. Write two detail sentences summarizing your opinion.
    c. Write a concluding sentence for the entire composition.

When you have completed the assignment, show it to your teacher.

For example, in grade 10 a possible topic for *Lord of the Flies,* by William Golding,[4] would be:

> You are Ralph, and you are trying to convince the boys on the island that you would be a more effective leader than Jack. Give at least two reasons why you believe that you have more to offer the group. Explain each reason.

For *The Diary of Anne Frank:*[5]

> You are Peter. Your father wants to kill Mouche so that she will not continue to eat food that the families need and so that she will not give their position away. Write a composition of about 150 words defending your desire to keep Mouche. Give at least three reasons why you believe she shouldn't be killed. Explain each reason. Keep in mind that the purpose of your composition is to persuade your father that you are right.

If you give writing assignments like these throughout the year, your students will have much writing experience in connection with the novels that they read. For each novel, the students should have practice with paragraph writing, compositions, and persuasive writing.

Report Writing

Another area emphasized on some competency tests and by English teachers everywhere is report writing. Our writing skills curriculum includes worksheets that we developed to help the students learn the skills of report writing.

We feel that students must learn the skills of categorizing and sequencing before they will be able to take a few notes and turn them into a usable report. Figure 62 shows the first introductory sheet in the report unit. If the students have not had categorizing exercises for vocabulary

Figure 62. Categorization Worksheet for Report Writing Unit (Grade 9)

Name: _____

The key to writing a good report is your ability to do two things:
   a. collect good, usable information
   b. organize that information logically

Once you have found a good source of information, collecting ideas to use in your report is not hard. The difficult part is organizing those ideas. The first step is to try to group ideas into similar categories. Here are some exercises to help you develop this skill.

[4]New York: Capricorn Books, 1954.
[5]*The Diary of Anne Frank,* rev. ed., trans. B. M. Mooyart (New York: Doubleday, 1967).

Figure 62. (*continued*)

I. Cross out the item in each group below that does not belong. On the blank line after each group, write the name of the category to which the remaining words belong.

Monte Carlo
Phoenix
~~Blood Sweat 'n Tears~~
GTO

Cars

Cape Cod
~~Durhamville~~
Florida
Bermuda

vacation spots

filling up with gas
~~getting back to work~~
packing a suitcase
making reservations

planning for vacation

~~getting a job~~
planning courses with goal in mind
meeting school board requirement
taking competency tests

Completing graduation requirements

II. Below are a list of words and three possible categories. Write each word in the list on a blank line under the appropriate category:

1. acrobat	9. scalp	17. joint
2. aluminum	10. abdomen	18. limb
3. attorney	11. aviator	19. marble
4. bone	12. beggar	20. nostril
5. cement	13. brick	21. spine
6. janitor	14. butler	22. asbestos
7. maid	15. chef	23. adobe
8. mortar	16. ebony	24. bishop

Parts of the Body	Professions	Building Materials
bone	*acrobat*	*aluminum*
scalp	*attorney*	*cement*
abdomen	*janitor*	*mortar*
	maid	
	aviator	
	beggar	

words, they can practice here. Some students may need more practice than is provided here, and you may have to devise more worksheets. Figure 63 shows exercises that give the students some practice in categorizing the kinds of notes they may collect in the process of writing their reports.

Figure 64 also shows how you can guide the students in organizing material. Since the purpose of these worksheets is to give the students some practice in the skill you wish them to master, they contain exercises, as well as explanations of the skill. By reading the explanation and then trying to use the skill, the students have a better chance of learning the idea you want to convey.

The final step in teaching report writing is showing the students what to do with the material they have collected and sequenced. There are not as many practice reports for the students to write. Writing a single paragraph or a three-paragraph composition is easier than a complete report. The students should have some practice, however. You can provide this practice in two ways. You can assign a topic and have the students gather their own facts, or you can give them a group of facts, as in figure 65, and ask them to sequence and organize the facts before writing them in final report form. If the students do this two or three times a year, they should have sufficient practice to pass a competency test or to write the longer reports often required of them as they move on to the higher grades.

(continued on p. 192)

Figure 63. Categorizing Worksheet for Report Writing (Grade 9)

Name: _____

Putting ideas into similar groups is part of organizing. For example, if you were writing a report on the steps of a camping trip, you would group all of the ideas that have to do with <u>preparation</u> under one heading. All the ideas that have to do with the <u>camping</u> <u>trip</u> <u>itself</u>, go under a second heading. The ideas that have to do with <u>cleaning</u> <u>up</u> or retelling some of the neat things which happened belong under a third heading.

Take the following list of ideas or items about a camping trip and put them under the proper headings.

toasting marshmallows	tied rack on car
raccoons invaded our garbage	hiked up to March
borrowed a knapsack	pressed leaves in book

Figure 63. (*continued*)

bought fuel for lantern
raked campsite
dug trench around tent
put in extra socks
froze water in old waxed milk
    containers
bought batteries for the radio
tied rope to tree for jumping in
    water
put rocks on garbage lid

left notches on trees
invited Mike to go with us next
    year
told kids about Joe losing his
    jeans
decided afterwards I'd like to be
    a ranger
filled in slop hole
wrote to grandmother to tell her
    about trip

THE CAMPING TRIP

1. Preparation: Getting ready to go camping

_____
_____
_____
_____
_____

2. Actual Camping Trip: While we were there

_____
_____
_____
_____
_____

3. Cleaning Up: What we did

_____
_____
_____
_____
_____
_____

Figure 64. Sequencing Worksheet for Report Writing Unit (Grade 9)

Name: _____

Sequencing is a very important step in report writing. For example, consider the following events:

arguing with parents
convincing father I should get
  a permit
driving home from
   Wampsville with Mother
studying Drivers' Ed book
I appeal to Dad to teach me

the day I take my permit test
Mother refuses to teach me
I go off the edge of the road
  with Mom
Dad starts lecture
I go to Drivers' Ed class
Dad backs into stop sign
Dad says I don't listen

In order to write a logical, step-by-step report using the above information, you will have to study all the items and arrange them into some kind of sequence.

Now look at the same events put into sequence:

1. arguing with parents
2. convincing father I should get a permit
3. studying Drivers' Ed book
4. the day I take my permit test
5. driving home from Wampsville with Mother
6. I go off the edge of the road with Mom
7. Mother refuses to teach me
8. I appeal to Dad to teach me
9. Dad starts lecture
10. Dad says I don't listen
11. Dad backs into stop sign
12. I go to Drivers' Ed class

Now that you have them sequenced, break the sequence up into thought units for paragraphing purposes.

1. Decision to allow me to get my permit

_____

_____

_____

2. Phase One: Mother as Teacher

_____

_____

Figure 64. (*continued*)

_____

3. Phase Two: Father as Teacher

_____

_____

_____

_____

Figure 65. Final Worksheet for Report Writing Unit (Grade 9)

Name: _____

Your school paper adviser has asked you to interview Mr. Banner about his trip to South Dakota and write a report for the school paper. While you were talking to Mr. Banner, you took notes. Some of the notes you took are in the box below.

NOTES

enjoyed ancient Navajo dwellings built into cliffs
no air conditioning in car
while climbing Mount Rushmore, met a man from Canastota
went down inside ceremonial room of Indian house
saw burned spots on cave roof as evidence of Indian fires
had to stop every hour to get a drink because of heat
certainly is a small world
only needed shorts and halters
people we met seemed just like folks back home
spent one week there in July
Mt. Rushmore carving really exciting
Crazy Horse is being carved next mountain over

Organize these notes into a written report. In your report be sure to:

• include <u>all</u> the information that is in the notes
• write complete sentences
• check your paragraphing, spelling, punctuation, capitalization, and usage

Letter Writing

One skill that generally appears on competency tests and that most every English teacher expects students to master is letter writing. We expect the high school graduate to be able to compose a coherent business letter. We teach the friendly letter and the social note also, but the one we stress is the business letter. It is through the business letter that the writer shows himself to be educated or not. As with the other units in writing, the ninth-grade curriculum contains the most material on writing letters.

Figures 66, 67, and 68 illustrate the progression of worksheets that the class follows in the letter writing unit. We begin with a lecture to give the class the basic facts about friendly letters, business letters, and social notes. The worksheets for this lecture (figures 66 and 67) are open outlines that help the students in several ways. First, they have something to which they can refer while we are talking. We don't give them a complete summary of what we plan to say, because if we did that, many of them probably wouldn't pay attention to the lecture. We leave some blanks in the outlines so that they can fill in the answers as we cover the material. This forces the students to listen carefully.

After the students have the basic facts about letter writing, we give them practice worksheets (figure 68). These worksheets have blank lines and exercises to guide the students in their work. They are not simply told to write a friendly letter about anything. Most slower students need structure and suggestions for topics. Our purpose is to help these students—not to create a mystery for them.

Most of our worksheets provide blank lines on which the students are to write. This gives a definite structure to the worksheets, and we have already discussed (chapter 4) how blank lines tell the students where to put their answers.

Figure 69 is an example of a tenth-grade review worksheet. You will note that these students aren't guided quite as much as the ninth graders. We hope that by this time the students have become more proficient in their letter writing and will not require as many review sheets. We do, however, continue with practice exercises throughout the tenth and eleventh grades.

The ideas discussed in this chapter can be adapted to many different curricula. Our worksheets can give you suggestions for your own worksheets. Your basic goal should be to give students continual writing instruction and practice throughout high school. With this practice, many students, including the slower students who benefit from structure and much attention from the teacher, *can* learn to write better, more varied papers. No longer will we be accused of graduating Johnnies who can't read or write!

Figure 66. Worksheet on Note Taking for Letter Writing Unit (Grade 9)

Name: _____

As you listen to the lecture on letter writing, fill in the blanks in this outline.

I. Types of Letters

    a. Friendly letter

    b. _____

    c. Business letter

II. Important Qualities

    a. Clarity

        1. _____

        2. _____

    b. Tone

        1. _____

        2. _____

    c. Appearance and form

        1. _____

        2. _____

        3. _____

            a. _____

            b. _____

        4. _____

III. Parts of a Letter

    a. _____

    b. _____

    c. _____

    d. _____

    e. _____

Figure 67. Worksheet on Note Taking for Letter Writing Unit (Grade 9)

Name: _____

As you listen to the lecture on friendly letters, fill in the blanks in this outline.

PARTS OF A FRIENDLY LETTER

  I. Heading
     a. Your complete address in top right-hand corner of the page
       1. Two lines
       2. No abbreviations
       3. Example: 14 Brown Street
                 Dayton, Ohio 35476
     b. Date

  II. Salutation

     a. _____

     b. _____
     c. Examples: Dear Dad,
               Dear Dr. White,
               Dear Bill,
     d. Comma punctuation

  III. Body of Letter

     a. _____

     b. _____

  IV. Closing

     a. _____
     b. _____
     c. Examples: Sincerely,
               Affectionately,
               Love,

  V. Signature

     a. _____

     b. _____
     c. Example: *Sue*

Figure 68. Worksheet on Friendly Letter for Letter Writing Unit (Grade 9)

Name: _____

Label the parts of this friendly letter on the blank lines in parentheses. Note spacing and punctuation.

FRIENDLY LETTER

(_____) 2674 Smithhaven Avenue
                     Noxire, Minnesota 76240
                     January 23, 1980

Dear Hubie, (_____)

_____(Indent to start paragraph)_____

_____

_____

_____

_____

_____(_____)_____

_____

_____

_____

_____

_____

_____

_____

_____

_____

_____

_____

_____

                    Sincerely, (_____)

                    Mary (_____)

_____

Figure 69. Review Sheet for Letter Writing Unit (Grade 10)

Name: _____

In last year's class, you learned that there are three types of letters:

> friendly letter
> social note
> business letter

You were taught that it was important to do the following:

> say what you mean in a tactful way
> keep letters neat by:
>   writing legibly
>   using appropriate stationery
>   using adequate margins

Here are the parts of a letter:

a. <u>Heading</u> (address of sender)

> 201 Main Street
> Oneida, New York 13421
> January 20, 1982

b. <u>Inside Address</u> (address to which letter is sent)

> Mr. John Smith
> Ford Motor Company
> 14 Lark Avenue
> Detroit, Michigan 06356

c. <u>Salutation</u> (greeting)

> Dear Tom,
> Dear Mr. Roth,
> Gentlemen:

d. <u>Body of Letter</u> (actual letter)

e. <u>Closing</u> (goodbye)

> Your friend,
> Sincerely,
> Yours truly,

f. <u>Signature</u> (handwritten)

Punctuation and closings are more formal in business letters than in friendly letters. There should be no abbreviations in either business or friendly letters. The format for envelopes is the same for both business and friendly letters. A friendly letter has no inside address. There are two spaces between the inside address (in a business letter) and the salutation, between the salutation and the body, and between the body and the closing. The closing should be lined up vertically with the heading. Below are samples of the two kinds of letters.

Figure 69. (*continued*)

Business Letter

560 Seneca Street
Oneida, New York 13421
January 20, 1982

Mr. Calvin Brewster
Brewster Insurance Agency
113 Farrier Avenue
Oneida, New York 13421

Dear Mr. Brewster:

Enclosed you will find my check for $27.50 to cover the additional insurance coverage on my trailer. From our conversation on the phone, I understand that this coverage will be added on to my automobile policy no. 13609.

Will you please forward the amendment to my policy for my signature. Thank you for taking care of this matter.

Sincerely,

Thomas Jones

Thomas Jones

Friendly Letter

560 Seneca Street
Oneida, New York 13421
January 25, 1982

Dear Cal,

It was great to see you at the picnic the other day. Since you moved away it has been difficult to keep track of what you are doing, so I enjoyed the chance to catch up on all the news.

I was particularly interested in hearing that your brother is playing ball for Ohio State. Do you remember the time we stole his collection of trading cards and set them on fire behind Smith-Lee? Those were the days!

Hey, it was good to see you. Now that we know that neither of us has changed all that much, how about keeping in touch? You might even want to drive over for the VVS game. Just let me know and you can stay here.

Your friend,

Tom

Figure 69. (*continued*)

Friendly Letter and Social Note Review

Fill in the missing information in the letter below.

_____

_____

_____

_____

 Andy and I are planning a party for Mom and Dad's twenty-fifth wedding anniversary. We are planning a <u>surprise</u> picnic out at Verona Beach State Park in the pavilion to the left of the parking lot. The date is Saturday, August 3, 1980, at 4:30 pm. Dress is casual, and you are asked to bring nothing but yourselves! We hope that you will be able to share this exciting time with us.

_____

_____

Now, <u>answer</u> the above invitation as if you were the person to whom it is addressed.

_____

_____

_____

_____

_____

_____

_____

_____

_____

_____

_____

_____

Curriculum 10

A few teachers think that simply placing all the students with skill deficits in one class will be the answer to their problems. Certainly, it helps. Instead of five classes with four or five stragglers in each room, you would have four classes moving right along, and a fifth class also moving forward but marching to the beat of a different drummer! But establishing homogeneous classrooms (see chapter 5) is only the beginning. Putting the right kids into the hands of the right teachers is only two thirds of the triangle. The all-important base is the appropriate curriculum.

In years past, classroom teachers faced with large teaching loads and multiple preparations have solved the problem of slow learners by "watering down" traditional curriculum. This meant teaching the same stories, but with fewer vocabulary words, more reading aloud, and one fewer essay on the final unit test. Generally, this meant less student involvement with the material and more teacher input. It meant less work for the classroom teacher but also less reward, because student progress was often negligible.

In chapters 6 through 9, we have introduced strategies designed to enhance affective concerns, vocabulary, comprehension, and writing, all necessary components of a carefully structured curriculum. Much of the curriculum for the slower learners has emphasized these skills only haphazardly. It is essential that goals and objectives be clearly spelled out for grades 9 through 12. Our suggestion is to discard most of the traditional curriculum and start from scratch. Develop your own curriculum based on the following guidelines.

MAJOR GUIDELINE FOR CURRICULUM DEVELOPMENT

We suggest that you base your criteria for curriculum selection on the following three guidelines:

1. Does the material build on interests the students already have?
2. Does the reading level of the material suit the abilities of the students?
3. Is the material appropriate in terms of departmental, school district, and state requirements?

Student Interests

This may well be the most important guideline for selecting material for students who are "turned off" by school. It just makes sense. How can you put *A Tale of Two Cities*, by Charles Dickens, into the hands of a seventeen-year-old boy who loves to build cars, hates school, and reads on the fourth-grade level? There is no one more stubborn than a student who has had years of remedial reading, has been identified and diagnosed to the point that everyone calls him "the 'tard" (short for *retard*), and has been made the brunt of jokes by parents, teachers, and peers. The adage about leading a horse to water has never been more true. No one enjoys being a poor reader. If this student could have taken a pill a long time ago and awakened as a good reader, he certainly would have. We must, therefore, forgive him if he does not rush enthusiastically into another year of English or social studies. The term *reluctant reader* is very appropriate. He *is* reluctant, and for obvious reasons. He has had books that were too difficult for him before. He also has had books that, even when read aloud, bored him to death. He has slept through monotonous period after monotonous period. He stopped trying a long time ago. He is now a passive member of the teaching-learning team rather than an active participant.

The key to turning this situation around is the interests of these students. Traditionalists will cry, "We can't teach all that trash! Our job is to help youngsters develop good taste." We couldn't agree more; however, unless you can awaken your students' desire to learn, you won't have much chance to elevate their taste. You might have Herman Melville's *Moby-Dick* in mind, but what's wrong with starting with *Jaws*[1] by Peter Benchley and moving up to Ernest Hemingway's *The Old Man and the Sea* en route to Ishmael's crisis? Having failed for so long, these students need some motivation before they will be willing to risk failure again, so start with something that has a chance of interesting them.

[1] New York: Doubleday, 1974.

When developing thematic units or choosing novels, start with subjects, authors, and characters that reflect the problems your students face. Make a list of television programs adolescents like, and try to identify the factors about those programs that appeal to them. What are their hobbies? Which films do they like? What do they talk about all the time? What topics appear most frequently in their journals?

For a tenth-grade class, you might develop a list somewhat like the following one:

problems with	football	weightlifting
parents	runaways	money
drugs	teen-age pregnancy	dieting
cars	shoplifting	"hoods" vs. "jocks"
sex	divorce	law
emotions	school	alcohol
mental health	dropping out	

List these themes on the board, and have the students rank them in order of interest. It is much more effective if you determine the interest of your own students instead of using the topics suggested in publishers' catalogs. In most cases, publishers have responded to the interests of young people and have prepared material on topics you will find to be of concern to your students, but if you start with the students, they will feel that they, and not the publishers, are your prime source of information. Right there is the secret! You will get more response to material that the students believe they had a part in choosing. In addition, you will want them to evaluate a unit when you have completed it. These evaluations can help you decide whether to use it again the following year or to discard it as dated. You can also present your current class with comments on several units by former students, and allow the class to determine which units it wants to study based on those student opinions. If the material really reflects the interests of your class, they may well trust you enough to risk failure once more!

Student Abilities and Reading Level of Material

The second guideline for curriculum development is to match the abilities of your students with the reading level of the material. Based on the diagnosis you have done as suggested in chapter 3, you have developed a skill chart that shows the strengths and weaknesses of your pupils (see figure 70). Under the heading *Physical*, you would record the results of the students' Snellen Chart and A.M.A. Rating Card tests in the column marked *Vision*. In the *Hearing* column, you would record the data from the students' acuity tests (e.g., the Maico Audiometric Screening) done by your school nurse. Speech information is available

Figure 70. Student Skills Composite Form for Use in Setting Curriculum Goals

Student	Physical					Reading															Spelling	Writing								Organizing					
						Decoding			Vocab.			Comprehension																								
	Vision	Hearing	Laterality	Speech	Penmanship	Vowels	Blends	Final Consonants	Prefixes	Suffixes	Meaning	Main Idea	Sequence	Details	Cause/Effect	Contrast	Inference	Conclusion	Judgments			Punctuation	Capitals	Sentences	Paragraphs	Social/Friendly Letters	Business Letters	Compositions	Reports	Self-starting	Research	Note Taking	Outlining	Completing Tasks	Proofreading

from the speech therapist, while laterality testing and penmanship observations are usually handled by the classroom teacher. Under *Reading*, the Decoding and Vocabulary columns may be completed by using the data obtained from the Individual Secondary School Inventory. The *Comprehension* column items may be obtained from teacher observation or an informal inventory as suggested in chapter 3. The first four columns under *Writing* would be completed with information obtained on the ISSI, and the remaining columns would be checked if the teacher noted through observation that these were areas requiring remediation. There are literally hundreds of skills that you could include. When working with weaker students, however, keep your list of skills relatively small, and keep your objectives within the realm of possibility. Figure 70 shows one kind of class skills composite that you might use to determine your objectives for your class. Of course, you should feel free to develop your own version of this composite. At any rate, you should have a list of specific skills in mind *before* you try to write curriculum.

Now, use your list of student interests. (See the section on student interests earlier in this chapter.) Choose those themes or unit topics that you feel have the most appeal to your students. Keeping interests and the skill needs in mind, begin your search for appropriate material. Almost all publishing companies have responded to the need for material for the student with learning deficits. The catalogs may list this material under such headings as high interest/low vocabulary, reluctant reader, drop-out prevention, easier reading, classics-made-easy, or young adult libraries. Whatever they call it, the material is still geared to the high school student who doesn't like to read and isn't crazy about school. To look for titles to match interests, the catalogs are the best source.

One word of caution, gauge the reading level of this material yourself (see figure 9 and the discussion in chapter 4). Do not rely solely on the catalog descriptions. When you are matching student interests and abilities with actual texts, the question of reading level is very important.

A classic example of *not* matching students' abilities and reading level to the material is Dickens's *A Tale of Two Cities*. Since Charles Dickens is reputed to have been paid by the word, it is easy to see why *A Tale of Two Cities* was written using a college-level vocabulary! While the romance and excitement are set against the violence of the Reign of Terror, the "humongous" vocabulary level puts this work out of the reach of students with reading problems. Yet, *A Tale of Two Cities* has for years been one of the classics forced on students with poor skills. Some teachers may think, "Oh, they love it! It has all that gory violence!" For a person reading on the fourth-grade level, reading *A Tale of Two Cities* is like taking physics in Russian without any knowledge of the Russian language! It's one thing to have a book replete with pictures, maps, and graphs. It's quite another to have nothing but text, and all of that written about seven grade levels higher than one can read! Poor readers have difficulty tracking through multisyllabic words. The more syllables a word has and the more complicated words a text has, the higher the reading level. Poor readers might not mind stumbling and trying to decode an occasional word like *insurgent.* But a whole paragraph about *irrefutable insurrectionaries* may overwhelm them. The task becomes so impossible that even trying seems like a waste of time!

A few teachers may say, "Well, that text has been used in eleventh-grade social studies for years." That does not justify its continued use with your students if their reading level is too low for them to have a chance of success with it. This does not, however, mean you should throw the books out, because next year's class may have readers with more skill. That's why it is important to have alternative texts available. One year you may have a class in which the students' ability is too high for *The Outsiders,* by S. E. Hinton. Another year, *The Outsiders* may be the perfect novel with which to finish up a year's curriculum. Several years ago, we ordered a class-size set of *Take 12/Action,*[2] a series of open-ended plays for high school students reading on or about the second- and third-grade levels. We have only used those paperbacks twice, but they were just the thing for the two classes in which they were used. Each year the ability levels change, and you cannot say, "Next year, I know my ninth-grade class will average a 3.2 reading level." Instead, you have to deal with a wide variety of possibilities. This year's 3.2 class may be replaced by a class whose average reading level is 6.3; and yet, both are well below grade level if we are talking about an eleventh- or twelfth-grade class.

For specific skill areas, your best answer may still be to prepare your own material. It is cheaper than a commercially prepared workbook and is more likely to meet the exact needs of your students, since you are writing it especially for them. Each time you write a new unit or alter an old one, you are adding to the flexibility of your program. You can pull out a unit on sentences that you haven't used in two years because it is appropriate to the needs of your students this year, while it wasn't needed last year. In some instances, you may wish to avoid "reinventing the wheel." There's nothing wrong with purchasing book 2 from one publisher's series and book 3 from another. This is particularly true for workbooks on competency skills and coping with the work world. You may not want a whole series. Write to the publishers requesting samples and select carefully material that fits your needs. If there is nothing, then don't be afraid to sit down to write your own!

[2]New York: Scholastic Book Services, 1970.

Departmental, School District, and State Requirements

The third guideline you should consider when developing curriculum is the appropriateness of that curriculum in terms of fulfilling the requirements of your department, your school district, and your state department of education.

While most courses of study established by a department will allow for some flexibility and the addition of new material, it would be unwise for a new teacher to eliminate an entire unit without clearing this decision with the department head. Not everything that has *always* been included in a standard curriculum should be treated as sacrosanct, but be sure to have good reasons for discarding old units, particularly if you are new. You may find that some material has long been taught simply because no one ever questioned it before. On the other hand, there may be a sound educational reason for its inclusion. For example, a unit on public speaking is included in our eleventh-grade second semester English curriculum because our state-mandated final exam has a required public speaking question. Likewise, the play *Twelve Angy Men*,[3] by Reginald Rose, is included to coordinate with a social studies unit on courts and the law. A new teacher might not realize why that particular play was chosen.

A social studies department may have decided to include specific topics such as geography, economics, and culture regardless of the area of the world being studied. Teachers of world history, Middle Eastern history, Far Eastern history, and American history would all feel an obligation to cover these three topics because of departmental policy.

Also, checking with your department head is just good personal relations! He or she should know what you are doing. This is important because you will be developing that good rapport that you will need later on if you decide to initiate more radical innovations. There is no substitute for good communications.

There will be many times in your career when someone will say to you, "Use your head. Use common sense." Nowhere does this apply more than in the selecting of curriculum that tastefully reflects the thinking of the rest of your school and of your school district's board of education. Most school districts have a policy for the selection of school texts and paperbacks. Along with that, they have developed a policy on how to handle criticism of the choices their staff has made. (If your district does not have such a policy, gently suggest to your superior that this is a committee on which you would like to work!) Wisdom, however, consists of choosing wisely in the first place. While teachers have the

[3]In G. Robert Carlsen, Richard Ludwig, and Edgar Schuster (eds.), *American Literature* (New York: McGraw-Hill, 1967).

responsibility of challenging their students and stimulating them to new levels of inquiry and awareness, it is still important that this inspiration come from within the framework of the community mores. Just as it is not necessary for teachers to swear in the classroom in order for them to enjoy the respect of their students, it also is not necessary that every novel include obscenities and pornography. Good stories, be they adolescent or classical literature, can interest students in learning without becoming the focal point of community controversy. No one profits from agitated parents' groups or censorship committees. We teachers can avoid unnecessary conflict by using discretion.

The third component of this guideline for curriculum selection is the state syllabus for your content area. This is, perhaps, the easiest because it is usually carefully spelled out in some type of handbook put out by your state department of education. Ask your department chairman for a copy of the syllabus, and proceed from there. What is required? What is currently being included? What would you like to add? Usually, the syllabus will state that English classes must teach correct English grammar and usage. The exact course of study and text, however, may be left up to you. If the syllabus suggests that a unit on public speaking be included, and you choose to leave it out, you will be open to censure. *How* you teach public speaking may be something you can decide; *that* you teach it, however, has been predetermined.

SPECIFICS OF CURRICULUM FOR STUDENTS WITH LEARNING DEFICITS

Sequencing

After you have chosen your curricular materials, you must arrange the units in the order in which you want to teach them. We suggest that you proceed from simple to complex, literal to applied, oral to written.

In our tenth-grade English curriculum, for example, we start out with a five-day unit in which the class develops a disc jockey radio program. The topic allows for originality, humor, music of the students' choice, and a minimum of writing and reading. The unit teaches organizational skills and provides opportunities for students to work together in groups. With no text to read and little emphasis on formal writing techniques, most students have a chance of succeeding. Have the students think of the parts of a radio show, and write their suggestions on the board: DJ, weather, time, national news, sports, commercials, contests, and local news. Divide the items among the students so that two pupils are assigned to each item. Each pair then develops the script for its segment of the show. While writing the material together, they help one another out with spelling as well as with ideas. Imagination is catching. If one student has an inspiration, the other will be able to enlarge the original concept. The students enjoy working together, and the result is usually of a high calibre. When all of the scripts are finished, the class sequences the material and chooses the music. After several rehearsals, and some confidence-gaining practice with the microphone, they are ready to tape the entire radio program. The pride the students take in such a finished product is alone worth the effort. This short unit follows the suggested format of proceeding from simple to complex, literal to applied, and oral to written.

It's a good idea to start the year with plays or scripts of radio or TV shows.[4] This gives you the opportunity to hear all the students read orally, and the skill weaknesses that you diagnose can help you plan later curriculum. No one has to read too much or for too long, and plays allow the entire class to get involved immediately. If you have a class of poor readers, you can keep the pace of the play moving right along by reading the stage directions, set and character descriptions, and background information. In the ninth grade we start out with a playlet version of *West Side Story* that appears in *Loyalties*.[5] This version is simplified and has a fourth-grade reading level. It is still compatible with the recording of the music from the original full-length play and yet is within the ability of poor readers.

Reinforcement

Another point to keep in mind when you are developing curriculum for students with learning deficits is that every skill or concept you introduce must be reinforced, and reinforced, and reinforced some more! In working with advanced students, we have often been struck by the observation that even the best students do not internalize oral directions the first time they are given. Students with learning problems are even worse!

Our writing curriculum (see chapter 9) has been designed to provide much reinforcement. We introduce a skill in the ninth grade and provide extensive practice at the ninth-grade level. The same topic is then reintroduced at the tenth-grade level, followed by more practice sheets. The eleventh-grade curriculum reviews the topic and is accompanied by further reinforcement material. The same basic paragraph structure is followed in all three grades. Three years of concentrated effort to teach a paragraph style with consistent reinforcement will pay off! We don't claim that every student coming out of your classes will be able to write a solid paragraph if you follow this idea, but we can tell

---

[4]*Capital Cities Television Reading Program* (Princeton, N.J.: Capital Cities Communications, 1980).
[5]William Goodykoontz (ed.), (New York: Scholastic Book Services, 1970).

you that more of the students will be able to write a decent paragraph than would if you didn't use reinforcement.

Many teachers want to provide reinforcement, but it's quite another thing to actually build reinforcement material into each curricular unit. Since we are all busy people, many times we don't pursue our best intentions. We may believe in reinforcement sheets but just never get around to writing them. When you sit down to plan and develop curriculum, be sure to include reinforcement material. After you have chosen the vocabulary words you wish to stress in a novel, develop several reinforcement sheets to accompany the initial introductory sheets on those words. Once you have introduced new vocabulary words, you must provide opportunities for your students to use them on other worksheets, or they will not remember the definitions. Keep in mind, too, that your goal must be to reinforce not only the immediate material but also concepts learned previously. For example, since many civil service exams and other entrance tests include analogies, we try to provide frequent practice with analogies. Then when the students face testing situations important to their futures, they will not be baffled by analogy questions. Our reinforcement sheets on vocabulary words sometimes use the analogy format to both reinforce the immediate vocabulary words and provide experience with analogies.

Another student who profits from reinforcement materials is the "late bloomer." Just because a youngster is six years old, he is not necessarily ready to read. By the same token, not all students in high school are necessarily skilled enough to handle high school work. Some misperception can occur and block learning. All of a sudden, what was once a very clouded concept can become crystal clear. In one instance, we had a student who was being instructed in the correct use of *lie* and *lay* for the third time. For some reason, this third explanation got through, and he said, "Why didn't you tell me that the first time?" He simply hadn't been ready to receive the information the first two times. Without the reinforcement, he might never have understood the concept.

Content Coordination Across Subject Areas

Coordination of material across subject areas is another important concept to keep in mind when you are writing new curriculum. Working with another content teacher on both skills development and subject matter is mutually reinforcing to both of you. In tenth grade, for example, our social studies department teaches world history, ending with World War II in May. We selected *Anne Frank: The Diary of a Young Girl* (abridged edition)[6] to go along with the social studies program.

[6]Melinda Blau (ed.), (Los Angeles: Bowmar-Noble, Falcon Books, 1969).

(The abridged edition is much better for students with reading deficiencies than the traditional version.) The social studies background expands on and amplifies the historical period in which Anne Frank wrote her diary. The references used in the book are more familiar to the students because they have discussed them in social studies class. This historical perspective seems to make the diary come alive.

In our eleventh-grade curriculum, we coordinate our use of the film *Black Like Me* for film critiquing with the civil rights unit in social studies. In addition, we schedule the play *Twelve Angry Men*, by Reginald Rose, to coincide with the social studies unit on the courts and the legal system. This kind of reinforcement strengthens both the social studies and the English curricula. In addition, coordination gives the students more exposure to the concepts and thus more reinforcement. Repeating the material doesn't bore the students; instead, it means that they can bring some knowledge to the second situation, thus appearing quick and bright!

Skill Coordination Across Subject Areas

The advantages of content coordination should be apparent. Skill coordination across subject areas can also provide benefits from repetition and frequency of exposure. If, early in the fall, for example, social studies, English, science, and math teachers all agree that they will emphasize the teaching of main idea in all reading assignments, the students will have reading comprehension instruction in main idea four times a day! As the year progresses, emphasis can be placed on reading for details, sequencing, comparison and contrast, and cause and effect. (See chapter 8 for a discussion of these reading comprehension skills.)

While content coordination may be handled through rather loose arrangements or through remarks shared in passing, skill coordination requires much more deliberate planning. First of all, you have to find other teachers who are willing to take the necessary time. Each teacher must start by listing all of the content material he or she wishes to cover. Then you must all agree on the skills you wish to stress and, after sequencing them, adjust individual curricula so that the content will lend itself to the skill chosen for that time slot. Make sure you all agree on the definitions of the skills, so that *reading for details* means the same thing to all of you.

The teachers must know their material well, so that they will know if the material lends itself to the particular skill to be emphasized. For example, cause and effect is more appropriate for studying the Civil War or World Wars I and II than for an analysis of Wilson's Fourteen Points. Sequencing is more pertinent to solving word problems in math and to a physics unit in general science than it is to graphing or a nutrition unit. In some cases, materials may have to be rewritten to focus on the selected skill, but the extra effort will pay off. With four major subject teachers all emphasizing the same skill, certainly no student can say that he wasn't taught that! A united effort may mean more work, but it also means more rewards!

Preparation for Competency Testing

Another focus to keep in mind when designing curriculum is that this curriculum, particularly in the case of students with learning problems, is the preparation for state competency testing. As the number of states requiring competency in reading, writing, and mathematics increases, the number of states requiring correlating remedial programs increase also. If teachers keep competency goals in mind as they develop new curriculum, the new material can become the core of preparation and the base on which the remedial program is built. For example, test-wiseness and experience with the format of the state competency

Figure 71. Worksheet in Competency Test Format

Name: _____

Several words have been omitted from the passage below. Under the passage, you will find four choices for each of the five missing words. Circle the letter of the word that best fits the passage.

What Is Illiteracy?

It is many ___1___ . It is one out of every five ___2___ in the world; it is one out of every three adults in the ___3___ . It is a child unable to ___4___ markings on a poster that have the magic to ___5___ others laugh, point, chatter together.

1. a. people
   b. books
   c. things
   d. puzzles

2. a. people
   b. countries
   c. things
   d. books

3. a. books
   b. newspaper
   c. school
   d. world

4. a. speak
   b. list
   c. interpret
   d. sing

5. a. keep
   b. make
   c. stop
   d. read

tests can be included right in your curriculum. If your state uses a modified cloze or degrees of reading power format, there is no reason why you cannot develop study guides in the same style as the competency tests. Take a sample reading from a social studies text or a magazine article that is appropriate to your content. Delete several words from the article. Provide three or four alternatives in a multiple choice question, including the correct word as one option. Figure 71 shows a sample exercise.

Building in "Crutches"

Don't forget that your materials are being designed for students who have learning problems. Most high school students with reading problems have had enough remedial reading instruction for a lifetime, and they do not want any more *b*, *d*, or *p*. You can, however, build aids to reading improvement right into the study guides and exercises themselves.

For example, putting page numbers and paragraph numbers in parentheses next to your questions provides a starting point for the students. It makes the task seem possible by removing the barrier that an entire page of print represents. As the students' skills improve, drop the paragraph numbers, but leave the page numbers for as long as you feel your pupils can profit from them.

Another important idea to keep in mind is to limit the amount of content realistically. Don't expect that a class of poor readers will be able to cover as much material as an average or above-average class. In addition, the longer you teach a given unit, the more material you acquire to expand that unit. Don't fall into the trap of thinking that everything you have used in the past is essential. Learning to be our own editors is a tough assignment but a necessary one if our students are to have a chance of success.

If the material you are writing is designed to accompany a text, be sure that your material is presented in the same sequence as in the text. The same suggestion holds true for evaluation and testing materials. Review in the same sequence in which the ideas were originally presented, and write the test questions in the same order also. Students are more likely to recall material taught, reviewed, and tested in the same sequence.

Other "crutches" can be built into the material in the format of presentation. For example, when writing vocabulary reinforcement sheets, try providing slash marks for syllabication and a blank line for each letter in the word. If, for instance, you are looking for the antonym of *passionate*, you can help by writing the answer space this way:

__ __ __ __ / __ __   (*f* r i g / i d)

Assuming that the student had already been given the word *frigid* for vocabulary, the slashes and blank lines serve as clues. At the same time, they are reinforcing the skill of syllabication. On a later reinforcement sheet you can change the blank lines to a solid line for each syllable:

_____ / ____

You are reducing the "crutches" to a "cane." The final step, of course, is to take away the syllabication line. This process of walking students through exercises with aids built in puts the task within the realm of possibility for them.

While you are writing this new curriculum, it is important to keep in mind the teaching techniques you plan to use in its delivery. One suggestion, for instance, would be to teach the regular examples of rules and skills first, and teach the exceptions later. As an example, if you were using Glass Analysis[7] techniques to teach *ab* words in spelling, you would start with three-letter words like *cab* and *nab* and move along to *fabric* and *cabin*. Eventually, you would get around to *laboratory* and *prefabrication*. As long as the *ab* is consistent and follows the rules, that's fine. Of course, there is the exception in the word *about*. Teach all the regular *ab* (short ă) words first, and then teach *about* for what it is—an exception. The same is true with "*i* before *e*, except after *c*." There are several exceptions, but teach the words that follow the rule first. Then make up a saying to cover the words that break the rule. For example, "Neither of the boys had either the height or the weight to bring the foreign receipt home to the neighbor."

The need for other crutches becomes evident when we consider that often these students have huge gaps in time and order. World War I and World War II become one and the same, a typographical slip of the Roman numeral rather than twenty-one years! Distance loses perspective, and Japan, Nepal, and Zimbabwe all become neighbors as "one of those countries over there." The distance lines on a map may really represent inches, rather than miles, to these students. One way to help is to take a local point as a focus, and then translate in terms of local distance: "That would be the same as if you walked from here to downtown fifty times."

When you are presenting lists of just about anything—words, phrases, ideas, concepts, causes and effects, good and bad points—the method you use is very important. Studies in learning techniques show that people tend to have better recall if items are presented vertically rather than horizontally. As you write material, be sure to list items you

---

[7]Gerald Glass (Adelphi University, Garden City, N.Y.) has developed a technique for teaching word recognition and spelling through the recognition of vowel/consonant clusters that remain similar in pattern.

want to emphasize for recall. The careful and attentive use of space, indentations, boxes, dark lines, and other attention-getting devices can make all the difference. For example:

Be sure to remember use of
- space
- indentations
- boxes
- dark lines

In addition, the presentation of important material at least three times is essential for students who have difficulty learning. If, for example, you included the list in the text of the paragraph above, followed later by the indented list summarizing the items, and then, again, in the review of the material for a test, you might expect that your students would remember two of the four items! Repetition and review are absolutely critical. While you are working your way painfully through multiple presentations, do remember that while variety may enliven your lesson, consistency and sameness are the essential ingredients for slow learners. If, for example, you are teaching a lesson on World War II and Roosevelt, and your first study guide is headlined "Franklin Delano Roosevelt and World War II," keep the same headline for all review materials. Don't change the headline to read "WWII and FDR." You destroy all sense of carryover if you change from the original model.

These technical gimmicks may seem relatively unimportant to you as you begin writing new curriculum, but they provide the "crutches" necessary for your students' success. By building aid right into the curriculum, you are telegraphing the message that you believe the students can handle the material. You are proving to them that you want to help and have, indeed, provided some assistance.

Spelling

Spelling is one of those areas that everyone agrees need to be improved. Unfortunately, very little is actually done to try to improve the spelling of poor readers. Most secondary-level poor readers demonstrate little understanding of spelling rules.

We suggest that you follow the principles used in *Spelling the Basics,* by Mary Jeanne Bialas and Susanne Miller.[8] The words selected for use were obtained from English, social studies, and science teachers

---

[8]Oneida, N.Y.: Oneida-Madison BOCES, 1978.

in grades 9 through 12. The words were ranked from the most frequently misspelled to the least frequently misspelled. Those words that appeared on the teachers' lists most consistently were incorporated into the spelling lessons in the book. The lessons themselves rely heavily on the study guide principles discussed in this book: plenty of white space, lines dividing tasks, much repetition, and consistency in format. Holidays, dates, and numbers, which are part of each lesson, also become spelling words. While we recommend correcting misspelled words in the margins of writing assignments rather than in the body of the paper, we do not take away credit for all misspelled words—only for assigned spelling words. For example, *probably* is a spelling word. A pupil may misspell *California* in his journal entry and lose no credit, but if he writes the spelling word as *probly*, he will lose a point. Once a word has been taught, the students are considered responsible for it. We recommend following the traditional sequence of spelling assignments: new words (with some repeats) introduced on Monday, reinforcement exercises and spelling bees during the week, with unit tests on Friday. This type of regularity and consistency shows the students how much emphasis you put on spelling. The students may complain that the words are too easy, but since the words are the ones that the students actually missed themselves, it should be clear that they do need to master these assigned words.

NINTH- THROUGH TWELFTH-GRADE CURRICULUM

Now that you have considered the interests and abilities of the students and departmental, district, and state requirements, it's essential that you put your curriculum into a framework that focuses on the entire ninth-through twelfth-grade years. This overall pattern should include a heavy emphasis on spelling, writing, and reading in ninth and tenth grades. In the eleventh grade, it is possible to include more coordination between English and social studies because there is more literature available dealing with American history and contemporary issues. As the students move into the twelfth grade, the needs of the class will dictate that you spend more time on life-coping skills and career preparation.

The major point that we wish to emphasize is that whatever material you select should be selected with specific goals in mind and *not* as an isolated grade-level decision. All teachers working with these students should take part in the sequencing of curriculum and should be aware of how their particular curricula fit into the total high school picture. Material should be selected because it meets the criteria discussed earlier in this chapter, and because it reflects the sequencing of skill development from ninth grade through twelfth grade.

Ninth Grade

Our ninth-grade program commences in September with diagnostic testing, particularly, the Individual Secondary Skills Inventory (see appendix A) and daily journal writing (see chapter 9). The reading teacher who is teamed with the classroom teacher does all group and individual testing (chapter 3). While individual testing is going on, the classroom teacher works with the class on journal entries, since this does not require that all students be present at all times. The information gleaned from this initial diagnostic testing provides the basis for the prescription for the remainder of the year, and the journal writing immediately tells the students that good and frequent writing is valued and will be emphasized.

Plays are generally a good vehicle for establishing rapport in a classroom. They involve everybody, reduce the teacher's role as authority figure, and provide a nonthreatening oral reading opportunity. They tend to aid in establishing that very elusive thread of good chemistry that is needed in order to have a successful year. We start off with the abridged version of *West Side Story* in *Loyalties*, because the play itself has high interest, speaks to adolescent concerns, and has lots of action. The abridged version has an adjusted vocabulary level so that the lines are short and easy to read. Daily journal entries are developed around topics suggested by *West Side Story*.

Following this play, we immediately move into the sentence structure unit of our writing skills curriculum. (See chapter 9 for a description of our writing skills curriculum, which is referred to frequently in this discussion of curriculum.) The students have done enough journal writing so that we are well aware of their writing problems. While the sentence unit provides for formal instruction, it has plenty of material that can be used for homework or supplemental exercises.

Our next literature unit is *Point 31*[9] which allows for individualized instruction in a short story unit. The stories are very brief, written on an appropriate reading level, and varied in subject matter. We often contract with the students individually regarding the number of stories each pupil will be required to complete. With the use of good management materials, it is possible for the classroom teacher and the assisting reading teacher to juggle an entire class reading different stories and working at different paces. The rules for any individualized unit must, however, be very specific. By setting up absolute requirements, such as three stories and accompanying study guides by the end of the week, with additional credit given for stories completed beyond the requirements, we keep everyone working.

Following the short story unit, we move immediately into the para-

[9]Pleasantville, N.Y.: Reader's Digest Services, 1975.

graph writing unit, which is the next logical step in writing skills. A few days spent in complete-class-period instruction in writing paragraphs is sufficient, since there is ample material to assign for homework or as part of the next literature unit, the novel *Rumble Fish*, by S. E. Hinton. This novel has very high interest, and like others of Ms. Hinton's books, *Rumble Fish* has a highly readable style with a vocabulary level appropriate for poor readers.

Following a novel on which the entire class has worked, we generally move into an individualized unit that allows for frequent interaction with the pupils on a one-to-one basis. The short novelettes from Scholastic Book Services' *Action Library* (*Libraries IA* and *IIA*)[10] allow for this very important teacher-student contact. This is immediately followed by a brief unit on myths, for which we use *Social Science Reader (9)*[11] This reader presents myths and legends from China, Japan, Pakistan, India, and Africa, which are the parts of the world ninth graders are studying in social studies class. This unit allows for good coordination between social studies and English, and thus provides excellent reinforcement for the students.

Throughout the remainder of the school year, we alternate between novels (*This School Is Driving Me Crazy*, by Nat Hentoff;[12] *The Skating Rink*, by Mildred Lee; *A Patch of Blue*, by Elizabeth Kata) and the writing units devoted to letter writing and compositions. Regularly scheduled spelling lessons from *Spelling the Basics* and frequent journal writing round out the ninth-grade curriculum.

Tenth Grade

Generally, the disciplined structure to which the ninth graders had become accustomed disappears over the summer, and the students return in the fall in the usual September chaos. While their ninth-grade experience may have been a good one, they are restless again, and they face tenth grade with apprehension. We try to allay this tentativeness by starting out the tenth-grade curriculum with the disc jockey radio program unit (see p. 226), which allows the students to work in pairs on writing creatively and has little grading pressure attached to it. The result is usually a product of which the class, as a whole, can feel proud, and the unit is a nonthreatening written and oral language experience from which the individual students can profit.

After any unit that emphasizes pairing, grouping, or individualization, we feel it is important to proceed to a project that requires class unity. Varying teaching style this way provides a different kind of learn-

[10]New York, 1975.
[11]Pleasantville, N.Y.: Reader's Digest Book Services, 1970.
[12]New York: Dell, 1976.

ing environment. While some students do best in a small-group or individualized setting, others need the structure of a large-group activity. For our first whole-class project in tenth grade, we use *That Was Then, This Is Now*,[13] another of S. E. Hinton's novels, which portrays teenagers in an honest and believable fashion. Since most students love this book, it is a good choice for opening the year. A combination of journal writing and tenth-grade review material from the paragraph writing unit refresh writing skills as the class reads this interesting novel.

Following *That Was Then, This Is Now*, we move into an individualized grammar unit and the review material from the composition writing unit. While most students claim to detest grammar, it has been our experience that teaching the grammar unit as we suggest in chapter 9 results in very little resentment. The students' distaste for grammar is usually acquired with repetition of information they already know. Inasmuch as our approach is built on the idea that no student need spend time on an area already mastered, the youngsters can move rapidly along.

Since we generally take our own advice about varying teaching styles, we move from the concrete ideas of grammar to the abstract concepts of a unit on values, symbolism, and awareness. In this unit, we deal mainly with symbolism and the use of tangible objects to stand for intangible ideas. The primary medium we use here is film, with some poetry added. The Center for Humanities[14] produces a series of film shorts and excerpts from full-length features that have high interest for high school students. In "I Who Am, Who Am I?" Burt Lancaster portrays a lost middle-aged man who has difficulty dealing with his life realistically. The film is an excellent example of the subtlety of symbolism. Broderick Crawford's portrayal of Willie Stark in "Power Politics" and Peter O'Toole's "Lord Jim" are both effective in gaining the students' attention as well as in helping them develop an awareness of the use of symbolism. The poem "Don't Be Fooled by Me" (see chapter 8) also lends itself well to this unit.

Next we proceed to *Lord of the Flies*, by William Golding. Depending on the abilities of our students, we use the novel itself or the film version. Either way, the story is an excellent example of the use of symbolism, and it certainly offers a strong lesson in values.

For a break from this large-group work, we then move into an individual interest unit. The theory behind this unit is simple: Have students choose material in an area that interests them, and they won't mind using that material to develop skills. For example, we might provide material such as magazines, films, paperback books, experts, pamphlets, videotapes, and cassettes in six areas: snowmobiles, music, teen-

[13]New York: Dell, 1971.
[14]White Plains, N.Y.: Center for Humanities, 1976.

age problems, sports, cars and racing, and motorcycles (An excellent working relationship with the librarian or media specialist is essential to the success of this unit.) Each student contracts to review one book from his area of interest, compare two magazine articles, review one piece of audiovisual material, interview one expert in the field, develop a list of ten vocabulary words having to do with the topic, design a set of five questions indicating competency in the area, and, finally, present a project or demonstration having to do with the topic. The materials that we provide are very carefully structured to help the students walk themselves step by step through this unit, which takes about four weeks to complete. Each packet of interest unit materials has a pupil management sheet (figure 72) so that the students can keep track of where they

Figure 72. Pupil Management Sheet for Individual Interest Unit

Name: _____

Interest Area _____

Contract Grade _____

Item	Outline		Final Copy	
	Date	Grade	Date	Grade
Book Review				
Magazine Comparison				
Audiovisual Review				
Interview				
Vocabulary				
Test Questions				
Demonstration				

are and what is required of them. For each of the reviews, they are required to fill out an outline (figure 73) that asks very specific questions. After we have gone over the outlines with the students, they use the outlines to write prose style reviews. This unit incorporates many skills including organizing, reading, outlining, writing, comparison and contrast, researching, listening comprehension, interviewing, working with an adult other than a teacher, spelling, and pursuing a task through to completion. It also insures regular teacher-student contact on an individual basis. Because this unit lends itself to a great deal of latitude, it is essential that we run a ''tight ship'' with expectations clearly defined and goals specifically set up with accompanying due dates.

After this unit of complete individualization, we pull back into the security of a class project with everyone focused on one novel, *Snowbound*, by Harry Mazer.[15] We chose this novel because the two main characters are so realistic, with all the strengths and weaknesses of young people: pompous arrogance tempered with lack of confidence, chicanery enobled by innovation, pilfering changed into sharing, and self-centeredness enriched by genuine concern for others. The students can identify with the plight of the two characters and can enjoy trying to match wits with Cindy and Tony as they try to extricate themselves from their predicament.

A brief unit on poetry, including a creative filmstrip that the students design to accompany the lyrics of a song, is inserted between *Snowbound* and *Anne Frank: The Diary of a Young Girl*, which is chosen to complete the tenth-grade curriculum so that it will coordinate with a social studies unit on World War II. Through the entire tenth-grade curriculum, there is regular reinforcement of writing skills from the units on sentence structure, compositions, report writing, and letter writing, along with consistent presentation of spelling.

Eleventh Grade

As the youngsters move into eleventh grade, our efforts with basic skills continue, but more emphasis is put on career goals and coordination with social studies. We usually open the year with *The Outsiders*, another popular novel by S. E. Hinton.[16] This book was chosen because of its high interest to the students. If the social studies class starts with a unit on social services or mental health, however, we might commence with *Lisa, Bright and Dark*, by John Neufeld. Since the social studies class next works with persuasive public opinion, we coordinate with a mass media unit, which concentrates on editorials and television.

Since these students will probably rely heavily on movies and television for information following graduation from high school, we feel it

[15]New York: Dell, 1973.
[16]New York: Dell, 1967.

Figure 73. Outline for Individual Book Review

Name: _____

Contract Grade: _____

Book Title: _____

Author: _____

<u>While</u> reading the book, think about these questions:

    a. What is the main idea of the book?
    b. Why does it fit into my unit?
    c. What new vocabulary words have I seen?
    d. What new ideas am I learning while reading the book?
    e. Why do I like or not like this book?

<u>After</u> reading the book, fill in this outline:

1. This book was (fiction, nonfiction). I know this because

    a. _____
    b. _____
    c. _____

2. The main idea of my book was _____
   Some details from the book that show this main idea are

    a. _____
    b. _____
    c. _____

3. I learned several new things from this book, such as

    a. _____
    b. _____
    c. _____
    d. _____

4. Some things I don't like about the book are

    a. _____
    b. _____
    c. _____
    d. _____

Figure 73. (*continued*)

5. I (would, would not) recommend this book to someone else because

 a. _____

 b. _____

 c. _____

<u>Now</u>, take the ideas you have listed in statements 1–5 above and write the book review in composition form. Talk to the teacher before you begin this task.

---

is important to help them develop some critiquing skills and awareness of propaganda. Consequently, when the social studies class proceeds to study civil rights, we use the film "Black Like Me" as the vehicle for a unit on critiquing. Although this film is somewhat dated, the message is contemporary, and the examples of stereotyping are excellent. The lighting, camerawork, and symbolism are well done and provide a good example of how a director can manipulate an audience.

When the social studies class starts work on civil liberties, law, and the courts, the English class reads *Twelve Angry Men*, by Reginald Rose.

After three units handled primarily as class projects, we relax into individualization with report writing and letter writing review units. The review is needed at this level for skill reinforcement, but it also helps to prepare the students for the New York Statewide Achievement Exam in June, as well as the Regents Competency Exams. In addition, the letter writing unit provides a natural transition to the career unit. Probably our most practical curriculum choice, the career unit covers applications, interviews, resumes, and career counseling to match interests and skills with areas of employment. We use this material to create the opportunity for participation by community resource people. A panel composed of graduates of our high school represents the military, trade schools, clerical and mechanical jobs, construction trades, and the self-employed. While our students may not know these young people personally, they will have heard their names, and they enjoy meeting our guests, who are only a few years older than our students and who speak from experience. Somehow, their advice is far more credible than ours!

We open second semester with *Hey, Dummy*, by Kin Platt. This novel is an excellent choice for developing sensitivity to mentally handicapped students and exceptional adults in the working world.

Perhaps the unit that meets with the strongest opposition is the one on public speaking. Almost without exception, our students detest speaking in front of their peers. Like castor oil, public speaking may be distasteful, but it is "good for them," and we start out by never telling the students what we are leading them into! Opening with charades and role playing helps relieve jitters about performing in front of an audience. Theatre games also help to break the ice. We are always the first to do the charade or game, because the class appreciates the fact that we are willing to be foolish in front of them. The unit moves gradually toward the major speeches, which are always demonstrations of topics students have chosen. Since they can pick the subjects, they are comfortable with them and generally bring a great deal of information to the task. In spite of student distaste for this unit, the resulting poise and confidence are well worth it.

The eleventh grade usually finishes up with *The Man Without a Face*, by Isabel Holland,[17] and some science fiction, including the first four expeditions of *Martian Chronicles* by Ray Bradbury.[18] For variety, we introduce several root words having to do with science, such as *solar, lunar, planetary,* and *celestial.* The students then brainstorm many prefixes and suffixes onto the board, and the class creates its own vocabulary for the future: *transsolarize, relunarization,* and *subcelestial* are examples. The students have fun doing this, and they gain good experience with prefixes and suffixes as well. We have also made a tape of the *Martian Chronicles* expeditions with "Martian" voices and appropriate sound effects. We think this broad-based eleventh-year curriculum is good preparation for twelfth grade.

Twelfth Grade

When we decided to develop a new curriculum for our lower-ability seniors, we were determined to establish a program that would have maximum interest for young people finishing up their high school education and would provide them with good, solid information for the years immediately following high school. Keeping this in mind, we divided the curriculum into two distinct semesters. The first semester deals with identity and seeks to answer the question "who am I?" in terms of male and female roles.

All of the motivational materials that lead into the unit are teacher-designed and are accompanied by extensive discussion and group work. The first piece of literature we use is *A Raisin in the Sun*, by Lorraine Hansberry. This play contains some classic examples of stereotyped roles and lends itself easily to discussion of women's rights, traditional female roles versus modern ones, and male responses to changing female roles.

[17]New York: Bantam, 1973.
[18]New York: Bantam, 1951.

Our next unit is one of the favorites with the students, and it allows for real individualization. We provide a choice of five novels: *The Bridges at Toko-ri,* by James Michener;[19] *Dinky Hocker Shoots Smack,* by M. E. Kerr;[20] *If I Loved You, Am I Trapped Forever?,* by M. E. Kerr;[21] *Lilies of the Field,* by William Barrett;[22] and *The Boy Who Could Make Himself Disappear,* by Kin Platt.[23] Since each student chooses the novel of his or her choice, it is possible for you to steer the weaker reader to *Lilies of the Field* and the better readers to *Bridges at Toko-ri.* For each of these novels, we have prepared a vocabulary worksheet, a study guide, review materials, and quizzes. The students read at their own pace. As a student completes the written work, we grade the work individually with the student.

Following the novels, we take the class back to a group activity, reading the play version of *Of Mice and Men,* by John Steinbeck.[24] This play takes a very candid look at an all-male world of "barley buckers" living on a remote ranch. The caring relationship between George and his retarded friend Lennie provides a welcome contrast to the typically "macho" male image. If you feel the language in this play might be objectionable to your community and would like an alternative, try *The Crucible,* by Arthur Miller.[25] Also a play, this piece of literature has stereotypes of authoritarian males and devious females. Despite its seventeenth-century setting, the play speaks to very contemporary qualities of character.

With the roles of men and women in society as the basis, the second-semester curriculum constitutes a very practical and natural extension of the first semester's material. We open in January with a unit on engagement and marriage. All of the materials are either teacher-designed or collected from nontextbook sources. We gather articles from such magazines as *Redbook, Time, Life,* and *Psychology Today* and use a variety of readings and poetry: "On Marriage" from *The Prophet,* by Kahlil Gibran;[26] "Surfaces"[27] and "The Lover,"[28] by Peter Meinke. Lyrics from love songs by contemporary groups and discussions of alternatives to marriage are added to the curriculum. In addition, we make use of community resource people whenever possible: a priest, a minister, a rabbi, and a lawyer come to share their views with the class. Among the highlights of the unit are the step-by-step discussions on how to plan a

[19]Greenwich, Conn.: Fawcett, 1953.
[20]New York: Dell, 1972.
[21]New York: Dell, 1973.
[22]New York: Popular Library, 1962.
[23]New York: Dell, 1968.
[24]Harold Clurman (ed.), *Famous American Plays of the 30's* (New York: Dell, 1959).
[25]New York: Bantam, 1959.
[26]New York: Knopf, 1953.
[27]*The Night Train and the Golden Bird* (Pittsburgh: University of Pittsburgh Press, 1977), p. 45.
[28]Poems by Peter Meinke: A Reading, presented by the Student Board of Governors, Hamline University, May 18, 1968, p. 10.

wedding, including arrangements with the church or synagogue, and which family has which obligations. The discussions in this unit are generally quite candid, and while we avoid any conflicts with individual mores or ethics, we are proud of the honest exchange of ideas which the seniors seem to want and need.

No discussion on engagement and marriage would be credible if we did not also discuss the disintegration of the family unit. We invite police officers and social service caseworkers to talk to the class about child and spouse abuse. Tapes and filmstrips from *Parents' Magazine's* "Children in Crisis"[29] are excellent. There are also many good feature films available through your interlibrary loan system on the subjects of marriage, the family, and divorce.

From here, we move into aging. Generally we start out with "The Stringbean,"[30] a short black-and-white/color film with only music for the soundtrack. This film depicts an elderly woman who lives alone and and nurtures a salvaged bean plant into a lovely, healthy plant and then selflessly gives up her enjoyment of it to transplant it out in a public garden where it will have more sun to thrive. All of the indoor and depressing scenes are in black and white. The happy life-commitment scenes are filmed in color. It is a very poignant and sensitive portrayal of the life cycle.

After this film and ensuing discussion, the class begins work at an individual pace on the novel *The Pigman*, by Paul Zindel.[31] There is an excellent ten-minute film vignette on *The Pigman* in the kit "Contemporary Novel," prepared by Center for Humanities. After this brief opening sequence, the students continue to work on our vocabulary sheets and study guides at their own paces. This unit again allows much time for teacher-student interaction during the grading of these materials.

The Pigman provides a natural transition from aging to death and dying. A virtual plethora of material is available on this topic, and while some of the students groan when we start the unit, it usually earns more kudos on the year-end evaluation than any other. Probably the most attention ought to be given to the selection of material, since it is the initial impression that helps the class establish its attitude toward the study of death and dying. We usually start with a reading from Ecclesiastes 3:1–8, "To everything there is a season. . . ." We also use the poems "Richard Cory," by E. A. Robinson,[32] and "To an Athlete Dying Young," by A. E. Houseman.[33] A kit called "Funeral Customs from Around the World" by Guidance Associates,[34] readings from Elisabeth

[29]Vincent J. Montana (New York: Parents Magazine, 1975).
[30]New York: McGraw-Hill, 1964.
[31]New York: Dell, 1968.
[32]I. Kincheloe and L. Cook (eds.), *Adventures in Values* (New York: Harcourt, Brace, 1969), p. 619.
[33]Carl E. Bain, Jerome Beaty, and J. Paul Hunter (eds.), *The Norton Introduction to Literature* 2nd ed. (New York: Norton, 1977), p. 557.
[34]George Daugh and David Berg, filmstrip from *Perspectives on Death* (Baltimore: Waverly Press, 1972).

Kübler-Ross's "A Time for Grief and Growth,"[35] films such as "The Garden Party"[36] and "Bang the Drum Slowly"[37] add a variety of material to the unit. Visits from a local funeral director, clergy, and lawyers round out the presentation and involve differing points of view.

Following the material above, we move into an individualized novel unit again, this time with all the novels having something to do with death: *Sunshine*, by Norma Klein;[38] *Brian's Song*, by William Blin (screenplay);[39] *Bang the Drum Slowly*, by Mark Harris;[40] *I'm Fifteen, and I Don't Want to Die*, by Christine Arnothy;[41] *Love Is a Blanket Word*, by Honor Arundel;[42] *I Heard the Owl Call My Name*, by Margaret Craven;[43] and *Death Be Not Proud*, by John Gunther.[44] While these books are carefully selected because of the subject matter and the range of reading levels, the format is fairly structured. On the other hand, the students feel that because they have chosen the novel (with some firm guidance in individual cases), they have selected the unit themselves; therefore, they have a strong commitment to the material. Each book has a packet containing vocabulary material, study guide, reinforcement and review exercises, and quizzes. All of these choices have been well received.

To finish out our twelfth-grade year, we choose from two alternatives: one is a unit on comics and how they reflect change in society; the other is a potpourri called "Where Do We Go from Here?" The comics unit provides an interesting change of pace and an historical, as well as a sociological, perspective. It does, however, require a good collection of old comics. It can be taught without the actual comics, but it is more effective with the old *Wonder Woman* and *Superman*. Without the original material something is missing. There are several kits and films on comics that provide some interesting asides, but the most creative part is having the students develop their own original comic strips to make satirical comment on contemporary life styles. Many profound observations can be made in a humorous way.

"Where Do We Go from Here?" was originally designed to provide some levity at the end of the year. We use selected readings from *What Really Happened to the Class of '65?*, by Michael Medved,[45] and *Class Reunion*, by Rona Jaffe.[46] We've had a great deal of fun writing self-descriptions of what we would look like twenty-five years from now at

[35]In Roy and Jane Nichols, *Death: The Final Stage of Growth* (Human Development Series) (Englewood Cliffs, N.J.: Prentice-Hall, 1975).

[36]New York: ACI Films, 1974.

[37]Wilmette, Ill.: Films Inc., 1973.

[38]New York: Avon, 1974.

[39]New York: Bantam, 1972.

[40]New York: Dell, 1956.

[41]New York: Scholastic Book Services, 1974.

[42]New York: Scholastic Book Services, 1973.

[43]New York: Dell, 1973.

[44]New York: Perennial Library, 1965.

[45]New York: Random House, 1976.

[46]New York: Delacorte Press, 1979.

Figure 74. Sample Four-Year Curriculum

Month	Grade 9	Grade 10	Grade 11	Grade 12
SEPTEMBER	Diagnostic testing Spelling *Scope* magazine Basic grammar	Journals Radio program Sentence structure *That Was Then, This Is Now*	*The Outsiders* *Lisa, Bright and Dark* Spelling	Roles of men and women *A Raisin in the Sun*
OCTOBER	*West Side Story* Sentence structure Spelling	*That Was Then, This Is Now* Individualized grammar unit Paragraph writing Spelling	Mass media *Black Like Me* Spelling	Individualized novels: *The Bridges at Toko-ri* *Dinky Hocker Shoots Smack* *If I Love You Am I Trapped Forever?* *The Lilies of the Field* *The Boy Who Could Make Himself Disappear*
NOVEMBER	*Point 31* (short stories) Paragraph writing Spelling	Values, symbolism, and awareness Spelling Composition writing	*Twelve Angry Men* Report writing Letter writing	
DECEMBER	Journals *Rumble Fish* Spelling	*Lord of the Flies* Report writing Individual interest unit	Career unit	*Of Mice and Men*
JANUARY	*Rumble Fish* Review Exams	Individual interest unit Review Exams	Career unit Review Exams	Review Exams

FEBRUARY	Journals Action Library *This School Is Driving Me Crazy*	Journals Spelling *Snowbound*	*Hey, Dummy* Public speaking	Engagement Marriage Child abuse Divorce
MARCH	Social studies reader: myths and legends Spelling Journals Letter writing	*Snowbound* Journals Spelling Poetry	*Man Without a Face*	Aging "Stringbean" *The Pigman* Death and Dying
APRIL	*The Skating Rink* Composition writing Journals Spelling	Poetry *Anne Frank's Diary of a Young Girl*	Composition writing Science fiction	Individualized novels: *Sunshine* *Brian's Song* *Bang the Drum Slowly* *I Heard the Owl Call My Name* *A Figure of Speech*
MAY	Journals *A Patch of Blue* Writing review Spelling	*Anne Frank's Diary of a Young Girl* Spelling Letter writing review	*Martian Chronicles*	
JUNE	*A Patch of Blue* Review Exams	Review Exams	Review Exams	Where Do We Go from Here? Review Exams

reunion time. We have also used this as a means for evaluating the current school environment. For example, we have the students write compositions on the kinds of things they would look for if they were to return to the school on Back-to-School-Night for their own children twenty years from now. While this short unit was initially intended to be fun, we have found in actual practice that it has very serious overtones. In spite of their strongly expressed desires to get out of high school, when faced with the immediate prospect of graduation, many of our students are unsure of themselves and reluctant to leave the safety of familiar ground. This unit provides a background against which some genuine fears can be allayed and realistic alternatives for the future considered. The whole thing can be wrapped up in three or four days, but those few sessions have a valuable place in the twelfth-grade curriculum.

The chart in figure 74 shows how our ninth- through twelfth-grade curriculum is actually scheduled within the framework of the school calendar. Of course we do not mean to suggest that these are the only possible curriculum choices for poor readers, and you should certainly make your own selections.

When you develop strategies keeping the students' interests, needs, and abilities in mind, you should experience some of the success we have had with our secondary slow learners. Instead of the frustration of students who cannot cope with assignments and the disillusionment of teachers who cannot reach unmotivated students, both students and teachers should develop improved attitudes. Build on the students' strengths, remediate their weaknesses, and reinforce their skills. Remember to use structural and psychological "crutches" to help the students along. These strategies require more work for you initially, but the progress of the students makes it well worth the effort.

Appendices
Selected Bibliography
Index

Appendix A
Individual Secondary Skills Inventory

by SUSANNE MILLER

This basic skills inventory is to be administered to secondary-level students. Test 1 is to be administered individually to each student. Test 2–8 may be administered individually or in groups. The results for each student should be recorded on the Teacher's Recording Copy. Class results may be entered on the Composite Record of Diagnosis.

Individual Secondary Skills Inventory   *Teacher's Reading Copy*

Test 1

(Purpose of this subtest is to determine student's ability to read unfamiliar words using long and short vowel rules. This must be administered individually to each student.)

<u>Directions to student</u>: "The words on this sheet are not real words. Please read these words to me even though they do not make sense."

(As student reads these words, record his accuracy on the individual student recording sheet.)

1. mife	6. dace
2. dest	7. hude
3. lete	8. paff
4. pode	9. sop
5. fub	10. jitt

Test 2

(Purpose of this subtest is to determine student's ability to hear initial blends.)

<u>Directions to student</u>: "I am going to read a list of words. On your answer sheet I want you to write the first two letters you hear at the beginning of each word. For example, if I said *protect*, you would write down *pr*."

1. black	6. transfer
2. brackish	7. fracas
3. plague	8. smattering
4. slurp	9. clientele
5. drainage	10. strangulation

Test 3

(Purpose of this subtest is to determine student's ability to hear final consonants.)

<u>Directions to student</u>: "I am going to read a list of words. On your answer sheet I want you to write the letter you hear at the end of the word. For example, if I said *occupation*, you would write down *n*."

1. amuck	5. protocol
2. tether	6. antihistamine
3. intercom	7. recess
4. acrid	8. subterfuge

Test 4

(Purpose of this subtest is to determine student's ability to divide words into syllables.)

<u>Directions to student</u>: "On your answer sheet you will find a list of ten words. On the blank line next to each word, rewrite the word, dividing it into syllables."

1. fol ly	6. se lec tion
2. bas ket	7. un com mon
3. pa per	8. dis ap pear
4. foot ball	9. in ter lock ing
5. play ground	10. trans por ta tion

Test 5a

(Purpose of this subtest is to determine student's ability to recognize prefixes. If necessary, you may read these words out loud, but be careful that your voice inflection does not identify the prefix.)

Directions to student: "On your answer sheet you will find a list of words. Underline the part of the word which is a prefix."

1. <u>un</u>fasten
2. <u>mis</u>understand
3. <u>semi</u>annual
4. <u>sub</u>way
5. <u>pre</u>view
6. <u>super</u>human
7. <u>re</u>seed
8. <u>trans</u>port

(You may not define *prefix*, but you may ask students if they know the difference between a *pre-test* and a *post-test*. You may continue giving examples as needed.)

Test 5b

(Purpose of this subtest is to determine student's ability to understand the meaning of basic prefixes.)

Directions to student: "On your answer sheet, you will find two blank lines next to each number. In the first space, write the letters you chose as prefixes for the words in Test 5a. In the space next to it, write the meaning of the prefix. For example, in the word *postoperative*, *post* is the prefix. *Post* means *after*. Your answer would look like this: <u>post</u> *after*."

1. un—*detract, take away*
2. mis—*not*
3. semi—*half*
4. sub—*under*
5. pre—*before*
6. super—*extra, outstanding*
7. re—*do again*
8. trans—*across*

Test 6

(Purpose of this subtest is to measure student's ability to spell ten basic but frequently missed words. The mastery of these words is essential for paragraph writing.)

Directions to student: "This next test is a short spelling test. I will say the word once, use it in a sentence, and repeat it."

1. their
2. a lot
3. because
4. any

5. thcro   8 too
6. enough   9. everything
7. together   10. they're

Test 7

(Purpose of this subtest is to measure student's ability to capitalize, and use commas, periods, and quotation marks correctly.)

Directions to student: "On your answer sheets are five sentences. I will read the sentences aloud. You are to correct these sentences using the necessary punctuation."

1. Bob and Jane rode into Oneida.
2. I want a new book, a dress, and a record for my birthday.
3. He went swimming, and Tom went bike-riding.
4. School starts in September and ends in June.
5. Mary said, "Go to the store."

Test 8

(Purpose of this subtest is to obtain a sample of the student's writing.)

Directions to student: "Write a paragraph answering this question: Do you think school is necessary?"

1. mife

2. dest

3. lete

4. pode

5. fub

6. dace

7. hude

8. paff

9. sop

10. jitt

Individual Skills Inventory   *Student's Answer Sheet*

Name: _____

Test 2

Write the first two letters you hear at the beginning of each word.

1. _____   6. _____

2. _____   7. _____

3. _____   8. _____

4. _____   9. _____

5. _____   10. _____

Test 3

Write the letter you hear at the end of each word.

1. _____   5. _____

2. _____   6. _____

3. _____   7. _____

4. _____   8. _____

Test 4

Divide the words listed below into syllables by rewriting the word on the line.

1. folly _____   6. selection _____

2. basket _____   7. uncommon _____

3. paper _____   8. disappear _____

4. football _____   9. interlocking _____

5. playground _____   10. transportation _____

Test 5a

<u>Underline</u> the part of each word below that is the prefix.

1. unfasten	5. preview
2. misunderstand	6. superhuman
3. semiannual	7. reseed
4. subway	8. transport

Test 5b

On the first space next to each number, write the letters you chose as prefixes from the words above. In the space next to it, write the <u>meaning</u> of that prefix.

1. _____   _____

2. _____   _____

3. _____   _____

4. _____   _____

5. _____   _____

6. _____   _____

7. _____   _____

8. _____   _____

Test 6

Spelling

1. _____

2. _____

3. _____

4. _____

5. _____

6. _____

7. _____

8. _____

9. _____

10. _____

Test 7

Punctuate the sentences below.

1. bob and jane rode into oneida
2. i want a new book a dress and a record for my birthday
3. he went swimming and tom went bike-riding
4. school starts in september and ends in june
5. mary said go to the store

Test 8

Writing. Write a paragraph answering this question: "Do you think school is necessary?"

_____

_____

_____

_____

_____

_____

_____

_____

_____

Individual Secondary Skills Inventory   *Teacher's Recording Copy*

Student _____   Grade _____   Section _____

Test 1

Ability to use long and short vowel rules.

1. mife _____   6. dace _____

2. dest _____   7. hude _____

3. lete _____   8. paff _____

4. pode _____   9. sop _____

5. fub _____   10. jitt _____

Test 2

Ability to hear initial blends.

Score: _____ out of 10 correct.

Missed blends: _____

Test 3

Ability to hear final consonants.

Score: _____ out of 8 correct.

Test 4

Ability to divide words into syllables.

Score: _____ out of 17 correct.

Test 5a

Ability to identify prefixes.

Score: _____ out of 8 correct.

Missed prefixes: _____

_____

Test 5b

Ability to identify meaning of above prefixes.

Score: _____ out of 8 correct.

_____

Test 6

Basic spelling list.

Score: _____ out of 10 correct.

1. their _____   6. enough _____

2. a lot _____   7. together _____

3. because _____   8. too _____

4. any _____   9. everything _____

5. there _____   10. they're _____

_____

Test 7

Punctuation

Score: _____

capital letters: _____ out of 11

periods: _____ out of 5

commas: _____ out of 4

quotation marks: _____ out of 2

Test 8

Test 8 should be graded on the basis of the number of points out of 5. Give one point for a paragraph main idea statement, one point for an example, one point for a paragraph conclusion statement, one point for grammar and sentence construction, and one point for spelling.

Score: _____ out of 5.

Composite Record of Diagnosis

Student	9th Grade N.Y. PEP	Gates Voc. Comp.	Maico Audiometric Screening	Wepman	A.M.A. Rating Card	Snellen Chart	Keystone	Preferred Hand	Preferred Foot	Preferred Eye	Speech	Motor	Handwriting	ISSI 1. Use of L & S, Vowels	2. Initial Blends	3. Final Consonants	4. Syllables	5a. Recognizing Prefixes	5b. Meaning of Prefixes	6. Spelling	7. Punctuation	8. Written Paragraph	Commen s

Appendix B
Informal Reading
Inventory, Grades 7–12

by SUSANNE MILLER

An informal reading inventory is just that: an informal, nonstandardized, quick assessment. This inventory provides sample passages taken from texts commonly used in grades 7 through 12, in social studies, science, and English classes. Each sample is followed by six to eight questions designed to measure a student's literal, interpretive, and applied levels of understanding of what he has read.

The line next to *Word Recognition Errors* in the upper right-hand corner is for you to record the number of oral reading errors the student accumulates on that passage. Next to *Comprehension Errors*, record the number of questions on which the student was CORRECT.

If you have no reading test score available to you, use your own judgment about where to start. If you have a score, start one level below. Have the student read the passage while you mark the oral reading errors he makes. Remove the passage, and ask him the comprehension questions. Go on to the next passage and continue in this fashion until the student scores *less than five* comprehension questions correct. The last passage on which he scores *five or more* correct would be considered his instructional level.

It is important for you to note that the reading level of the passage in some instances is actually higher or lower than the grade level at which the text is used. In using this inventory, you will not be determining the student's reading level as much as whether or not he can handle the text material commonly in use at his given grade level. Note that the grade level for usage as well as reading level appears in the lower left-hand corner.

Word Recognition Errors _____

Comprehension Errors (5) _____

Jet fighter Number 313 taxied onto the end of the runway, cleared for takeoff. The pilot, a young major, fastened his safety belt, set his brakes and ran up 100 percent rpm on his engine. Then he released his toe brakes. The wheels rolled the first inch. And in that first inch, the pilot of Number 313 was doomed. In effect, he was already dead.

A mile and a half of smooth, white concrete runway narrowed into the distance in front of the nose of the gleaming fighter plane. The runway was 8,000 feet long, more than ample for the 6,700 foot take-off distance calculated in the flight plan.

The weather was good, a clear bright morning with a hot sun beating down on the shimmering California desert. Surface winds were nearly dead calm. The J-79 engine was in perfect condition and turning up normal thrust. No mechanical defect lurked anywhere within the complex innards of the aircraft. The pilot was highly experienced and could point to a spotless safety record and superior past performance.[1]

QUESTIONS

1. Why did the jet fighter taxi onto the runway? (*cleared for take-off*)
2. What are *two* of the procedures the pilot went through at the end of the runway? (*fastened safety belt, set brakes, ran up to 100 percent rpm, released brakes*)
3. How would you describe the runway? (*1½ miles of smooth, white concrete, 8,000 feet long*)
4. What synonyms could you use for the word *calculated* in this passage? (*plotted, planned, estimated*)
5. Describe the day. (*good weather; clear, bright morning; hot sun; calm winds*)
6. Give two reasons why you might think this is the right pilot to have on a difficult mission. (*highly experienced, perfect safety record, superior past performance*)

Seventh-grade English anthology
Ninth-grade reading level

[1]Bradley Robinson, "Matthew Henson," in Eghert Nieman, Elizabeth O'Daly, and Thomas Folds (eds.); *Adventures for Readers* (New York: Harcourt, Brace and World, 1968), p. 110.

Word Recognition Errors _____

Comprehension Errors (5) _____

The judicial branch is made up of the state courts. In New York state we have three kinds of state courts: the Supreme Court, the Appellate Division of the Supreme Court, and the Court of Appeals.

The Supreme Court is the lowest of the state courts, the Appellate Division is next, and the Court of Appeals is the highest court in the state. This is hard to get used to because we know that the Supreme Court of the United States is the highest in the land.

The state is divided into ten judicial districts. In these ten districts there are 130 Supreme Court justices (another name for judge). The justices are elected by the voters in their judicial district. Each justice serves for a term of 14 years.

The Supreme Court may hear civil and criminal cases. It may also judge cases which have been appealed from the lower courts.

Appellate means "appeal," and that is just what the Appellate Division is—an appeals court. It hears cases which have been appealed from the Supreme Court. There are four of these Appellate Division courts. The judges are appointed by the governor, with the consent of the senate, from among the 130 Supreme Court justices. Each judge serves for a term of 5 years.

The highest court, the Court of Appeals, has a chief judge and six associate judges. These judges are elected by the people. Each judge serves for a term of 14 years.[2]

QUESTIONS

1. In New York state we have three kinds of courts. What are they? (*Supreme Court, Appellate Division, Court of Appeals*)
2. What is the lowest state court? (*Supreme Court*)
3. Why is this hard to remember? (*because we know that the Supreme Court is the highest in the U.S.*)
4. What is another name for court justice? (*judge*)
5. How does a person get to be a justice? (*he is elected*)
6. What does the word *appellate* mean? (*appeal*)
7. In what way do the judges of the appellate division courts differ from the state Supreme Court justices? (*they are appointed by the governor*)
8. What does *highest court* mean? (*the last court of appeal—a case must go through the other two courts before reaching the Court of Appeals*)

Seventh-grade social studies text
Sixth-grade reading level

[2]David M. Ellis, James A. Frost, and William Fink, *New York, the Empire State,* 4th ed. (Englewood Cliffs, N.J.: Prentice-Hall, 1975), p. 35.

Word Recognition Errors _____

Comprehension Errors (5) _____

Centuries passed. . . . Pompeii was forgotten. Then, fifteen hundred years later, it was discovered again. Beneath the protecting shroud of ashes, the city remained intact. Everything was as it had been the day Vesuvius erupted. There were still loaves of bread in the ovens of the bakeries. In the wine shops, the wine jars were in place, and on one counter could be seen a stain where a customer had thrown down his glass and fled.

To go to Pompeii today is to take a trip backward in a time machine. The old city comes to life all around you. You can almost hear the clatter of horses' hoofs on the narrow streets, the cries of children, and the laughter of the shopkeepers. You can almost smell the meat sizzling over a charcoal fire. The sky is cloudlessly blue, with the summer sun almost directly overhead. The grassy slopes of great Vesuvius pierce the heavens behind the city, and sunlight shimmers on the waters of the bay a thousand yards from the city walls. Ships from every nation are in port, and strange languages can be heard in the streets.[3]

QUESTIONS

1. How much time elapsed before Pompeii was rediscovered? (*1,500 yrs*)
2. What is Vesuvius? (*volcano*)
3. What signs would indicate to you that Pompeii is the same as it was the day Vesuvius erupted? Give at least *two*. (*bread in ovens, wine jars, stain on counter*)
4. What does "take a trip backward in a time machine" mean?
5. What is the geography of the area surrounding Pompeii? (*mountains near coast, well protected*)
6. Give me *two* clues which told you people from all over the world visited Pompeii. (*strange languages, ships from every nation are in the port*)

Eighth-grade English anthology
Seventh-grade reading level

[3]Pliny, "The Eruption of Vesuvius," in Eghert Nieman, Elizabeth O'Daly, and Thomas Folds (eds.), *Adventures for Readers* (New York: Harcourt, Brace and World, 1968), p. 97.

Comprehension Errors (4) _____

Word Recognition Errors _____

"Lay on the horns!" he shouted, so that Joel Nichols and the other highway trooper stationed on the grade would be alerted to the emergency. He swung out of the bunk. Ahead, sharp red clusters of taillights and beady truck markers brokenly traced the dropping twists of the divided highway. It was the Corkscrew, all right. And worse, they were already past the patrol-car spot!

Fingers of fear squeezed his stomach. It was a sickness worse than the indigestion he'd been trying to sleep off—the only reason he'd let the kid drive up the hill, with a strict order to wake him at the top. But the kid hadn't obeyed. He'd boomed across the ridge's level four miles. Now the Corkscrew had him.

But this was no time for jawing. Not with five miles of murderous downgrade ahead of the runaway rig loaded with tons of machine parts.

Barney shouted, "Let me have it!"

"Barney, I didn't mean to take her down. But you looked so comfortable I thought I'd take her across the top and then—"

Barney jammed his left forearm on the wheel ring. He hoped the blasting air horns would carry back to the patrol-car station. Ahead, the driver of a hay rig heard it and changed his mind about cutting out to pass a tanker.[4]

QUESTIONS

1. What does "Lay on the horns" mean in this story? (*toot the horn*)
2. Why does Barney shout, "Lay on the horns?" (*so troopers will be alerted to emergency*)
3. Describe the road they were on. (*dropping twists of a divided highway, Corkscrew, murderous downgrade*)
4. Why had Barney let the kid drive up the hill? (*indigestion*)
5. In this context, what does the word *jawing* mean? (*talking*)
6. Why would the driver of the hay rig change his mind about passing a tanker? (*to leave one lane open for the truck in trouble*)

Ninth-grade English anthology
Sixth-grade reading level

[4]Carl Henry Rathjen, "Runaway Rig," *Adventures for Today* (Henry I. Christ and Herbert Potell), New York: Harcourt, Brace, and World, Inc. 1968, p. 127.

Word Recognition Errors _____

Comprehension Errors (5) _____

As trade among nations increased, it developed into what was called "the great circuit," or "triangular trade." Ships sailed from Europe to Africa with cargoes of cheap goods, beads, trinkets, and guns. At the trading posts that dotted the coastline the goods were exchanged for captives—at first mainly strong young men—to be sold as slaves in the West Indies. From the West Indies the ships returned to Europe with cargoes of sugar and tobacco.

Britain's New England colonies set up their own triangular trade—rum from New England for slaves in Africa; then on to the West Indies to sell the slaves; finally pick up sugar and molasses to be made into rum back home.

After buying the slaves, the European traders kept them in stockades until a slave ship arrived. The longer the wait, the more crowded the prisons became. Under such horrible conditions, many Africans died of beatings, disease, sickness, and a lack of food and water.[5]

QUESTIONS

1. What was the *triangle* of the trade route? (*Europe to Africa to the West Indies and back to Europe*)
2. What is a synonym for the word *captive* as used here? (*slaves*)
3. Where were the slaves sold? (*West Indies*)
4. The New England colonies set up their own triangle of trade. What was that route? (*New England to Africa to the West Indies and then home to New England*)
5. Name *two* items in the cargo used for trade (*slaves, beads, guns, trinkets, sugar, molasses*)
6. What is the author suggesting when he says ". . . at first mainly strong young men . . . ?" (*perhaps later slaves were women, children, or older people*)
7. To what country did the New England colonies owe their loyalty? (*Britain, England*)
8. Why did so many of the slaves die? (*crowded conditions in prisons, beatings, disease, sickness, and lack of food and water*)

Eighth-grade reading level
Ninth-grade social studies text

[5]Milton Jay Belasco, Harold E. Hammond, *Africa*, History, Culture, People series (New York: Cambridge Book Company, 1975), p. 53.

Word Recognition Errors _____

Comprehension Errors (5) _____

If the nerves were not connected to some central place, the body would really not have control. Your left leg would operate separately from your right leg; your fingers would not work together, which would make grasping hard. There would be no coordination. But if you look, you will see that all nerves are connected. We call this cord in which all the nerves are brought together the spinal cord. The spinal cord runs up and down the length of your backbone and enters the skull. It is protected from injury by a series of bones called vertebrae. Inside the skull, the nerve tissue forms a large organ, the brain.[6]

QUESTIONS

1. To what central place are the nerves connected? (*brain*)
2. If you had no *coordination*, what would be your problem? (*couldn't move your arms or legs together gracefully*)
3. Why are vertebrae important? (*protect the spinal cord*)
4. Are the nerves in your fingers independent from the nerves in your toes? (*no, connected to spinal cord*)
5. Who would be most interested in this passage? (*doctor, therapist*)
6. If you had a spinal cord injury, what might be a result? (*no feeling in arms, legs; paralysis*)
7. What is the function of the brain? (*to coordinate the action of the nerves*)

Ninth-grade biology text
Seventh-grade reading level

[6]Joseph M. Oxenhorn, *Pathways in Science: Built for Living* (New York: Globe Book Company, 1975), p. 151.

Word Recognition Errors _____

Comprehension Errors (5) _____

The red-coated, many-antlered buck acknowledged the lordship of the spirit of the place and dozed knee-deep in the cool, shaded pool. There seemed no flies to vex him and he was languid with rest. Sometimes his ears moved when the stream awoke and whispered; but they moved lazily, with foreknowledge that it was merely the stream grown garrulous at discovery that it had slept.

But there came a time when the buck's ears lifted and tensed with swift eagerness for sound. His head was turned down the canyon. His sensitive, quivering nostrils scented the air. His eyes could not pierce the green screen through which the stream rippled away, but to his ears came the voice of a man. It was a steady, monotonous, singsong voice. Once the buck heard the harsh clash of metal upon rock. At the sound he snorted with a sudden start that jerked him through the air from water to meadow, and his feet sank into the young velvet, while he pricked his ears and again scented the air. Then he stole across the tiny meadow, pausing once and again to listen, and faded away out of the canyon like a wraith, soft-footed and without sound.[7]

QUESTIONS

1. How do you know that this is a mature buck, probably several years old? (*many antlers; implied lordship, leadership*)
2. What human qualities does the author attribute to the stream? (*whisper*)
3. What disturbs the buck's peaceful browsing? (*sound of man*)
4. Why does he turn his head down the canyon? (*to gain the scent because of the direction of the wind*)
5. To what is the author probably referring when he says that the buck's feet "sank into the young velvet?" (*moss, slippery mud, or marsh*)
6. On what senses does the buck rely the most? (*hearing, smelling*)
7. Provide a synonym for the word *wraith* as used here. (*ghost, vision*)

Seventh-grade reading level
Tenth-grade text

[7]Jack London, "All Gold Canyon," in *Exploring Life Through Literature* (Chicago: Scott, Foresman and Company, 1964), p. 129.

Word Recognition Errors _____

Comprehension Errors (5) _____

The most sweeping reforms of the French Revolution were made at the very beginning of the National Assembly. Frightened by rioting in the provinces, the upper classes suddenly agreed to give up most of their privileges. This dramatic scene described below is by an eyewitness.

During the evening, a member of the National Assembly read a proclamation. This announcement had been prepared to stop the attacks on the nobles' castles. It ordered the payment of taxes, rents, and feudal dues, which the people were refusing to pay. This led to a great debate. It was pointed out that the peasants were refusing to pay feudal dues and were burning feudal title deeds. They were doing these things because they hated the feudal regime and the burdens it placed on them.[8]

QUESTIONS

1. From what country's history is this passage taken? (*France*)
2. Why did the nobles agree so quickly to give up most of their privileges? (*fear of the rioting*)
3. What is the source of the information in the above paragraph? (*an eyewitness*)
4. What is a *proclamation*? (*an order, an announcement*)
5. What were some of the burdens placed on the peasants? (*payment of feudal dues, rents, and taxes*)
6. Provide a synonym for the word *burden*. (*load, responsibility*)
7. If you were a peasant, what would have been your response to this proclamation?

Tenth-grade social studies text
Ninth-grade reading level

[8]Sidney Schwartz and John R. O'Connor, *Democracy and Nationalism,* Inquiry: Western Civilization series (New York: Globe Book Company, 1976), p. 32.

Word Recognition Errors _____

Comprehension Errors (5) _____

Photosynthesis is a process by which green plants use carbon dioxide and water, with the energy from light (usually sunlight), to produce carbohydrates and oxygen. During this process light energy is converted into the chemical-bond energy of organic compounds.

Most of the photosynthesis (80%) which occurs on this planet is carried on by algae (one-celled green plants) which live in the oceans and fresh water. It is also carried on by multicellular green plants—the familiar low plants, shrubs, and trees of the land. The chemical process of photosynthesis is essentially the same in both the one-celled protists and the multicellular plants.

Chlorophyll acts as a catalyst—a substance which promotes (or hinders) a chemical reaction but does not itself become changed as a result of the reaction. The light energy becomes converted to the chemical bond energy of the glucose molecule (one of the products of photosynthesis). The glucose formed may be used by the plant as a source of energy in cellular respiration, or it may be converted into other compounds such as starch, proteins, or fats.[9]

QUESTIONS

1. What gas do plants produce that is essential for humans? (*oxygen*)
2. Name three kinds of plants that carry on photosynthesis. (*algae, low plants, shrubs, trees*)
3. What is a main difference between algae and multicellular plants? (*algae have only one cell*)
4. What kind of people might be interested in photosynthesis? (*botanists, florists, gardeners*)
5. What is a catalyst? (*substance which promotes—or hinders—a chemical reaction but does not itself become changed*)
6. What natural element is necessary for the photosynthesis process? (*sunlight*)
7. Can photosynthesis take place in water? (*yes, oceans and fresh water*)

Tenth-grade biology text
Twelfth-grade reading level

[9]David Kraus, *Concepts in Modern Biology* (New York: Cambridge Book Company, 1974), p. 222.

Word Recognition Errors _____

Comprehension Errors (5) _____

New England was in Nathaniel Hawthorne's blood, but rarely has an American writer been so consciously tied to his birthplace and his ancestry and, at the same time, so aware of his aversion to both. Born in Salem, Massachusetts, on Independence Day, 1804, he was descended from wealthy and influential citizens who, in spite of their prominence, left a blot on the family's history which Hawthorne spent a lifetime trying to atone. William Hathorne (Nathaniel changed the spelling), arriving in the American colonies in 1603, a soldier and eventually a judge, condemned a Quaker woman to be whipped in the streets of Salem for holding to a religion the Puritans strongly opposed. "Grave, bearded, sable-cloaked and steeple-crowned," Hawthorne described him. . . . Intolerance, cruelty, pride—these sins obsessed the young Hawthorne as he listened to the history of early Salem and his ancestors.[10]

QUESTIONS

1. How does Nathaniel Hawthorne feel about his ancestors? (*disliked*)
2. What was the blot on the family's name? (*his ancestor had ordered a Quaker woman whipped publicly*)
3. Can you suggest a reason Hawthorne may have wanted to change the spelling of his last name? (*perhaps didn't wish to be associated with his relatives*)
4. What proof do you have that Hawthorne considered his ancestor somber? (*grave, bearded, sable-cloaked and steeple-crowned*)
5. Distinguish between the word *pride* as it is used in this passage and the more traditional use. (*one is negative and one is positive; pride as in arrogance, and pride as in pleased*)
6. There is a quote "The sins of the fathers are visited on their sons." How does this quote apply to this passage? (*Hawthorne was obsessed by the cruel and intolerant behavior of his family.*)

Eleventh-grade English text
College reading level

[10]G. Robert Carlsen (ed.), *American Literature: Themes and Writers* (New York: Webster Division, McGraw-Hill, 1967), p. 225.

Word Recognition Errors _____

Comprehension Errors (5) _____

What are the major arguments of the NCBH (National Committee to Ban Handguns) and the NRA (National Rifle Association)?

NCBH arguments for the bill:

1. Guns in the home are a constant danger to those who possess them. They often lead to fatal accidents and murders. Besides, the bill does not prevent hunters from owning rifles for sporting purposes.

2. The Supreme Court has ruled that Congress does have the right to pass gun-control laws. The Second Amendment to the Constitution, said the Court, gives people the right to establish *militias*. That does not mean that all individuals have the constitutional right to own a gun.

3. The ownership of handguns is a poor protection against robbery, rape, and other violent crimes. An experienced criminal can shoot you before you shoot him or her.

NRA arguments against the bill:

1. Despite what the Supreme Court has said, the bill takes away a citizen's "right to bear arms" as guaranteed in the Second Amendment to the Constitution. Every citizen has a right to own a gun for his or her self-defense.

2. Criminals will always be able to get handguns in illegal ways. Knowing that citizens are now defenseless will only make criminals bolder.[11]

QUESTIONS

1. What is the position of the NCBH on hunting? (*doesn't oppose it*)
2. Cite an example of what the author might mean when he says guns in the house are a constant danger. (*children, guns not unloaded*)
3. What is the position of the Supreme Court on Congress's right to pass gun-control legislation? (*approves*)
4. Why does the author think that ownership of handguns is poor protection from violent crimes? (*an experienced criminal can shoot you before you shoot him or her*)
5. What does the NRA contend is the main purpose for an individual citizen owning a gun? (*self-defense*)
6. According to the author, what will be the attitude of the criminal if the innocent citizen has no firearms? (*criminal will be bolder*)
7. What solution can there possibly be for this controversy? (*any logical answer is acceptable*)

Eleventh-grade social studies text
Eighth-grade reading level

[11]Steven Jantzen, Carolyn Jackson, Norman Lunger, Diana Reische, and Phillip Parker, *Scholastic American Citizenship Program* (New York: Scholastic Book Services, 1977), p. 318.

Word Recognition Errors _____

Comprehension Errors (5) _____

Suppose we place a cover over a container partially filled with a liquid. It appears that evaporation of the liquid continues for a while and then ceases. Let us examine this apparent situation in terms of the kinetic theory. The temperature of the liquid is proportional to the average kinetic energy of all the molecules of the liquid. Most of these molecules have energies very close to the average. However, as a result of collisions with other molecules some have very high energies and a few have very low energies at any given time. The motions of all are random.

Some high-energy molecules near the surface are moving toward the surface. These molecules may overcome the attractive forces of the surface molecules completely and escape, or evaporate. But some of them then collide with molecules of gases in the air or other vapor molecules and rebound into the liquid.[12]

QUESTIONS

1. Based on the information in the passage, what might you think is a meaning of the word *kinetic*? (*moving*)
2. If the liquid is hotter, what happens to the molecules? (*they move or evaporate faster*)
3. What are two things that can happen to the molecules? (*escape into the air; rebound into the liquid*)
4. What is a synonym for *vapor*? (*gas, air*)
5. Where might you witness the escape of vapor molecules? (*steam in kitchen, sauna, shower in bathroom*)
6. Do all molecules move at the same rate? (*no, random movement*)
7. What profession might be interested in this passage? (*chemist*)

Eleventh-grade chemistry text
Twelfth-grade reading level

[12]M. Clark Metcalfe, John E. Williams, and Joseph F. Castka, *Modern Chemistry* (New York: Holt, Rinehart and Winston, 1978), p. 227.

Word Recognition Errors _____

Comprehension Errors (5) _____

He was in a high, exalted mood, flying the flags of rebellion against authority. No one attempted to stop him and he took five cans of soup out of his locker, a can of peaches, a can opener. He saw Mother Maria Marthe bearing down on him as he started back to the house and his flags drooped on the flagstaff. He pretended that he did not see her and lengthened his stride. He piled his cans on the table, resisting the impulse to look over his shoulder. He went through the pantomime of opening the cans for the benefit of Sister Albertine.

"Soup," he said.

"Ja. Thank you."

She looked interested, but she also looked fearful. She did not have the authority to accept gifts, but she lacked the vocabulary necessary to refuse acceptance or to explain her dilemma. Homer sensed it.[13]

QUESTIONS

1. What does the expression "flying the flags of rebellion" mean? (*going against authority; disagreeing; resisting*)
2. What can you tell about the relationship between Mother Marthe and Homer from the statement ". . . and his flags drooped on the flagstaff?" (*she is overbearing; he is intimidated by her*)
3. What language does Sister Albertine speak? (*German*)
4. Why does Homer have to go through the pantomime of opening the cans for Sister Albertine? (*she can't understand him*)
5. Why does Sister watch him fearfully? (*She can see Mother Marthe over his shoulder and is intimidated by her.*)
6. What is the meaning of the statement, "She did not have the authority to accept gifts?" (*She was probably not important enough in the convent to be able to decide what the nuns would take and what they wouldn't take.*)
7. What proof do you have that Homer is sensitive? (*Each person cannot understand what the other is saying, but·Homer can sense what Sister Albertine means.*)

Twelfth-grade English text
Seventh-grade reading level

[13]William E. Barrett, *The Lilies of the Field* (New York: Popular Library, 1962), p. 138.

Word Recognition Errors _____

Comprehension Errors (5) _____

Battery is the actual striking or offensive touching of another person. For a battery to have been completed, a person must have intended to touch or strike the other person. The resulting injury need not have been intended.

An assault is an unlawful attempt to strike or touch someone. Thus, an assault may be an attempted battery. One necessary condition for an assault is that the assailant (attacker) have the ability to actually cause injury. Another condition is that the victim must have sufficient reason to believe that the threat of injury will be carried out.

If a person points a loaded gun at you and threatens to shoot—and you believe the threat—this is an assault. On the other hand, suppose you are bothering a friend who is trying to study. Finally, the friend says: "Stop it or I'll hit you with a chair." This is probably not a valid threat and, therefore, not an assault even though the chair is available and your friend is physically capable of picking it up. In general, words alone are not enough for an assault.[14]

QUESTIONS

1. What is battery? (*actual striking or touching*)
2. What is assault? (*attempted battery*)
3. What is a synonym for *valid*? (*reasonable*)
4. What are two conditions for an assault? (*assailant be able to cause injury; victim thinks that there will be injury*)
5. Where might battery take place? (*opinion*)
6. Which condition, battery or assault, would require prior intent? (*assault*)
7. What is another word for *sufficient*? (*enough*)

Twelfth-grade social studies text
College reading level

[14]Betty Gertz, J.D., *Understanding the Law* (Chicago: Science Research Associates, 1980), p. 279. © 1980, Science Research Associates, Inc. Reprinted by permission of the publisher.

Newton's first law of motion may be stated as follows: a body continues in its state of rest or uniform motion unless an unbalanced force acts on it. At first glance, this law seems to contradict our everyday experiences. If we want to keep a car moving with a constant velocity, we have to apply a constant force to it through the car's engine. If we stop applying this force, the car rolls to a stop. Only then does the car seem to obey the part of Newton's law that states that objects at rest will remain at rest unless acted upon by an unbalanced force.

Further study of the moving car will show, however, that it is the force of friction that brings the car to a stop, and not the absence of the force provided by the engine. If it were possible to remove this friction, it would be reasonable to assume that the car would keep rolling without the application of a constant force.[15]

QUESTIONS

1. Who discovered the laws of motion? (*Newton*)
2. What is a synonym of the word *velocity*? (*speed*)
3. What must you eliminate in order to have the moving car follow Newton's law? (*friction*)
4. What other kinds of objects would follow Newton's first law? (*any acceptable body that moves*)
5. Who might be interested in this law? (*physicist*)
6. What is an unbalanced force? (*force to cause motion*)
7. Without friction and without an opposing force, would the car keep moving indefinitely? (*yes*)

Twelfth-grade physics test
Tenth-grade reading level

[15]John E. Williams, Frederick E. Trinklien, and M. Clark Metcalfe, *Modern Physics* (New York: Holt, Rinehart and Winston, 1972), p. 95. Used by permission.

Appendix C
Sample Management Sheets

Teacher management is an essential part of any individualized instruction. Appendix C includes information on management materials for an independent novel unit, individualized grammar unit, and an individual interest unit. Management sheets allow the teacher the flexibility of working with students individually while, at the same time, seeing at a glance the progress of the class as a whole.

1. *Independent Novel Unit.* This management sheet is designed to accompany a short novel unit in which the class makes selections from *Action Libraries* (Scholastic Book Services) books (see chapter 4). Write each student's name and choice of novel in the columns at the left. Under each chapter heading are columns designated V (vocabulary) or SG (study guide). In each box, record the number of items a student gets correct over the possible number of correct items. At the end of the unit, add up the total correct items and divide it by the total possible items to obtain a percent. In the sample provided, Mary's scores in three boxes are unrecorded. The empty boxes have been outlined to emphasize to the busy teacher that this particular material is missing.

2. *Individualized Grammar Unit.* A discussion of this management sheet appears in chapter 9 and the sheet itself appears as figure 46 on page 163.

3. *Individual Interest Unit.* This unit is explained in chapters 4 and 10.

Independent Novel Unit

Student	Novel	Ch. 1		Ch. 2		Ch. 3		Ch. 4		Ch. 5		Ch. 6		Ch. 7		Ch. 8		Ch. 9		Ch. 10		Quiz	Final
		V	SG	V	SG	V	SG	V	SG	V	SG	V	SG	V	SG	V	SG	V	SG	V	SG		
Allen, Joe	Ratcatcher	4/5	2/3	4/5	6/10																		
Aris, Mary	no girls allowed	1/5				3/4	2/6																

KEY: V = Vocabulary, SG = Study Guide.

Individual Interest Unit Management Sheet

Student	Vocabulary		Book Report		Interview		AV Media		Demonstration	Craft Project	Article Comparison		5 Test Questions	Final Grade
	OL	FC	OL	FC	OL	FC	OL	FC			OL	FC		

KEY: OL = Outline, FC = Final Copy.

Appendix D
Glossary of Terms

affective concerns. improved motivation, emotional stability, and self-concept so that students can feel better about themselves and can do better in school.

alternating laterality. ability to grasp objects with one hand or the other.

analogy. determining the relationships between words.

applied level of comprehension. using a concept expressed by an author in a practical manner.

assumptive teaching. believing that students have learned all that they were taught the previous year.

auditory acuity. the ear's capability of hearing high- and low-frequency sounds.

auditory discrimination (perception). the brain's interpretation of what the ear receives.

auditory memory. remembering what is heard (for example, directions).

bilateral development. reaching for an object with both hands at the same time.

blend. two consonants that produce a single sound.

categorizing. placing groups of words under broad headings on the basis of shared qualities.

cause and effect. one of the organizational patterns that help the reader comprehend written material.

cloze technique. a test of reading skills in which every fourth or fifth word in a reading passage is deleted. The reader fills in a word that seems to fit the context of the whole passage.

comparison and contrast. an organizational pattern used to help the reader comprehend written material.

comprehension. understanding what has been read.

content material. material actually used in a subject area.

context. the paragraph or sentence in which a word appears.

cultural experience. an event in the larger society (for example, a visit to a firehouse, a library, a store) that broadens a reader's awareness of the world.

262

decode.   to take a word apart or sound out a word in order to be able to read the word correctly.

deduction.   discovering the answer to a question by moving from the general concept to the specific data.

details.   small facts in written material that are necessary for full comprehension.

diagnostic.   a test to help determine the strengths and weaknesses of the students.

drawing conclusions.   finding an idea by examining the facts.

drawing inferences.   coming to a conclusion about the reading based on something that is implied in the material.

heterogeneous class.   a class containing students of mixed abilities and reading levels.

homogeneous class.   a class containing students of the same abilities and reading levels.

individualize.   to gear the curriculum so that each student reads and does written work at his or her own level and pace. Methods are built in to deal with each student's weaknesses.

informal reading inventory.   a series of reading passages chosen from classroom materials to test the student's oral, silent, and listening comprehension.

interpretive level of comprehension.   determining what the author meant by what he said on the printed page.

key concept words.   in content area curriculum (for example, science, social studies), certain words that are important to the understanding of the subject matter.

literal level of comprehension.   understanding what the author said.

main idea.   a basic comprehension skill that a reader must develop; the major point the author is stressing.

making judgments.   deciding whether the concepts or values implied or stated in the written material are right or wrong.

mixed dominance.   a mixed preference for eye, hand, and foot use (for example, right-eyed, left-handed, and right-footed).

motor perception.   being able to coordinate the large and small muscles of the body for writing, reading, and movement.

organizational patterns.   the methods by which an author organizes material so the reader can follow his or her ideas more easily.

perseveration.   repeating an idea, word, or concept indefinitely and without purpose.

prefix.   a group of letters that always comes at the beginning of a word and adds meaning to the word.

prescriptive.   a program or technique devised after diagnosing a student's problems, to strengthen the weak areas.

preteach.   to teach, *before* the material is studied, certain words in a unit or piece of literature that are necessary for a basic understanding of the material.

reading readiness.   having the motor coordination, the cultural experiences, and the motivation to begin learning to read.

reasoning worksheets. guides given to the student to assist in reasoning and analysis of the reading assignment.

reinforcement worksheets. worksheets that give the student practice using the vocabulary words and key concepts in the material.

retention. how much the student remembers after teaching, reinforcement, and review.

reversal. reading words with the letters reversed (for example, *saw* for *was*).

root. the main part of the vocabulary word. The prefix and suffix are added to the root.

sequencing. putting details in order of occurrence.

standardized test. a test that has been given to a segment of the population and has a scoring system based on the "average" response.

study guides. worksheets containing questions that help the student determine what is important in the written material.

suffix. a group of letters added to the end of the word to enhance the meaning.

transition. a bridge (word, phrase, or sentence) that helps to connect sentences or paragraphs smoothly.

tracking. reading from left to right on the page.

visual acuity. the eye's capability of sighting an object or letter at both near and far point.

visual memory. the ability to recall material taken in visually.

visual perception sheet. a worksheet used with students who remember a word better if they have a visual image. The sheet contains several exercises designed to have a student repeat the shape and physical features of the word.

vocabulary wheels. vocabulary improvement exercises using words related to a given topic.

word attack skills. the skills used when approaching a vocabulary word that is unfamiliar (such as determining prefixes, suffixes, and roots; syllabication; and determining context).

Appendix E
Study Guides, Worksheets, and Tests

These study guides, worksheets, and tests are easy and inexpensive to use. All you need to do is photocopy or Thermofax those which fit into your curriculum. Answer keys to selected exercises begin on page 353.

They serve two purposes. First, they are complete models of the kinds of materials demonstrated in this book, and second, they can make your life easier by giving you a start at developing new curriculum for your low achievers while you are working on materials of your own creation. They are to be used in teaching five reading curriculum units: *Lisa, Bright and Dark; I Heard the Owl Call My Name; Hey, Dummy; The Pigman;* and *The Man Without a Face.*

Although this appendix may be used independently of the text of this book, the two are most effectively used together, as the study guides, worksheets, and tests illustrate the ideas presented throughout the text. Individual study guide questions are used in the text as examples, but complete study guides are included here.

Our study guides feature a variety of questions on the literal, interpretive, and applied levels of comprehension, and they measure comprehension skills ranging from main idea, details, and sequencing, on up to drawing conclusions and making judgments. (Comprehension levels and skills are discussed in detail in the text of the book. We always have our students read the study guide questions on a chapter before they read the chapter. The questions help focus their attention on certain ideas. When grading, we give a possible two points per question: one point for answering the question correctly and one point for writing the answer in a complete sentence. We have found that students with learning problems will often try to do as little work as possible. In their haste to finish an assignment, they tend to write phrases and single-word answers. Later they have difficulty writing complete sentences and paragraphs. For this reason, we require that all answers be in complete sentences.

Our vocabulary worksheets range from puzzles, unscrambling word games, and exercises on synonyms, antonyms, and parts of speech to a standard initial vocabulary sheet on which the students are asked to identify a word's part of speech and provide its definition and an example sentence. These worksheets demonstrate numerous ways of introducing, reviewing, and reinforcing vocabulary development and they will help you develop your own vocabulary worksheets for books not covered here.

In addition, we have included introductory material for two of the novels to illustrate our effort to relate literature to contemporary issues in music, magazines, or real life.

Finally, the quizzes and tests included here reflect our philosophy that a test should measure the skills as well as the content taught. If, for example, we stress cause and effect relationships in the study of the novel, our test will be designed to measure the same thing. Sequencing questions will appear on tests when we have emphasized sequencing throughout the instruction of the novel. In most cases we provide blank lines for answers on both the right and left sides of a question. We do this to enable right- and left-handed students to choose the side of the page on which they feel more comfortable writing. Note that this kind of aid is built right into the material.

We hope you find our strategies for success useful, and we hope they help you develop strategies of your own!

EXERCISES

Lisa, Bright and Dark
Study Guide

Write your answers on a separate sheet of paper. Be sure to put your name on the paper.

INTRODUCTION

1. Before reading this novel, describe what you think might be meant by the title.

CHAPTER 1

1. What does the word *indifferent* mean? Cite proof that it applies to Mrs. Schilling.

2. Discuss the attitudes that Mr. and Mrs. Schilling and Lisa each have toward psychiatric help.

3. Why do you think people find it hard to admit that they need psychiatric help?

CHAPTER 2

1. Who is the narrator? How does she describe herself?

2. Look up the word *realist.* Can you defend the statement that Betsy is a realist?

3. What does the expression *basking in her reflection* mean?

4. What kind of economic background do you think these girls come from?

CHAPTER 3

1. *Selective inattention* is defined as choosing what you want to hear. How does this apply to Lisa's friends?

2. Discuss the meaning of the word *hindsight.* How does it apply to Betsy and M.N. in their dealings with Lisa?

CHAPTER 4

1. Divide Lisa's appearance and behavior into two columns. Head the columns "Good Days" and "Bad Days."

2. Can you explain why Lisa's friends might question whether or not they were to blame for Lisa's behavior?

CHAPTER 5

1. What is meant by the statement: "Adults—real ones—insist on thinking soft"?

2. How does Betsy see the adult policy of protecting kids?

3. Why does Betsy see Lisa's parents as "phonies"?

4. How can the kind of family you are raised in determine your personality, hang-ups, and fears?

CHAPTER 6

1. How did the girls know that Lisa's trip to Florida had not helped?

2. What does the word *rebuff* mean? Can you cite an example of when you have been rebuffed?

3. The girls tried to adjust to her so as not to jar Lisa any more than necessary. What does this tell you about her friends?

CHAPTER 7

1. Mr. Bernstein tries to avoid the problem. Can you find any explanation for this?

2. Can you tell why Lisa's illness is really so hard for Mrs. Schilling to accept?

CHAPTER 8

1. What are M.N. and Betsy really offering to do for Lisa?

CHAPTER 9

1. What is schizophrenia? How does it differ from paranoia?

2. Why could Lisa's home life make her paranoid?

3. What does Betsy mean by the following statement? "Dionne Warwick was still trying to get to San Jose, and we were trying to find Vienna. There was a big difference."

CHAPTER 10

1. What is the difference between *caring* and *understanding?*

2. How is Elizabeth's reaction puzzling to M.N. and Betsy?

CHAPTER 11

1. What is the danger you see in the girls' plans to help Lisa?

2. What is the most important thing to Lisa in trusting her friends in group therapy?

3. Can you explain Lisa's coming to Betsy's house and not to M.N. or Elizabeth?

4. Would you respond the same as or differently than M.N. did if your close friend lit into you as Lisa did to M.N.? Why?

CHAPTER 12

1. What is the meaning of the statement: "A little learning is a dangerous thing"?

2. React to this statement: "M.N.'s ego is at stake in dealing with Lisa."

CHAPTER 13

1. What strikes you as unusual about this chapter?

CHAPTER 14

1. Elizabeth makes an observation: "The trouble with reasonable adult human beings is that they collapse when they meet other reasonable adult human beings. We don't." What does she mean? Do you agree with this?

2. Can you find a statement that proves Betsy is perhaps the most honest in the group?

3. What does the term *free associate* mean?

CHAPTER 15

1. React to this statement: "The teachers and guidance counselor wanted to help but were afraid of Lisa's parents."

2. What does Betsy mean when she says, "I gave him my Joanne Woodward smile"?

CHAPTER 16

1. How does the expression "It takes one to know one" apply to this chapter?

CHAPTER 17

1. What does the expression *fighting herself* mean?

2. Betsy's definition of madness is "doing just the opposite of what you wanted to do, and having no control over any of it." React to her definition.

3. Look up the word *catatonic*. Why would this phase of Lisa's illness particularly frighten M.N.?

CHAPTER 18

1. What is the meaning of Elizabeth's statement: "You may have saved Lisa's life"?

2. Is Mrs. Schilling's reaction to Lisa's walking through the plate-glass door predictable? Why?

CHAPTER 20

1. How does Betsy explain the distant appearance that Elizabeth had shown earlier to the other kids? Would you have behaved as she did? Why?

CHAPTER 21

1. Does Betsy's insight in recognizing that Mr. Bernstein has problems surprise you? Do you know adults who you think could profit from psychiatric help?

2. Why does M.N. waste any sympathy on Mrs. Schilling?

3. Why is Elizabeth worried about their meeting with Lisa in the hospital?

CHAPTER 22

1. Dr. Donovan tells the girls that they will have a big job when Lisa comes home —"not to insulate Lisa but to educate the others." Explain what he means.

2. Can you explain "the one thought none of us needed to think"?

VOCABULARY

paranoia	regal	inaudible
manic-depressive	palsy	staunch
schizophrenia	hindsight	realistic
censorship	indecisive	psychiatrist
bask		

Lisa, Bright and Dark
Quiz No. 1 (Ch. 1–5)

1. What is the setting of the book (where does the story take place)?

   _____

2. Mr. and Mrs. Schilling are anxious to _____ (*Write the letter of the correct answer in space.*)

   a. impress their friends.

   b. get psychiatric help for Lisa.

   c. move to Florida.

   d. transfer Lisa to a better school.

3. Who is the narrator of the book? (full name) _____

4. Select the description that best fits each character and write the letter of that description on the blank line next to the character's name.

   _____ Mr. Schilling   a. insurance salesman

   _____ Mr. Fickett   b. a phoney

   _____ Mr. Goodman   c. understanding, intelligent

   _____ Mr. Frazer   c. minister

5. How does Betsy feel about *most* adults?

   _____

   _____

6. What kind of "hindsight" did the girls have concerning Lisa?

   _____

   _____

7. True or false:

   According to Betsy, listening to their children is the most important thing parents can do.

Lisa, Bright and Dark
Quiz No. 2 (Ch. 6–16)

1. After Lisa's return from Florida, M.N. and Betsy see she is no better so they decide to _____ .

2. Betsy tries to talk to Mr. Bernstein about helping Lisa. Mr. Bernstein's attitude is _____ .

3. M.N. tries to talk to Mrs. Schilling. Mrs. Schilling's attitude is _____

_____ .

4. M.N. and Betsy talk to Lisa about group therapy. Lisa thinks their idea

_____ .

5. The one person Lisa seems to trust above all the others is _____

_____ .

6. M.N. and Betsy ask Elizabeth to join their group therapy session for Lisa. Elizabeth acts like she _____

_____ .

7. M.N. and Betsy start reading psychology books for information about words like _____ and _____ .

8. Betsy watches the movie _____
on TV because it is about mental illness.

9. Lisa shows up at Betsy's house and makes Betsy promise always to be

_____ with her.

10. Betsy thinks Lisa has gone home but later finds she is _____

_____ .

11. While talking to M.N., Betsy, and Elizabeth, Lisa shows that there is a second person developing in her body. Some characteristics of the "other Lisa" (Lisa II) are:

    a. _____

    b. _____

12. _____ and _____ try to talk to Mr. Schilling about Lisa's problem.

13. Lisa begs for help, but _____ refuses to get involved.

14. M.N. is trying to be an amateur _____ , and this is dangerous.

15. Which Lisa (I or II) attacks Elizabeth? _____ Why?

    _____

16. Elizabeth seems to understand Lisa better than M.N. or Betsy because

    _____

Lisa, Bright and Dark
Quiz No. 3 (Ch. 17–22)

1. Why don't Lisa's parents ever see anything strange about Lisa's behavior?

_____

_____

_____

2. Who is the one person in Lisa's family who notices a change in Lisa?

_____

3. Which adult sees Lisa walk through the glass door? _____

4. Why does Lisa walk through the door? _____

_____

5. How does Mrs. Schilling react to Lisa's accident?

_____

_____

6. Betsy finally meets her "Paul Newman." His name is

_____ .

7. How else does Lisa try to get attention in order to get help and understanding from her parents?

_____

_____

8. What is Lisa's reaction to meeting Dr. Donovan? Why?

_____

_____

_____

9. Dr. Donovan thinks the three girls have been special in the way they have treated Lisa because

_____

_____

Lisa, Bright and Dark
Vocabulary Reinforcement Worksheet

Write the correct form of the vocabulary word on the blank line to complete the sentence.

1. I like to (basking, bask) _____ in the sun.

2. We knew she had (palsy, palsied) _____ by the way she walked.

3. The teacher (censorship, censored, censoring) _____ his paper.

4. The (psychiatrist, psyche, psychedelic) _____ talked to me and helped me solve my problems .

5. There was a (rex, rule, regal, regally) _____ air about the way she walked.

6. She walked (rex, rule, regal, regally) _____ .

7. His whisper was almost (inaudibility, inaudible, inaudibly)

_____ .

8. He was a (staunching, staunch) _____ supporter of the team.

9. He made a (realist, realistic, realistically) _____ decision.

10. He showed (indecision, indecisive, indecisively) _____ when he was unable to make up his mind.

Lisa, Bright and Dark
Vocabulary Crossword

Across

1. unsure; uncertain
3. split personality
5. sunbathe
7. kingly; royal
9. what you do when in a hurry
10. realizing something after it has occurred
11. doctor trained in dealing with mental illness
12. inability to move; paralysis

Down

2. not able to be heard
3. loyal; trustworthy
4. person who tells it like it is
6. something that opens doors
8. eliminating offensive parts of a movie
9. same as 4 down

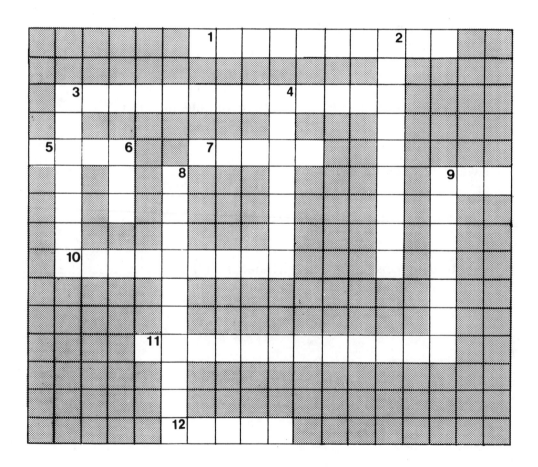

Lisa, Bright and Dark
Final Test

A. VOCABULARY

Choose from the list below the word that best completes each sentence. Write the word in the blank to the left of the sentence. A word can be used only once, and two words won't be used at all.

indifferent	hindsight	schizophrenia	associate
realist	rebuffed	paranoia	catatonic
bask	hysterical	persecution	chronic

_____ 1. Because of __1__ , Sue and Ellen were able to understand *after* the game why they had lost.

_____ 2. Joe is a __2__ . He's always trying to do things in a practical way.

_____ 3. If you __3__ in the sun for five hours you will certainly get a burn.

_____ 4. The dog coughed off and on for three months and the vet said she had a __4__ condition.

_____ 5. My neighbor suffers from delusions of __5__ because he thinks I throw rocks at his window at 3 A.M.

_____ 6. Jean was in a __6__ state—at lunch she threw her mashed potatoes at Mr. Willey and then sat rigidly in her seat staring at the clock on the wall.

_____ 7. Mrs. Sneed was __7__ when her son destroyed my new living room table—she pretended he wasn't there.

_____ 8. Heather was __8__ by the dog when the dog took his bone and ignored her.

_____ 9. Sheila curled up in a corner of the room, not caring about anything and thinking the world was against her. It was a perfect example of __9__ .

_____ 10. Jerry's mother yelled, "I don't want you to __10__ with Joey because he swears and rides a motorcycle."

B. TRUE-FALSE

Circle the *T* if the statement below is true. Circle the *F* if the statement is false.

T F 11. Elizabeth's parents were the richest of all the parents on the novel.
T F 12. Elizabeth didn't pay much attention to the other kids, because she was smarter than they were.
T F 13. The phrase "a little learning is a dangerous thing" describes M. N. and her reading about psychiatry.
T F 14. The kind of family a child comes from helps make the child the kind of person he or she is.
T F 15. Brian tried to understand Lisa and stood by her until she was better.

C. CHRONOLOGICAL ORDER

Column B contains a list of events in the order in which they happened in the novel, but some of the events are missing and are shown only by a letter. The missing events are given in column A. Place the letter of the missing event from column B next to the right answer in column A. Remember, you want all the events to be in order.

Column A

_____ 16. Lisa attacks Elizabeth.

_____ 17. For the first time M. N. hears Lisa plead with her parents for help.

_____ 18. Betsy tries to talk to Mr. Bernstein about Lisa.

_____ 19. Brian breaks up with Lisa.

_____ 20. Elizabeth tries to explain the nature of mental illness to Betsy and M. N.

Column B

a.

b. Lisa shows signs of her illness at Brian's and her anniversary party.

c.

d. Lisa goes to Florida for a rest.

e.

f. Betsy and M. N. try to talk with Lisa, but Lisa wants Elizabeth there too.

g.

h. Mr. Fickett and Mr. Milne try to talk to Mr. Schilling about Lisa.

i.

j. Lisa walks through the glass door in front of Mr. Goodman.

D. MULTIPLE CHOICE

Place the letter of the phrase that *best* completes the statement in the blank either to the left or to the right of the number.

_____ 21. Because the setting of the book is Long Island, you can guess   21. _____
that the girls
   a. are richer than most.
   b. go to school in New York City.
   c. are snobs and are selfish.
   d. would have no problems at all.

_____ 22. The theme of *Lisa, Bright and Dark* is   22. _____
   a. adults should get involved in the serious problems of
      their children.
   b. teen-agers shouldn't try amateur counseling.
   c. don't listen to your school guidance counselor.
   d. friends should stick together.

_____ 23. Smiling, Lisa walks through the glass doors. What part of the   23. _____
novel is this incident?
   a. setting
   b. point of view
   c. climax
   d. turning point

_____ 24. Lisa trusts Betsy and Elizabeth more than M. N. because   24. _____
   a. M. N. is playing a game with people's minds.
   b. Betsy and Elizabeth have less money than Lisa.
   c. both Betsy and Elizabeth have had counseling.
   d. Betsy and Elizabeth have more friends than M. N.

_____ 25. Several clues give Betsy the idea that Elizabeth has been men-   25. _____
tally ill. One of them is
   a. Elizabeth's coolness toward the kids at school.
   b. the knowledge that Elizabeth has when she talks about
      helping Lisa.
   c. the many days she is absent from school for no reason.
   d. the way Lisa always tries to be near Elizabeth, as if they
      have something in common.

_____ 26. Which character is most sincere and helpful to Lisa?   26. _____
      a. M. N.
      b. Elizabeth
      c. Mr. Goodman
      d. Mr. Schilling

_____ 27. Which of the following would *not* be a cause of the kind of   27. _____
      mental illness Lisa had?
      a. home life
      b. tension at school
      c. peer pressure
      d. brain damage at birth

_____ 28. Another title for this book that might mean the same thing as   28. _____
      Lisa, Bright and Dark and tell about the story is
      a. *Lisa, the Schizophrenic.*
      b. *Good and Bad Days.*
      c. *Lisa, the Black; Lisa, the White.*
      d. *The Glass Door.*

_____ 29. After reading the novel you can conclude that the author thinks   29. _____
      a. schools are very helpful to students' problems.
      b. mental illness should be ignored and not talked about.
      c. you should show care and understanding toward other
         people's problems.
      d. you should depend on your friends when you have a
         problem.

_____ 30. Who is the most mature person in the book?   30. _____
      a. Mrs. Schilling, because she is an adult
      b. M. N., because she reads a lot about mental illness
      c. Lisa, because she is trying to get people to help her
      d. Betsy, because she knows who she is and has insight into
         other people

_____ 31. How does the author feel about teen-agers?   31. _____
      a. Teen-agers are cruel and make fun of anyone who is
         different.
      b. Teen-agers will ignore the problems of their friends.
      c. True friends will try to help even if they are rebuffed.
      d. Most teen-agers will try to help a friend but if rebuffed
         they will stop.

_____ 32. Who is the most helpful adult to Lisa and the girls?   32. _____
        a. Neil Donovan
        b. Mr. Schilling
        c. Mr. Goodman
        d. Mr. Frazer

E. MATCHING

In section A are several concepts or main ideas that we discussed. In section B are events that happened in the novel or might happen in your daily life. Place the letter of the main idea in either blank next to the event in Section B that shows the idea best.

Section A. Main Ideas

a. Symptoms and causes of mental illness

b. Responsibility of parents to their child

c. Responsibility of the school to the child

d. Problems of amateur counseling (not knowing what you're doing)

Section B. Events

_____ 33. John's parents never care what time he comes home at night.   33. _____

_____ 34. Lisa thinks she is going out of her mind and asks her parents to   34. _____
help her.

_____ 35. When Sally was afraid she was pregnant, her friends told her   35. _____
not to worry because they had read about how to perform an
abortion.

_____ 36. Every day Eric came to school with another incredible story   36. _____
about his world adventures that everyone knew was a lie.

_____ 37. Sam couldn't read well so he failed in most of his subjects, but   37. _____
he was promoted from one grade to the next anyway.

_____ 38. Mr. Bernstein doesn't feel he can do anything to help Lisa. He   38. _____
doesn't want to upset Lisa's parents.

_____ 39. Barbara can't be in any after-school clubs. She must go right home to babysit, clean the house, and make supper for her younger brothers while her mother goes to art class.

39. _____

_____ 40. In one of their group therapy sessions, Lisa tries to kill Elizabeth.

40. _____

F. ESSAY

Write your essay on a separate sheet of paper. You will be graded on writing a *complete* paragraph (at least four sentences) and on what you say.

Why were Betsy, Elizabeth, and M. N. lucky that everything turned out all right for Lisa?

I Heard the Owl Call My Name
Study Guide

Write your answers on a separate sheet of paper. Be sure to put your name on the paper.

VOCABULARY

Look up each word and write its definition *before* starting to read.

ordinand	potlatch	myth	primitive
vicar	vicarage	matriarch	hospitable

INTRODUCTION

Knowing that his new young priest will die soon, the Bishop sends him to his most difficult parish? Why?

CHAPTER 1

1. What does Caleb mean when he tells Mark that the Indian boy, Jim, will shake his hand, but it is a gesture which he has learned, and it has no meaning?

2. Caleb suggests that Mark should feel sorry for the Indians. "You know nothing, and they must teach you." What does he mean?

3. In describing the setting for this novel, Mark says, "If man were to vanish from this planet tomorrow, here he would have no trace that he ever was." (p. 17) What is he telling us about the setting?

4. When a language has no word for "thank you," what can we tell about the tribe that speaks the language?

CHAPTER 2

1. How can you tell that the village has temporarily accepted Mark?

CHAPTER 3

1. What is the author's purpose in putting in the cook in this particular chapter?

CHAPTER 4

1. The Bishop wrote Mark a letter suggesting that he must start by working with his hands. What was his purpose in suggesting this?

CHAPTER 5

1. What is the first sign that the Indians are warming to Mark?

CHAPTER 6 and 7

1. At the close of Chapter 7, we recognize that Mark has developed a deep commitment to the people of his village. List three events or incidents that have led to this commitment.

CHAPTER 8

1. How can you explain the uneasy feeling in the village when the young people are home from school?

2. What does Mrs. Hudson mean when she says of her granddaughter and her approaching marriage to a white man: "What I fear is that we will be ashamed of her"?

CHAPTER 9

1. Of what importance are the myths and dances to the tribe?

CHAPTER 10

1. What was it that *really* caused the death of Keetah's sister? (not OD)

CHAPTER 11

1. What is the meaning behind the Bishop's statement: "You suffered with them, and now you are theirs, and nothing will ever be the same again"? (p. 87)

CHAPTER 12

1. Why do the elders feel a sense of urgency about keeping alive the old myths?

2. Why do Jim and the elders stay away from the vicarage when Gordon is home?

CHAPTER 13

1. What does Mark mean when he tries to tell the women that "no village, no culture can remain static"? (p. 103)

2. What is the real message behind Bishop's advice to Mark on how to handle the problems that will arise after the Indians are allowed to buy liquor? (p. 105)

CHAPTER 14

1. What is the shocking realization that confronts Mark when he visits his old friends?

CHAPTER 16

1. Explain what the author means by the following: "Here every bird and fish knew its course. Every tree had its own place upon this earth. Only man had lost his way." (p. 120)

CHAPTER 17

1. What does Caleb suggest will happen to his village?

CHAPTER 18

1. What effect does winter have on the attitude of the villagers toward one another?

2. What evidence do we have in this chapter that Mark has come to think like an Indian?

CHAPTER 19

1. Why is it important to the villagers to notice how Mark accepts Keetah's return?

2. Why had Keetah deliberately waited to return until she was sure she was pregnant?

CHAPTER 20

1. The theme of this novel can be found on p. 144. State it below.

CHAPTER 21

1. What is Marta's response when Mark tells her he thinks he heard the owl call his name?

CHAPTER 22

1. On p. 151, we have the final proof that Mark has been fully accepted by the village. What is that proof?

CHAPTER 23

1. Why does the school teacher not run down to the bank to see who has survived the accident?

2. Describe the Indians' philosophy of life, which can be found in the last short paragraph on p. 159.

I Heard the Owl Call My Name

Final Test

A. MULTIPLE CHOICE

Place the letter of the word or phrase that *best* completes the statement in the blank either to the left or to the right of the number.

_____ 1. The Bishop sends Mark to the Indian village because   1. _____
     a. Mark needs to understand more about primitive people.
     b. Mark is sick and the Bishop doesn't want to expose him to the pressures of city life.
     c. the Bishop feels that the lessons of life in the village will prepare Mark for death.
     d. Mark needs to learn about himself before he will be ready for a city parish.

_____ 2. The title of this book comes from an Indian myth or story that   2. _____
suggests that
     a. the owl will call the name of a person who is soon to die.
     b. the owl used to call the name of a person who is the most beloved person in the village.
     c. the soul of a person who dies returns to the village in the form of an owl.
     d. the owl is the tribe's sacred bird.

_____ 3. The matriarch of the village is   3. _____
     a. Marta.
     b. Mrs. Hudson.
     c. Keetah.
     d. Mr. T. P. Wallace.

_____ 4. The setting of this story is   4. _____
     a. Mexico.
     b. Northeast Canada.
     c. West coast Canada, south of Alaska.
     d. a pueblo in Arizona.

_____ 5. The climax of this story occurs when
    a. Calamity dies.
    b. Keetah returns.
    c. the tribe gives Jim a potlatch.
    d. Mark discovers he is going to die.

5. _____

_____ 6. The myths are important to the tribe because
    a. they tell the tribe's history and are the heritage and tradition that gives the tribe its identity.
    b. this is how the young know what is expected of them as adults.
    c. these stories mark the difference between the Indians and the white man.
    d. they are something no one can ever prove wrong.

6. _____

_____ 7. The theme of this story is
    a. old customs keep one from being able to adjust to new ways.
    b. every man must learn enough of the meaning of life to be ready to die.
    c. before someone can be a good priest, he must understand nature and primitive society.
    d. going back to nature is the only way to add meaning to one's life.

7. _____

_____ 8. When Mrs. Hudson suggests at the end of the story that they feed the Bishop carrots, she is
    a. trying to apologize to the Bishop for serving him turnips in the past.
    b. feeling guilty for her stubborness in insisting that Mark eat turnips.
    c. showing her willingness to adjust to the white man's way.
    d. trying to teach the younger women to be more hospitable.

8. _____

_____ 9. The salmon play an important part in the village myths, dances, and economy. They symbolize
    a. the role of men and women in the village's life.
    b. the loss of the young to white civilization.
    c. the order and consistency of nature.
    d. the hopelessness of trying to live the old Indian life.

9. _____

_____ 10. The most important idea about death that the Indians in the story   10. _____
teach us is that
   a. death leaves everyone sad.
   b. living is more important than dying.
   c. death is natural and a part of the continuity of life.
   d. a good person can always be replaced.

B. ESSAY

On a separate sheet of paper, write a two (2) paragraph essay to answer
one (1) of the following questions.

1. From the beginning of the book to his death, Mark makes many attempts to
adjust himself to the life style of the village. In your first paragraph, discuss
why this effort on his part was necessary to make his ministry successful. In
your second paragraph, discuss at least three examples of his adjustment to
their life style.

2. In your first paragraph, discuss the Bishop's reasons for sending Mark to the
Indian village. Please be specific in your use of examples. In your second
paragraph, discuss how effective you feel his decision was.

Hey, Dummy
Introductory Worksheet

I. Responsibility

  A. Definition: _____

  _____

  B. People, society, and leaders have responsibilities toward others. List some pairs of people who have responsibilities. What are some of their responsibilities?

  EXAMPLE *Parents* have a responsibility toward *children.*
  What? *Parents must clothe, protect, teach values, and feed their children.*

  1. _____ have a responsibility toward _____ .

  What? _____

  2. _____ have a responsibility toward _____ .

  What? _____

  3. _____ have a responsibility toward _____ .

  What? _____

II. Intelligence

  A. Definition: _____

  _____

  B. I.Q. tests are ways to compare your thinking with that of the rest of society. The following table gives the general categories of I.Q. scores.

Genius:	130+
Gifted:	110–130
Average:	90–110
Educable:	50–75
Trainable:	30–50
Custodial:	0–30

C. We have some stereotyped ideas about certain I.Q.s. If you heard what a person's I.Q. was or heard him or her described by one of the words above, what would you think of the person without knowing him?

1. Genius: _____

_____

2. Gifted: _____

_____

3. Educable: _____

_____

4. Custodial: _____

_____

D. Ideas about I.Q.s and their meanings are changing. How?

_____

_____

III. Involvement

A. Definition: _____

_____

B. Many people argue about the degree to which they should be involved with things and people around them. Below are listed several life situations. Explain what kind of involvement, if any, there should be by the people.

1. You know one of your friends is cheating on an exam. _____

_____

_____

2. Your father comes home drunk every night and beats up your mother.

_____

_____

3. Your car hits a cat running across the road, and you aren't sure if it is dead.

_____

_____

4. A friend is being hassled to try pot at a party and doesn't want to.

_____

_____

5. Someone broke into the school over the weekend and did about $2,500 worth of damage. You have heard, through a friend, who probably did it.

_____

_____

Hey, Dummy
Vocabulary

Word	Definition	Sentence
1. intercept		
2. monotony		
3. humanity		
4. ridicule		
5. detached		

Word	Definition	Sentence
6. sarcastic		
7. aloof		
8. mentality		
9. solidarity		
10. manipulating		

Hey, Dummy

Vocabulary Worksheet (Root Derivatives)

Choose four words from the vocabulary words. Write as many words as you can find that are built from the same root word as the one you have chosen. You may use the dictionary. *Monotony* is used as an example. Find the meaning of the root you choose.

1. monotony

monogram

monologue

monoplane

monopoly

monosyllable

monotheism

monotone

monarchy

monastery

monk

monotonous

mono = one _____ = _____

2. _____ _____ _____ _____ _____ _____ _____ _____ _____ _____ _____ _____ _____ =

3. _____ _____ _____ _____ _____ _____ _____ _____ _____ _____ _____ _____ =

4. _____ _____ _____ _____ _____ _____ _____ _____ _____ _____ _____ _____ =

5. _____ _____ _____ _____ _____ _____ _____ _____ _____ _____ _____ _____ =

Hey, Dummy
Study Guide

Write your answers on a separate sheet of paper. Be sure to put your name on the paper.

CHAPTER 1

1. What are Charley, Dave, and the narrator doing when they meet the Dummy?

2. What traits would a foreigner and Dummy have in common?

CHAPTER 2

1. How does Neil's behavior make it hard for his parents to understand him?

2. By listening to Mr. Comstock make a reference to "Danny," what do we learn about Neil?

3. To what is Neil referring when he says, "That was a hundred years ago; what's that got to do with now?" (p. 22)

CHAPTER 3

1. Why does the woman in the bakery let the Dummy take the sweet cakes without paying for them?

2. Why does Neil wish he hadn't slapped the Dummy?

CHAPTER 4

1. Why might you expect Mr. Alvarado to have sympathy with Alan Harper?

2. What does the following statement mean: "They hold up to ridicule what neither they nor their audience can understand. The level of intelligence in most rural areas is low to begin with, so they have no problem at all manipulating their listeners"?

CHAPTER 5

1. In your experience, you have probably played a game like "grab his hat," or "grab his lunch bag." Why do we play these games, and how do we pick our victim?

2. The author uses a phrase to describe Dummy: "He was like a bee buzzing from flower to flower sampling the nectar." Why does the author use this phrase and how does it apply to Alan?

3. What is Neil discovering about his hometown as he walks Alan home?

4. What does Neil mean when he says, "I sort of wondered who was the real Dummy, after all"?

CHAPTER 6

1. Can you explain why Neil feels self-conscious with Alan?

CHAPTER 7

1. How is knowing Alan like dropping a stone into still water?

2. Would you rather not talk or talk and sound like a moron? Why?

CHAPTER 8

1. Can you tell in this chapter how Susie feels about her brother's sticking up for Alan?

CHAPTER 9

1. "If you don't reach out to people, you can't get hurt." How might this statement apply to Desdemona?

2. When Neil finally finds Alan, an angry man has Alan by the arm. What is the problem?

3. How would your family react if you brought home a moron?

CHAPTER 10

1. Explain why Neil feels both relief and shame at his father's statement that Alan could not visit their home.

CHAPTER 11

1. List four kinds of "cripples."

2. Why is Mr. Alvarado pleased with Neil?

3. Does the word *involvement* have any meaning in your life? How?

CHAPTER 12

1. How is the game of "tease" in this chapter different from the game earlier in the book?

2. The author could have had several things in mind when he ended this chapter saying, "All I had to do was keep running." What does he mean by this?

CHAPTER 14

1. What does the term *mob rule* mean? How does it apply to this chapter?

2. How can you explain that people will do things in a mob that they wouldn't do if they were alone?

3. What are the circumstances in this chapter that help Neil to see that Mr. Alvarado is right, that he (Neil) is in over his head?

CHAPTER 15

1. In this chapter, Neil's efforts to get help are blocked. What are some of the choices open to Neil?

2. What are Mr. Alvarado's reasons for not getting involved?

3. What might he (Neil) be thinking as he runs through the streets looking for Alan?

CHAPTER 16

1. Alan *trusts* Neil. What does *responsibility* have to do with *trust?*

CHAPTER 17

1. What is the major discovery that Neil makes in this chapter about Alan?

CHAPTER 18

1. What importance can you give to the statement: "The drum gave Alan an identity"?

2. What are the two reasons Neil starts to talk to Alan and tell him stories?

3. What does this chapter tell us about Neil and his parents?

4. Does this chapter help you to understand why there is so little communication between Neil and his parents? Why, or why not?

5. What is the *irony* in this chapter?

CHAPTER 19

1. Where do you think Neil is in this chapter?

2. The diagnosis of Neil's condition is "altered personality due to an existing anxiety state from unknown psychogenic causes." What does this mean to you?

3. Look up the medical terms in question 2 and restate the problem in your own words.

4. There are several unsolved details in this story. *Predict* what you think may happen or guess what has happened in each of the following cases.
   a. Who hurt the girl in the park?
   b. Why was there such a change in Mr. Alvarado?
   c. What response do the Comstocks have to Neil's difficulty?
   d. How does Neil learn to live with his crisis?

5. What causes Neil's emotional and mental change?

6. Can you think of an incident in your life that made you think you'd crack up because of the pressure? Explain.

Hey, Dummy

Quiz No. 1 (Ch. 1–7)

1. _____ is Neil's sister.

2. _____ is Neil's English teacher.

3. The name Desdemona comes from a famous Shakespearean play called

    _____. *Write the letter of the correct answer in space.*
    a. *King Lear.*
    b. *Othello.*
    c. *Romeo and Juliet.*
    d. *Henry IV.*

4. Neil's English teacher belongs to a minority group called _____

5. Why is Mr. Comstock disappointed in Neil? _____

    _____

6. One of Desdemona's main problems is that _____.
    a. she is poor and goes barefoot.
    b. she is a dummy (retarded) like Neil.
    c. she never talks or looks at anyone.
    d. she is dumb in school and fails all the time.

7. Alan's father is _____

8. Name one thing Neil guesses is worse than being poor. _____

    _____

9. Alan can help himself to anything in the bakery because _____

    _____

10. What does Alan mean when he says, "Look things my number-one-hit throw-

    kick-funny-what-boy"? _____

    _____

Hey, Dummy

Quiz No. 2 (Ch. 8–14)

For numbers 1–7 choose the correct answer and write its letter in either space provided. For numbers 8–10 write your answer on the line that follow each question.

_____ 1. Susie is _____ about her brother's involvement with Alan. 1. _____
     a. happy
     b. unhappy

_____ 2. Alan is yelled at by a man because he 2. _____
     a. killed a girl.
     b. broke a window.
     c. stole some cakes.
     d. stole some money.

_____ 3. Neil's parents don't want Alan to come to the house 3. _____
     a. because they don't like him.
     b. because they are afraid he will break things in the house or mess up.
     c. because they don't know what the neighbors will say.
     d. because they are worried about Neil's involvement with Alan.

_____ 4. When Susie sticks up for Neil and Alan, her mother 4. _____
     a. says Neil is cracking up.
     b. is angry with Susie for sticking up for Alan.
     c. ignores her.
     d. tells Susie to do what she wants but to be quiet.

_____ 5. Alan falls into a category of children called 5. _____
     a. gifted.
     b. special.
     c. exceptional.
     d. dumb.

_____ 6. Desdemona's medical problem is known as 6. _____
     a. schizophrenia.
     b. autism.
     c. manic-depression.
     d. brain-damage.

_____ 7. Neil loses his best friends because 7. _____
     a. he doesn't have time for them.
     b. he chooses his involvement with Alan over them.
     c. he tells them they are cruel.
     d. Mr. Alvarado tells them not hang around with Neil anymore.

8. Where does Mr. Alvarado live? _____

9. Why does the mob stone Desdemona? _____

   _____

10. What is the setting of this book? _____

Hey, Dummy
Review Sheet (Sequencing)

Part B has the events listed in the order in which they happened. Fill in the blanks with the correct event from Part A.

PART A

- Neil cracks up and becomes like a dummy.
- Susie shows she is proud of Neil and brings him lemonade.
- Neil sees Dummy stealing cakes and not getting caught.
- Neil sees Alan's house, sees how poor he is, and meets Desdemona.
- Mr. Alvarado lectures Neil and his English class about not taking advantage of retarded people.
- Neil hears his parents' opinions about retarded kids and not bringing them home.
- Neil ties Alan's feet together.
- The mob stones Desdemona.
- Neil loses his best friends because he refuses to tease Alan with the drum.
- Neil and Alan steal a ride on a moving van.

PART B

1. Alan steals a football from Neil, Dave, and Charley.

2. _____

3. Susie explains to Neil that Alan is retarded.

4. _____

5. Neil walks home with Alan and sees things in a new light.

6. _____

7. Neil gets beaten up trying to save Alan from being teased and pushed around.

8. _____

9. Neil gives Alan a drum.

10. _____

11. Neil goes to talk to Mr. Alvarado about his problem.

12. _____

13. Alan is accused of murdering a girl in the park.

14. _____

15. Neil and Alan go to Mr. Alvarado's house for help to get away.

16. _____

17. Neil and Alan stay near a supermarket to get food from the garbage.

18. _____

19. Alan is shot.

20. _____

Hey, Dummy

Review Sheet (Applying Themes)

Below are several statements. In *Column A,* place the *number of the character* who probably made the statement. In *Column B,* place the *letter of the theme* that applies to the statement and character. There may be more than one theme for a statement.

Characters

1. Mr. Comstock
2. Mrs. Comstock
3. Neil Comstock
4. Mr. Alvarado
5. Alan Harper
6. Susie Comstock

Themes

a. Alienation
b. Responsibility
c. Involvement
d. Intelligence
e. Loneliness

Column A   Column B

_____   _____   1. I'm proud that you got beat up.

_____   _____   2. Aaaah!

_____   _____   3. Watch out! My foot just turned into a claw.

_____   _____   4. We don't want any creepy morons in this house.

_____   _____   5. Danny would have held the bat this way.

_____   _____   6. Exceptional children are hard to understand. When we don't understand, we are afraid.

_____   _____   7. Dave and Charley have neat parents who talk to them.

_____   _____   8. I can't be an accessory to the crime; don't you see?

_____   _____   9. There's no place to go or no one to talk to to get advice.

_____   _____   10. My number-one-boy-mad-no-no.

Hey, Dummy
Review Sheet (Concepts and Vocabulary)

A. CONCEPTS

Explain each item as we have used it in class discussions.

1. phony liberal _____

_____

2. autism _____

_____

3. identity _____

_____

4. maturity _____

_____

5. symbolism _____

_____

6. dummy/Dummy _____

_____

7. Danny's death as a contributing cause of Neil's hospitalization after Alan's death

_____

8. Purpose of random phrasing at the beginning of each chapter _____

_____

B. VOCABULARY

Define these words.

1. monotony _____

2. minority _____

3. subside _____

4. lynch _____

5. contempt _____

6. pathetic _____

7. hysterical _____

8. solidarity _____

9. malady _____

10. tantalize _____

11. manipulating _____

12. bawled _____

13. raved _____

14. maniac _____

15. stowaway _____

16. humanity _____

17. tantrum _____

18. intersection _____

19. intercept _____

20. sarcastic _____

21. mentality _____

22. detached _____

23. aloof _____

Hey, Dummy
FINAL TEST

A. VOCABULARY

In each blank in the right-hand column, write the vocabulary word that correctly completes the sentence.

intercept	hysterical	sarcastic	aloof	mentality
monotony	manipulating	bawled	tantrum	solidarity
humanity	detached	ridicule	subside	contempt

1. The Air Force hopes its missile will be able to ___1___ the rocket.

1. _____

2. He was so ___2___ when he spoke to us that we thought he hated us.

2. _____

3. He had such a limited ___3___ that we thought he was retarded.

3. _____

4. All he did all day long was label bottles. This is an example of ___4___ .

4. _____

5. The new teacher never spoke to anyone. He was considered ___5___ .

5. _____

6. When I told him he failed, he just ___6___ .

6. _____

7. He threw such a temper ___7___ that we thought he was ___8___ .

7. _____

8. _____

9. Because they all worked together as a team, they showed great ___9___ .

9. _____

10. The wind began to ___10___ when the hurricane passed over and moved out to sea.

10. _____

11. He had such a chip on his shoulder that he always treated everyone with __11__ .

11. _____

12. He did such crazy things that it was hard not to __12__ and mock him.

12. _____

13. We could get into her locker because the lock had been __13__ .

13. _____

14. By __14__ the skeleton key carefully, we could get in the back door.

14. _____

B. MULTIPLE CHOICE

Choose the answer which best completes each of the following statements.

_____ 15. Who was the first one to give Alan Harper the nickname Dummy?
    a. Mr. Alvarado
    b. Neil Comstock
    c. Desdemona
    d. the kids in the neighborhood

15. _____

_____ 16. How does Neil treat Alan in the beginning of the book?
    a. as a friend
    b. indifferently
    c. makes fun of him
    d. as a brother

16. _____

_____ 17. Why does Neil help the Dummy when he is being teased by the other kids?
    a. He thinks of how it would be if he were in Alan's place.
    b. Neil can identify with Alan because he has a brother who is mentally retarded.
    c. He doesn't think it is right for people to be mean to the mentally retarded.
    d. He wants to get Alan alone so he could really be mean where no one would see them.

17. _____

_____ 18. How do Neil's parents treat Neil?
    a. They give him lots of attention.
    b. They treat him almost as a nonperson.
    c. Neil is the pet in the family.
    d. They blame him for Danny's death.

18. _____

_____ 19. Why don't Mr. and Mrs. Comstock understand Neil?   19. _____
    a. They have not gotten over Danny's death and expect too
       much from Neil.
    b. They are selfish and materialistic.
    c. They can understand no one; they are retarded.
    d. They are against all young people.

_____ 20. How does Mr. Alvarado react to Neil's composition?   20. _____
    a. He is angry.
    b. He understands what Neil is trying to say.
    c. He has no reaction at all.
    d. He bursts out laughing.

_____ 21. What type of person is Mr. Alvarado?   21. _____
    a. He is unpredictable.
    b. He is upset over the way minorities are treated.
    c. He is a phony liberal.
    d. All of the above.

_____ 22. Which statement best tells us what type of character Alan is?   22. _____
    a. Alan has adjusted to the world because he has been picked
       on so often.
    b. In some unexplained way, Alan has learned to live with his
       handicap.
    c. Alan has mysteriously been able to discover beauty in the
       world despite his limited mentality.

_____ 23. How does Neil's attitude toward Alan change?   23. _____
    a. He is more sympathetic to Alan.
    b. Neil begins to understand how difficult it is for Alan to
       adjust to life with such a poor family life.
    c. Neil does not treat Alan as if he were a dummy but starts to
       treat him as a human being with needs.
    d. All of the above.

_____ 24. Where does Neil get the drum?   24. _____
    a. from Alan
    b. from his father
    c. from the store
    d. He steals it.

_____ 25. What does Neil learn about the Harper family?   25. _____
    a. Alan had been born with brain damage.
    b. Mr. Harper is in a mental institution.
    c. Mrs. Harper is the sole support of the family.
    d. All of the above.

_____ 26. Which event occurs *first?*   26. _____
    a. Alan gets the drum from Neil.
    b. Mr. Alvarado refuses to let Alan in the apartment.
    c. Alan's hat is grabbed by the school children.
    d. Alan and Neil hide in the Bekin moving van.

_____ 27. Which event occurs *last?*   27. _____
    a. Alan steals donuts from the store.
    b. Alan pounds the drum as he walks down the street.
    c. Neil and Alan are caught in the rain running from
       Mr. Alvarado's.
    d. Neil finds out about the incident in the park.

_____ 28. What is the reaction of the Comstocks to Neil's suggestion
    that he bring Alan home?   28. _____
    a. They don't want Neil to be involved with a dummy like
       Alan.
    b. They don't want Neil to bring Alan home, but they change their
       minds.
    c. They think it is a fine idea.

_____ 29. Why do the people chase Alan Harper?   29. _____
    a. They want to make up for how they treated him and his
       family.
    b. They believe he had something to do with the girl in the
       park.
    c. They want to give him the money they have collected to send
       him to a special school for exceptional children.

_____ 30. How has Neil matured?   30. _____
    a. He can see the value behind a good education.
    b. Neil can now say he has helped a good cause.
    c. Neil has been able to judge people.
    d. Neil has been able to accept people for what they really are.

_____ 31. How is Neil in over his head with Alan?   31. _____
    a. He has made Alan feel so close to him that now he can't shake
       him.
    b. Neil cannot get his friends to understand why he is helping
       Alan.
    c. Neil cannot reason out what to do now that he is on his own.

_____ 32. What does the drum that was given to Alan symbolize?   32. _____
    a. love
    b. brotherhood
    c. friendship
    d. all of the above

_____ 33. Why is Neil in a state of confusion at the end of the novel?   33. _____
      a. Mr. Alvarado lets him down.
      b. Neil is unable to gain help from anyone he approached.
      c. Neil finds himself separated from his former world. He had seen
         how happy Alan had been in his world and he thought perhaps
         he could feel the same peace of mind Alan had shown.
      d. All of the above.

_____ 34. Who actually was the Dummy?   34. _____
      a. Mr. Alvarado, for not getting involved
      b. Neil, for getting involved
      c. All the people who were insensitive to Neil's and Alan's needs

C. SEQUENCING

Arrange the four items in each group in the order in which these events happened in the novel. Write the number 1 next to the item that occurred first, and so on.

35. _____ Alan is shot.

    _____ Neil alienates himself from everyone.

    _____ Desdemona sits on the porch.

    _____ Alan and Neil hide out on the porch.

36. _____ Alan is teased by the children at school.

    _____ Neil nicknames Alan "Dummy."

    _____ Mr. and Mrs. Comstock reject Neil's suggestions that Alan visit.

    _____ Neil reads his theme in front of the class.

37. _____ Mr. Comstock gives Neil the drum.

    _____ Susie tells Neil that Alan has had brain damage since birth.

    _____ Mr. Alvarado complains about Neil's composition.

    _____ Neil gives Alan the drum.

38. _____ Neil and Alan hide out near a shopping center.

_____ Mr. Alvarado tells Neil to leave his neighborhood.

_____ The mob throws stones at Desdemona.

_____ Neil arrives at the Harper home to warn Alan.

39. _____ Neil visits Alan's home and sees what Alan's home is like.

_____ Neil takes on Alan as his friend.

_____ Neil recognizes what a peaceful and happy world Alan lives in.

_____ Neil recognizes that Alan's life is really a better life than his own.

D. ESSAY

Choose *two* of three questions. On a separate sheet of paper, write at least *two* complete paragraphs for each question you choose. Be sure that you answer the question completely and use examples from the novel to prove your points.

1. Neil Comstock had a poor home life because of his parents' inability to adjust to the death of their older son, Danny. Explain how this fact contributed to the ending of the story.

2. Discuss the importance of the random phrasing and words at the beginning of each chapter. What is the author's purpose, and what information do we get from Alan's comments?

3. As the protagonist, Neil carries out the author's several themes in the novel *Hey, Dummy.* In your essay, discuss how Neil changes from the beginning of the story to the conclusion. You must cite at least four specific observations on Neil to answer this.

The Pigman

Vocabulary

Word	Part of speech	Definition	Sentence
gestapo			
avocation			
subliminally			
thrombosis			
repress			
philanthropy			
syndrome			

Word	Part of speech	Definition	Sentence
patron			
maternal			
disdain			
antagonistic			
nocturnal			
perpetual			
interrogate			
ingrate			

NUMBER 4.A, PAGE 2

Word	Part of speech	Definition	Sentence
mundane			
transformation			
infantile			
hovel			
incongruous			
edited			
proficiency			

The Pigman
Study Guide

Write your answers on a separate sheet of paper. Be sure to put your name on the paper.

CHAPTER 1

1. Define "memorial epic."

2. How would you describe John?

3. Why doesn't John give the signal for the fruit roll when the retired postman is substituting?

CHAPTER 2

1. According to Lorraine, why does John get away with all his pranks?

2. "The fact that I'm his best friend shows he isn't as insensitive to Homo sapiens as he makes believe he is." (p.16) Using the context of this sentence, define *Homo sapiens*.

3. What does Lorraine think of Miss Reillen? What does John think of her?

CHAPTER 3

1. What does "paranoia" mean?

2. How does John get along with his parents?

3. What can you tell about John's character from the opening of this chapter?

CHAPTER 4

1. Why do John, Lorraine, Morton, and Dennis invent the "telephone marathon"?

2. Why does Mr. Pignati keep talking on the phone to Lorraine?

3. According to Lorraine, why does John lie so much?

4. What does Lorraine mean in the last two sentences in the chapter by saying that John *complicates* everything?

CHAPTER 5

1. Why do John and Lorraine tell Dennis and Norton that Mr. Pignati hung up? What does this tell you about their relationship?

2. What evidence do we have that John is feeling slightly guilty about Mr. Pignati?

3. For what reason does Lorraine finally consent to visit Mr. Pignati?

CHAPTER 6

1. Why does the author have John and Lorraine write alternate chapters of the story?

2. Describe Lorraine's mother.

3. What does Lorraine mean by saying that she is the type the boss's wife would hire as the secretary?

CHAPTER 7

1. What is John's home life like?

2. Why do John and Lorraine first suspect something is wrong about Mr. Pignati?

CHAPTER 8

1. Why does Mr. Pignati say his wife is in California?

2. What does Lorraine mean when she says that toy manufacturers could use a course in preventative psychology?

CHAPTER 9

1. According to John, why is his friendship with the Pigman so important?

2. Why do you think John and Lorraine spend so much time analyzing themselves and everyone else?

CHAPTER 10

1. Why does Lorraine's mother seem to hate men?

2. Do you think Mr. Pignati's personality test is valid? What do you think Mr. Pignati represents? Why is he magic to John and Lorraine?

3. What do you think Norton represents in the story (greed, loneliness, selfishness)?

CHAPTER 12

1. Why does Lorraine say that John is "maladjusted"?

2. If Lorraine's dream is an omen, what will happen in the last chapters of the story?

CHAPTER 13

1. Why did John tell Dennis not to invite Norton to the party?

2. What does Norton represent in the story?

CHAPTER 14

1. What is Lorraine's attitude at the opening of this chapter?

2. In this chapter, Lorraine mentions seeing a kitten play with a rubber ball. She goes on to suggest that play is preparation for life. Prove this statement with evidence from this chapter.

3. How have John and Lorraine hurt Mr. Pignati by play?

4. How does the relationship between John and Lorraine and Mr. Pignati change, or doesn't it?

CHAPTER 15

1. According to John, what is the secret of life?

2. Who is Kenneth?

3. What fact of life does John comprehend while holding Mr. Pignati's body?

4. Why does Lorraine think that she and John murdered Mr. Pignati?

5. What is the meaning of John's statement that Mr. Pignati was trespassing?

The Pigman
Vocabulary Worksheet (Antonyms)

From the list at the bottom of the page, choose the pair of antonyms that best matches each word.

1. avocation _____

2. patron _____

3. disdain _____

4. antagonistic _____

5. perpetual _____

6. ingrate _____

7. mundane _____

8. infantile _____

9. incongruous _____

10. proficiency _____

matched, same

job, work

enemy, opponent

pleasant, agreeable

awkward, clumsy

allow, permit

heavenly, special

praise, flattery

temporary, impermanent

mature, adult

harmony, understanding

conscious, aware

The Pigman

Worksheet (Characterization)

Character	An Action He/She Did	What He/She Said	What Others Say About Him/Her
John			
Lorraine			
Mr. Pignati			
Mr./Mrs. Conlan			
Mrs. Jensen			
Norton			

The Pigman
Worksheet (Characterization and Theme)

A. Match the characters with the conflicts they faced.

Conflict	Character
_____ 1. Guilt for Pignati's death (internal)	a. John
_____ 2. Difficulty of resigning self to death (internal)	b. Lorraine
_____ 3. Dissatisfaction with life style (internal)	c. Mr. Pignati
_____ 4. Lack of faith in people—especially men (internal)	d. Mrs. Jensen
_____ 5. Lack of communication (external)	e. Mr. Conlan
_____ 6. Reaching out to others and facing the consequences (external)	
_____ 7. Wish for better communication (external)	
_____ 8. Attempts to mold other's lives (external)	

B. Which of the characters would have said the following?

_____ 1. The living must forget the dead and go on with life.

_____ 2. Do unto others as you would have others do unto you.

_____ 3. Money counts and will give you the good life.

_____ 4. Do your own thing.

_____ 5. One bad apple spoils the whole bunch.

_____ 6. But *everyone* has gone into the family business.

_____ 7. Don't waste your time on things that don't pay well.

_____ 8. Even the smallest creature is of value.

_____ 9. All work and no play makes Jack a dull boy.

_____ 10. As the wind blows, so the tree is bent.

C. Put stars next to any conflicts or sayings in parts A and B on page 1
that might be themes of the book. Defend your choices below.

_____

_____

_____

_____

_____

_____

_____

_____

_____

_____

The Pigman
Final Test

A. MULTIPLE CHOICE

Choose the best answer and write it in one of the spaces provided.

_____ 1. The opening chapter tells us a lot about John as a person. We can   1. _____
tell that
   a. John is a mean troublemaker.
   b. John is not a very bright student.
   c. John has a good sense of humor and is full of the dickens.
   d. John basically hates all adults.

_____ 2. Lorraine says that it is important to write this story immediately 2. _____
because
   a. they will soon mature and forget the whole thing.
   b. they will look back on it and laugh.
   c. their parents will never believe it.
   d. they want proof of the problems they had as adolescents
      to show their own children.

_____ 3. Even though it is not always obvious, Lorraine feels that   3. _____
   a. John has the makings of becoming another Dennis or
      Norton.
   b. John has a lot of human compassion within him.
   c. John's parents really are proud of him.
   d. John is a genius.

_____ 4. John's stated purpose for writing the memorial epic is   4. _____
   a. to make himself not feel so guilty.
   b. to put everything in perspective and try to understand
      why they did what they did.
   c. to make Lorraine feel better.
   d. to prove to Dennis and Norton that they are all actually
      guilty for what happened.

_____ 5. The main impression Lorraine got of Mr. Pignati when she first   5. _____
called him was that he
   a. was a little senile.
   b. had a good sense of humor.
   d. liked kids.
   d. was lonely.

_____ 6. The first trip to the zoo gives us some insight into the character   6. _____
of Mr. Pignati. We can tell that
   a. he understands that Lorraine is not comfortable with ani-
      mals in cages.
   b. Mr. Pignati has a special relationship with Bobo.
   c. John has a gift for talking to animals.
   d. Mr. Pignati has made a friend out of a baboon because he
      is uncomfortable with people.

_____ 7. John's main concern in life is to   7. _____
   a. irritate adults.
   b. avoid being bored.
   c. find himself.
   d. get out of high school.

_____ 8. John decides to wear his roller skates out of the department store   8. _____
because
   a. he wants to prove that it isn't necessary for everything in
      the world to have a purpose.
   b. he knows he would embarrass Lorraine.
   c. he wants to make Mr. Pignati feel good.
   d. he needs to be important and get a lot of attention.

_____ 9. The main difference between John's father and Mr. Pignati is that   9. _____
   a. John's father is too concerned with money.
   b. John's father is older.
   c. Mr. Pignati allows John to be himself.
   d. Mr. Pignati behaves like a child, and John's father only
      talks like one.

_____ 10. John had told Dennis not to invite Norton to the party because
    a. John thought he was still mad at him for calling him the Marshmallow Kid.
    b. John didn't think Mr. Pignati would like him in his house.
    c. He was afraid that Norton would make a play for Lorraine.
    d. Norton had a reputation for going berserk at parties.

10. _____

_____ 11. Lorraine refuses to beg forgiveness from her mother because
    a. she only wants forgiveness from Mr. Pignati.
    b. the only thing that has really upset her mother is the possibility of Lorraine's having been with boys.
    c. she is so mad at John for getting them involved.
    d. her mother would not have let her go to the party in the first place.

11. _____

_____ 12. Mr. Piganti's death proves to John that
    a. older people cannot take the pace of keeping up with youth.
    b. life is only what we make it.
    c. Lorraine really didn't care about Mr. Pignati at all.
    d. Mr. Pignati had nothing to live for.

12. _____

_____ 13. Lorraine feels play is important because
    a. it releases tensions.
    b. kids have something in common then.
    c. it prepares you for life.
    d. all children do it.

13. _____

_____ 14. The climax of the book occurs
    a. when Mr. Pignati dies.
    b. when Mr. Pignati returns from the hospital to find the party.
    c. as Mr. Pignati realizes Bobo is dead.
    d. when Mr. Pignati says his wife is dead.

14. _____

_____ 15. Which of the following is NOT something that Lorraine feels is   15. _____
an omen during the book?
a. having the nightmare about the pigs being broken
b. being chased by a peacock with a low I.Q.
c. being taken home by the police.
d. having the small boy stare at her in the nocturnal animals' house at the zoo

B. VOCABULARY

Use the following words in the sentences below.

freak   berserk   hazardous   compulsive   mortified
antagonistic infantile   pathetic   abominable   prevaricate

16. Smoking may be _____ to your health.

17. The cat ate some catnip and went _____ .

18. Sucking your thumb is considered a (an) _____ habit.

19. John's mother is a cleanliness _____ .

20. John's father was _____ toward him because he wanted to
become an actor.

21. The death of the small helpless animal was such a _____
sight.

22. Many people who visit Las Vegas become _____ gamblers.

23. The teacher _____ the student; she made him sit in the
corner.

24. John learned to _____ from his parents.

25. Carol had a (an) _____ thought of cheating on the exam.

C. SHORT ANSWER

Name a conflict each of the following characters had.

26. John Conlan _____

27. Lorraine _____

28. Mr. Conlan _____

29. Mrs. Jensen _____

30. Mr. Pignati _____

D. MATCHING

Whom do you associate with the following descriptions or statements?

_____ 31. Fruit roll

_____ 32. Feeding Bobo

_____ 33. Nervous in hospitals

_____ 34. Wished to be a journalist

_____ 35. Paranoid

_____ 36. Maladjusted

_____ 37. "It was my wife's favorite joke."

_____ 38. Has made an art out of prevaricating

_____ 39. "Whenever my mother tells me to get a glass of milk, I feel like a Pepsi."

_____ 40. "I brought home some canned goods I 'borrowed' from the pantry."

_____ 41. "I was thinking maybe you'd like to work with me over at the Exchange."

_____ 42. Very concerned about omens

_____ 43. Wouldn't admit to death

_____ 44. Light-fingered

_____ 45. Super-clean nut

a. John

b. Lorraine

c. Mr. Conlan

d. Mrs. Jensen

e. Norton

f. Mr. Pignati

E. ESSAY

Choose *two* (2) of the following topics. On a separate sheet of paper, write at least one (1) paragraph for each essay. Back up your opinion with facts from the book. Each essay will be graded for the following:

Punctuation

Spelling

Complete sentences

Paragraph structure (at least four sentences)

Details from the book

1. How does John and Lorraine's relationship start out in the novel? How does this relationship change during the course of the novel? Be able to identify at least three (3) specific events that affect their relationship.

2. Choose either John *or* Lorraine. Discuss how his/her relationship with his/her parents and his/her home life have influenced his/her adolescence.

3. The relationship John and Lorraine have with Mr. Pignati changes. Discuss how it starts, changes, and ends. Why is the relationship so important to the kids? Why is it so important to Mr. Pignati?

4. Discuss how your attitude toward elderly people may have changed as a result of reading this book. How could society help retired people adjust to their new role in life? In other words, what is our responsibility to the elderly?

The Man Without a Face
Introductory Worksheet

There are many synonyms for *love*. Some of them appear in the list below. Choose the synonym that expresses best the kind of love described below and write the synonym on the blank line. The first one is done for you.

SYNONYMS FOR LOVE

sentiment	adoration
affection	tenderness
benevolence	attachment
rapture	passion
liking	

EXPRESSION OF LOVE

__affection__ 1. toward animals, small children, adults outside of family

_____ 2. toward lover, mistress, partner

_____ 3. toward foods, sports, acquaintances

_____ 4. toward babies, the sick, the unprotected

_____ 5. toward parents, friends, home

_____ 6. toward friends in need, the underprivileged

_____ 7. toward great teachers, wise friends, helpful relatives

_____ 8. toward a fantastic mental or sexual experience

The Man Without a Face

Vocabulary

Word	Definition	Sentence
Oedipus complex		
manipulate		
relevant		
amends		
priority		
inhibit		

Word	Definition	Sentence
speculate		
mull		
alternative		
pseudonym		
repress		
reactionary		
racist		

NUMBER 5.B, PAGE 2

Word	Definition	Sentence
hostile		
inequity		
deduction		
turmoil		
equivalent		

The Man Without a Face
Study Guide

Write your answers on a separate sheet of paper. Be sure to write your name on the paper.

CHAPTER 1

1. Why does Chuck want to be a pilot when he grows up?

2. Describe Chuck's relationship with his family. How does this influence his decision to want to go to St. Matthew's?

3. What effect did his stepfather have on Chuck?

4. Has the fact that he has no brothers made a difference in Chuck's personality?

5. The boys speculate about the appearance of Justin McLeod. What does the word *speculate* mean?

CHAPTER 2

1. Why is the phrase "I don't think it's his parasites that bug her" considered a pun? (p. 19)

2. What is the main difference between Gloria and Meg?

3. What action does Chuck take that shows he is really serious about getting into St. Matthew's?

4. McLeod writes under a *pseudonym.* What does that mean?

5. What are two things about McLeod's house and his pet that tell us about McLeod, the man?

6. Describe Justin McLeod's appearance.

7. What does Chuck mean when he says, "With my usual luck, I have found another Hitler"?

CHAPTER 3

1. What attitude does McLeod have toward tutoring Chuck?

2. How do you know McLeod may have taught before?

3. "Grammar is a racist device for repressing the language of the people." (p. 42) What does this sentence mean? What does *racist* mean?

CHAPTER 4

1. How does Chuck get around telling his friends where he is going during the days?

2. Why does Meg like "Barry Rumble Seat"?

3. Why does Meg come to talk to Chuck just before dawn?

4. What might McLeod and his horse, Richard, have in common?

5. Chuck finds it disconcerting that he is beginning to like McLeod. (p. 61) What does the word *disconcerting* mean?

CHAPTER 5

1. The school psychologist gives Chuck some Rorschach tests. What is a *Rorschach test?*

2. Why is Gloria asking Meg questions about where Chuck is studying?

3. Why does Gloria have so much against Chuck?

4. What is a *vendetta?* Use the word in a sentence.

5. How does Chuck feel about his natural father? How does Gloria feel about Chuck's natural father?

CHAPTER 6

1. Why does Chuck want to stay at McLeod's house to study after they are finished tutoring?

2. Who is Terence Blake?

3. Chuck says what he wants most is to be free from being crowded. What does he mean? (p. 81)

4. What is tragic about the cause of McLeod's disfigured face?

5. Why do you think McLeod reacts the way he does when Chuck reaches out and touches his arm?

CHAPTER 7

1. How does Chuck react to McLeod's apparent rejection?

2. To what does Chuck seem to be allergic?

3. Why does Chuck feel guilty about the afternoon he spent with his friends?

4. Why isn't Chuck excited about the news of his mother's engagement to Barry?

5. Meg says Gloria puts down Chuck and Meg because she has to be number one. Is there a child in every family who feels he or she has to be number one? Why?

CHAPTER 8

1. When McLeod sees Chuck is hung over, he stops the tutoring. What does this show you about McLeod's ability to understand people?

2. Chuck is a happy, euphoric person. What does the word *euphoric* mean? Use it in a sentence.

3. What causes Chuck to have a euphoric feeling?

4. How is Chuck feeling differently toward McLeod? Why?

CHAPTER 9

1. What events bring Justin and Chuck closer together?

2. What new things does Chuck learn about Justin?

CHAPTER 10

1. What might be a reason for Chuck's fainting in church?

CHAPTER 11

1. Why is this chapter the climax of the book?

2. Percy's boot kills Moxie, but Chuck is as much to blame. Why?

3. How does Gloria get even with Chuck for embarrassing her?

4. How is Chuck comforted by Justin? (p. 143)

5. Justin says, "The only thing you can't be free from is the consequence of what you do." How does this apply to Chuck's actions with Moxie and Justin?

CHAPTER 12

1. Who is the man without a face?

2. Why does Justin mention to Chuck that Barry has been in the Air Force?

3. What happens to the following characters: (a) Gloria, (b) Justin, (c) Chuck, and (d) Barry?

4. Is this book a tragedy or a comedy? Why?

The Man Without a Face
Review Sheet (Characters)

Choose the word or phrase in the second column that best describes each character in the first column. Write the letter of the description on the blank line.

Character	Description
_____ 1. Gloria	a. found by side of road
_____ 2. horse	b. unhappy without attention
_____ 3. Meg	c. Chuck's father
_____ 4. dog	d. pseudonym
_____ 5. Chuck's mother	e. Moxie
_____ 6. Terence Blake	f. doesn't like strangers
_____ 7. man without a face	g. former teacher
_____ 8. cat	h. puts Chuck down
_____ 9. Barry Rumbolt	i. fat and friendless
_____ 10. Justin McLeod	j. kind and understanding

The Man Without a Face
Review Sheet (Cause and Effect)

Match each *Cause* from Column A with its *Effect* in Column B. Write the number of the cause on the line in front of the effect. When you are able to locate the place in the novel where a cause is mentioned, jot down the page number so that you can refer to it later for review.

Page
Number   Column A—Causes   Column B—Effects

_____ 1. Chuck's feeling of affection, his   _____ a. Chuck's second try at
           relationship with McLeod   getting into St. Mat-
                                                                   thew's
_____ 2. Chuck's need to get into St.
           Matthew's   _____ b. McLeod's burned face

_____ 3. They are abused by people   _____ c. Chuck's being tutored
                                                                   by McLeod
_____ 4. The car accident
                                                      _____ d. Gloria's jealousy, her
_____ 5. McLeod rejects Chuck's gesture   hatred of Chuck and
           of sympathy, his hand on   his father
           McLeod's arm.
                                                      _____ e. McLeod, Richard, and
_____ 6. Chuck hates being "crowded."   Mickey are suspicious
           He dislikes his mother and   of people.
           hates Gloria.
                                                      _____ f. Meg's weight problem
_____ 7. Gloria is not going to the board-
           ing school.   _____ g. Chuck tells his friends
                                                                   about McLeod's past
_____ 8. Chuck was born.   while Chuck is under
                                                                   the influence of pot.
_____ 9. Chuck smokes pot.
                                                      _____ h. Chuck wonders if he is
_____ 10. The unhappiness of her home   a homosexual.
            life, her many stepfathers, and
            her mother's attitude toward   _____ i. Chuck wants to be free.
            marriage
                                                      _____ j. Chuck has a hangover.

The Man Without a Face
Vocabulary Review No. 1

Below are eighteen scrambled vocabulary words. Place the *number* and unscrambled word next to the correct definition below.

1. aelvertn
2. yueingti
3. piirroyt
4. teddicuon
5. bihinti
6. ssperre
7. ruilmot
8. luml
9. yspmndueo
10. siteloh
11. mdsena
12. mertoe
13. dtpiur
14. ecsutaepl
15. bllafiel
16. vnibeelait
17. sujicdiou
18. craafs

_____ a. stop, slow the growth of something

_____ b. false name

_____ c. to the point; important to what is going on

_____ d. distant; far off

_____ e. think over

_____ f. noisy fight

_____ g. can't be avoided

_____ h. angry; mean

_____ i. wise; showing sound judgment

_____ j. order of importance

_____ k. put down; stop

_____ l. able to make mistakes

_____ m. payment for injury or loss

_____ n. rotten; foul-smelling

_____ o. great confusion, turbulence

The unscrambled words will come from this list of vocabulary words:

Oedipus complex
manipulate
relevant
amends
priority
inhibit
speculate
mull

alternative
pseudonym
repress
reactionary
racist
hostile
inequity
deduction

turmoil
equivalent
mania
demented
remote
miffed
putrid

tactless
inevitable
fracas
fallible
debased
inhospitable
judicious

The Man Without a Face
Vocabulary Review No. 2

On the left is a column of definitions. The letter of each definition appears in a section of the puzzle on the next page. On the right is a column of vocabulary words. Match the words to the definitions, by writing the letter of the definition on the line next to the word. (Two of the words don't have definitions.) Then place the *number* of each vocabulary word in the appropriate box in the puzzle. One is done for you. When you have completed the grid, add the numbers vertically and horizontally. All eight totals should be the same. If they are not the same, you have made an error, and you should go back to check your answers.

Definitions	Vocabulary Words
A. very conservative; opposing progress	_____ 1. fracas
B. make guesses	_____ 2. reactionary
C. equal to	_____ 3. inhospitable
D. mentally ill	_____ 4. turmoil
E. made to feel inferior	___F___ 5. judicious
F. wise, sound judgment	_____ 6. alternatives
G. injustice; unfairness	_____ 7. speculate
H. excessive love of mother	_____ 8. debased
I. manage; good use of hands	_____ 9. mania
J. segregationist; prejudiced person	_____ 10. hostile
K. choices	_____ 11. inequity
L. not giving protection or refuge	_____ 12. demented
M. decide by weighing the facts	_____ 13. manipulate
N. angry; antagonistic	_____ 14. mull
O. great confusion	_____ 15. Oedipus complex
P. wild insanity; manic-depressive	_____ 16. deduce
	_____ 17. racist
	_____ 18. equivalent

A	B	C	D
E	F **5**	G	H
I	J	K	L
M	N	O	P

The total of each column is _____.

The Man Without a Face
Review Sheet (Concepts)

A. KINDS OF LOVE

> There are many different types of love. After each pair of names below, write the synonym of *love* that might apply. Why did you choose this word to describe their relationship?

1. Gloria and Percy _____ _____

_____

_____

2. Meg and Barry _____ _____

_____

_____

3. Meg and Chuck _____ _____

_____

_____

4. Chuck and Moxie _____ _____

_____

_____

5. Chuck and his mother _____ _____

_____

_____

6. Chuck and Justin _____ _____

_____

_____

7. Justin and Richard _____   _____

_____

_____

8. Justin and Barry _____   _____

_____

_____

9. Mother and Barry _____   _____

_____

_____

B. ALIENATION

People can be alienated for many reasons. Give examples of people in the novel who were alienated. Tell why they were alienated and from what.

1. Name _____

Why alienated _____

Alienated from what _____

2. Name _____

Why alienated _____

Alienated from what _____

3. Name _____

Why alienated _____

Alienated from what _____

C. LONELINESS

Give two examples of characters who were lonely. Tell why.

1. Name _____

   Why lonely _____

2. Name _____

   Why lonely _____

The Man Without a Face

Final Test

A. MULTIPLE CHOICE

Choose the answer that BEST answers the question.

_____ 1. Chuck's natural father was his mother's
    a. first husband.
    b. second husband.
    c. third husband.
    d. fourth husband.

1. _____

_____ 2. Justin McLeod remains a lonely and scarred man because
    a. he has no money.
    b. he feels most people are beneath him.
    c. he needs to feel self-punishment for the car accident.
    d. no one in the village has ever tried to be friendly toward him.

2. _____

_____ 3. What are two things that surrounded Justin McLeod that tell you about his personality?
    a. his face and his well-stocked refrigerator
    b. his cows and his horse
    c. his library and his antique car
    d. his forbidding house and his dog

3. _____

_____ 4. When Meg wants to talk seriously with Chuck, she comes to
    a. his room at dawn.
    b. McLeod's.
    c. the cove.
    d. the kitchen.

4. _____

_____ 5. Gloria hates Chuck because he
    a. is smarter than she.
    b. took his father's attention away from her.
    c. knows how to handle his mother.
    d. bugged her when she was making out with her boyfriend.

5. _____

_____ 6. Because Chuck was a loner at school, the psychologists gave him tests, such as
    a. Digit-span.
    b. Iowa I.Q.
    c. Rorschach.
    d. riddles.

6. _____

_____ 7. The tragedy behind McLeod's scarred face is that   7. _____
    a. he killed another boy at the same time.
    b. he was scarred over his entire body also.
    c. it was the first time he wasn't drunk.
    d. he killed his own son.

_____ 8. Chuck finally remembers why he repressed seeing his father   8. _____
at the church. Why?
    a. He wanted Justin to be his father.
    b. He remembers seeing his father dragged out of the church
       while drunk.
    c. His father died in church.
    d. He remembers his father beating him while he was drunk.

_____ 9. Gloria comes back early from Mexico because   9. _____
    a. her father decides she is old enough to live alone.
    b. her father pays her to get lost so he can be with his wife.
    c. Gloria gets in a fight with her stepmother.
    d. Moxie dies and Chuck finds out the truth about his father.

_____ 10. The turning point of the book is   10. _____
    a. Chuck's spending that final night at Justin's.
    b. Chuck's getting into St. Matthew's.
    c. Gloria's marriage to Percy.
    d. Moxie's death and Chuck's finding out the truth about his
       father.

B. COMPLETION

Fill in the blank with the word or phrase that BEST completes the
sentence.

11. McLeod dies of a _____ .

12. The setting of the book is _____ .

13,14. Two of Chuck's stepfathers are _____ and

_____ .

15. The Man Without a Face is _____ .

16. Chuck can never be free from _____ .

17. A flawed and fallen creature that Justin salvaged (or saved) is

_____ .

18. Justin tells Chuck not to idolize him because one day Chuck would see Justin had

_____ .

19. Gloria finally gets even with Chuck for embarrassing her and Percy by _____

_____ .

20. Chuck is _____ years old.

C. TRUE-FALSE

Place 0 next to the false sentences and + next to the true sentences.

21. A cause for Meg's weight problem was an overactive thyroid gland.

22. Justin wants Chuck to realize that his feeling of affection toward Justin doesn't make Chuck a homosexual.

23. Chuck tells Pete and Meg about McLeod's tutoring him.

24. Chuck compares McLeod to Hitler because he's such a hard teacher.

25. This book was written from the first person point of view.

D. MATCHING

_____ 26. Justin McLeod	a. two broken legs
_____ 27. pun	b. internal injuries
_____ 28. Eric	c. Terence Blake
_____ 29. Meg	d. had a strong need to feel loved
_____ 30. Barry Rumbolt	e. Chuck's father at the end of the book
_____ 31. Mickey	f. boys' hideout for smoking pot
_____ 32. Moxie	g. self-centered, insecure
_____ 33. Mother	h. Chuck's natural father
_____ 34. Gloria	i. understanding, sensitive
_____ 35. the cove	j. joke based on a word with two meanings
	k. pseudonym

E. VOCABULARY

Choose the word that best completes each sentence and write the word on the blank line.

amends	reactionary	putrid
inhibit	turmoil	speculated
repress	judicious	fallible
mull	tactless	debased

_____ 36. Chuck tries to make __36__ to Meg for calling her fat.

_____ 37. Sometimes you must __37__ a desire to hit your father.

_____ 38. When the teacher left, the study hall was in __38__ .

_____ 39. All humans make mistakes and are __39__ .

_____ 40. The __40__ decision was fair to all concerned.

_____ 41. Men who belong to the Ku Klux Klan are __41__ .

_____ 42. The white man has __42__ the black man for many years.

_____ 43. Some vaccines __43__ the growth of germs.

_____ 44. Men in the old West __44__ that they could find gold.

_____ 45. Most small children are __45__ and say exactly what is on their minds.

F. ESSAYS

Answer the following two essays. Write at least one paragraph for each question. You will have a minimum of eight sentences. Use specific examples to back up your opinion.

1. Was this book a tragedy or a comedy? Give at least two examples from the novel.

2. Many characters in the story were alienated. What does alienated mean? Name two characters who were alienated. Why were they alienated and what were they alienated from? Give examples from the book.

Answer Keys
to Selected Exercises

LISA, BRIGHT AND DARK

1.B. Quiz No. 1 (Ch. 1–5)

1. The story takes place in wealthy suburban Long Island.
2. a
3. Betsy Goodman
4. b,d,c,a
5. They are too soft, not reliable, afraid to get involved.
6. They felt they should have gotten help sooner.
7. true

1.C Quiz No. 2 (Ch. 6–16)

1. counsel her themselves
2. indifference. He puts her off because he's afraid of upsetting her parents.
3. one of "Mind your own business."
4. might work. Nothing is helping right now, so why not try group therapy.
5. Betsy
6. doesn't think it will work. She tells the girls they *can't* understand Lisa.
7. schizophrenia   paranoia
8. "Raintree County"
9. honest
10. hiding in the closet
11. a. She prefers to wear dark clothes.
    b. She is moody and withdrawn.
12. Mr. Fickett   Mr. Milne
13. her father
14. psychologist
15. Lisa II. She is crying out for help.
16. She has suffered from mental illness herself.

1.D Quiz No. 3 (Ch. 17–22)

1. They don't want to believe she is ill, so they have a vested interest in seeing her only as healthy and stable.
2. Tracy, her sister
3. Mr. Goodman
4. She has an adult as audience. She feels now her parents won't be able to ignore her bizarre behavior.
5. She treats it lightly and disregards its seriousness.
6. either Brian Morris or Neil Donovan
7. She takes an overdose of barbiturates.
8. She begins to cry gently; then she sobs as if relieved. She is glad to be getting help at last.
9. they were willing to be involved when the adults weren't.

1.E Vocabulary Reinforcement Worksheet

1. bask	6. regally
2. palsy	7. inaudible
3. censored	8. staunch
4. psychiatrist	9. realistic
5. regal	10. indecision

1.F Vocabulary Crossword

Across	*Down*
1. indecisive	2. inaudible
3. schizophrenia	3. staunch
5. bask	4. realist
7. regal	6. key
9. nay	8. censorship
10. hindsight	9. realist
11. psychiatrist	
12. palsy	

1.G Final Test

A. VOCABULARY

1. hindsight
2. realist
3. bask
4. chronic
5. persecution
6. hysterical
7. indifferent
8. rebuffed
9. paranoia
10. associate

B. TRUE–FALSE

11. true
12. false
13. true
14. true
15. false

C. CHRONOLOGICAL ORDER

16. i
17. a
18. e
19. c
20. g

D. MULTIPLE CHOICE

21. a
22. a
23. d
24. a
25. d
26. b
27. d
28. c
29. c
30. d
31. c
32. c

E. MATCHING

33. b
34. b
35. d
36. a
37. c
38. c
39. b
40. d

I HEARD THE OWL CALL MY NAME

2.B Final Test

A. MULTIPLE CHOICE

1. c
2. a
3. b
4. c
5. d
6. a
7. b
8. a
9. c
10. c

HEY, DUMMY

3.E Quiz No. 1 (Ch. 1–7)

1. Susie Comstock
2. Mr. Alvarado
3. b
4. Chicanos
5. He doesn't defend himself or fight back as Danny does.
6. c
7. in an institution
8. He guesses that not being able to talk or say what you want to say is worse.
9. his mother works there
10. "This is my friend who plays football."

3.F Quiz No. 2 (Ch. 8–14)

1. a
2. c
3. b
4. b
5. c
6. b
7. b
8. He lives in the barrio.
9. They want her to tell them where Alan is because they think Alan attacked a girl in the park.
10. It takes place in the Southwest United States.

3.G Review Sheet (Sequencing)

2. Neil sees Dummy stealing cakes and not getting caught.
4. Mr. Alvarado lectures Neil and his English class about not taking advantage of retarded people.
6. Neil sees Alan's house, sees how poor he is, and meets Desdemona.
8. Susie shows she is proud of Neil and brings him lemonade.
10. Neil hears his parents' opinions about retarded kids and not bringing them home.
12. Neil loses his best friends because he refuses to tease Alan with the drum.
14. The mob stones Desdemona.
16. Neil and Alan steal a ride on a moving van.
18. Neil ties Alan's feet together.
20. Neil cracks up and becomes like a dummy.

3.H Review Sheet

Character	Theme
6	b, c
3 or 5	d
6	a, e, c
1	a, e
1	a, c, b
4	a, c, e
3	a, e
4	a, b, c
3	a, c, e
5	c, d

3.J Final Test

A. VOCABULARY

1. intercept	8. hysterical
2. sarcastic	9. solidarity
3. mentality	10. subside
4. monotony	11. contempt
5. aloof	12. ridicule
6. bawled	13. detached
7. tantrum	14. manipulating

B. MULTIPLE CHOICE

15. b	22. c	29. b
16. c	23. d	30. d
17. a	24. b	31. c
18. b	25. d	32. d
19. a	26. c	33. d
20. a	27. c	34. c
21. d	28. a	

C. SEQUENCING

35. 3	37. 3	39. 1
4	2	3
1	1	2
2	4	4
36. 1	38. 4	
2	3	
4	2	
3	1	

THE PIGMAN

4.E Worksheet (Characterization and Theme)

A. MATCHING

1. a, b	5. a, e
2. c, a	6. c
3. c, d	7. a, b, c
4. d	8. c, d, e

B. BLANKS

1. John	6. Mr. Conlon
2. Mr. Pignati	7. Mr. Conlon
3. Mr. Conlon	8. Lorraine, John, Mr. Pignati
4. John	9. Mr. Pignati, John
5. Mrs. Jensen	10. Lorraine, John

4.F Final Test

A. MULTIPLE CHOICE

1. c	4. b	7. b	10. d	13. c
2. a	5. d	8. a	11. b	14. c
3. b	6. b	9. c	12. a	15. c

B. VOCABULARY

16. hazardous	20. antagonistic	23. mortified
17. berserk	21. pathetic	24. prevaricate
18. infantile	22. compulsive	25. abominable
19. freak		

D. MATCHING

31. a	34. b	37. f	40. d	43. a
32. f	35. b	38. a	41. c	44. d
33. a	36. e	39. a	42. b	45. d

THE MAN WITHOUT A FACE

5.D Review Sheet (Characters)

1. b	5. h	8. e
2. f	6. d	9. j
3. i	7. c	10. g
4. a		

5.E Review Sheet (Cause and Effect)

a.	7 (pp. 9, 2)	f. 10 (p. 52)
b.	4 (p. 83)	g. 45 (p. 92)
c.	2 (p. 2)	h. 1 (p. 114)
d.	8 (pp. 34, 72)	i. 7 (pp. 81, 91)
e.	3 (p. 57)	j. 9 (p. 95)

5.F Vocabulary Review No. 1

a. (5) inhibit
b. (9) pseudonym
c. (1) relevant
d. (12) remote
e. (8) mull
f. (18) fracas
g. (16) inevitable
h. (10) hostile
i. (17) judicious
j. (3) priority
k. (6) repress
l. (15) fallible
m. (11) amends
n. (13) putrid
o. (7) turmoil

5.G Vocabulary Review No. 2

1. —	7. B	13. I
2. A	8. E	14. —
3. L	9. P	15. H
4. O	10. N	16. M
5. F	11. G	17. J
6. K	12. D	18. C

5.I Final Test

A. MULTIPLE CHOICE

1. b	5. b	8. b
2. c	6. c	9. b
3. d	7. a	10. d
4. a		

B. COMPLETION

11. heart attack
12. the coast of Maine
13. Meg's father
14. Barry Rumbolt
15. Chuck's father
16. the consequences of his actions
17. Richard, Mickey, or Chuck
18. faults
19. showing him the clippings on his father
20. fourteen

C. TRUE-FALSE

21. 0	24. +
22. +	25. +
23. +	

D. MATCHING

26. c	31. a
27. j	32. b
28. h	33. d
29. i	34. g
30. e	35. f

E. VOCABULARY

36. amends	41. reactionary
37. repress	42. debased
38. turmoil	43. inhibit
39. fallible	44. speculate
40. judicious	45. tactless

Selected Bibliography

Action Libraries, I, II. New York: Scholastic Book Services, 1972.

Action Libraries, IA, IIA. New York: Scholastic Book Services, 1975.

BOND, GUY, and TINKER, MILES A. *Reading Difficulties.* New York: Appleton-Century-Crofts, 1967.

BRADBURY, RAY. *The Martian Chronicles.* New York: Bantam Books, 1951.

CEBULASH, MEL, and EDITORS OF *Scholastic Scope* MAGAZINE. *Take 12/Action Plays.* New York: Scholastic Book Services, 1970.

CULLUM, ALBERT. *The Geranium on the Window Sill Just Died, But Teacher You Went Right On.* Belgium: Houlen Quist, 1971 (distributed by Dial/Delacorte Sales).

FADER, DANIEL. *The Naked Children.* New York: MacMillan, 1971.

FADER, DANIEL, and McNEIL, ELTON B. *Hooked-on-Books.* New York: Berkley Publishers, 1977.

FRY, EDWARD. *Graph for Estimating Readability.* New Brunswick, N.J.: Rutgers University Reading Center, 1968; extended version, 1977.

GATES, ARTHUR L., and MacGINITIE, WALTER H. *Gates-MacGinitie Reading Test.* 2nd ed. New York: Teachers College Press, 1969 (now available exclusively from Riverside Publishing Co.).

GOODYKOONTZ, WILLIAM, ed. *Drugs: Insights and Illusions,* New York: Scholastic Book Services, 1971.

_____ *Loyalties.* New York: Scholastic Book Services, 1958.

HANSBERRY, LORRAINE. *A Raisin in the Sun.* New York: Signet Classics, 1966.

HENTOFF, NAT. *This School Is Driving Me Crazy.* New York: Dell, 1976.

HERBER, HAROLD. *Reading in the Content Areas.* Englewood Cliffs, N.J.: Prentice-Hall, 1970.

HINTON, S. E. *The Outsiders.* New York: Dell, 1961.

_____ *Rumble Fish.* New York: Dell, 1975.

_____ *That Was Then, This Is Now.* New York: Dell, 1971.

HINTZE, NAOMI. *You'll Like My Mother.* Greenwich, Conn.: Fawcett, 1969.

JAFFE, RONA. *Class Reunion.* New York: Delacorte Press, 1979.

JOHNSON, MARGORIE SEDDON, and KRESS, ROY A. *Informal Reading Inventories.*

IRA Service Bulletin. Newark, Del.: International Reading Association, 1905.

KATA, ELIZABETH. *A Patch of Blue.* New York: Popular Library, 1961.

LEE, MILDRED. *The Skating Rink.* New York: Dell, 1969.

LORGE, IRVING; THORNDIKE, ROBERT L.; and HAGEN, ELIZABETH. *Lorge-Thorndike Intelligence Test.* Boston: Houghton Mifflin, 1954 (rev. ed. 1966).

MADSEN, ALAN L., ed. *Tomorrow: Science Fiction and the Future.* New York: Scholastic Magazines, 1973.

MAZER, HARRY. *Snowbound.* New York: Dell, 1973.

MEDVED, MICHAEL. *What Really Happened to the Class of '65?* New York: Random House, 1976.

Nelson-Denny Reading Test. Boston, Houghton Mifflin, 1960.

NEUFELD, JOHN. *Lisa, Bright and Dark.* New York: S. G. Phillips, 1969.

PLATT, KIN. *Hey, Dummy.* New York: Dell, 1971.

Point 31 Magazine. Pleasantville, N.Y.: Reader's Digest Services, 1975.

Sequential Tests of Educational Progress. Princeton, N.J.: Educational Testing Service, 1959, revised 1971.

SLOSSON, RICHARD L. *The Slosson Intelligence Test.* Aurora, N.Y.: Slosson Educational Publishers, 1963.

Snellen Chart. Southbridge, Mass.: American Optical Company.

Social Science Reader (9). Pleasantville, N.Y.: Reader's Digest Book Services, 1974.

SPACHE, GEORGE. *Spache Diagnostic Reading Scales.* Monterey, Calif.: CTB/McGraw Hill, 1963.

Stanford-Binet Intelligence Scale. 3rd rev. ed. Boston: Houghton Mifflin, 1964.

SULLIVAN, ELIZABETH T.; CLARK, WILLIS W.; and TIEGS, ERNEST W. *California Test of Mental Maturity.* New York: CTB/McGraw-Hill, 1936 (rev. ed. 1965).

TIEGS, ERNÉST W., and CLARK, WILLIS W. *California Achievement Tests: Reading.* New York: CTB/McGraw-Hill, 1970.

Webster's Intermediate Dictionary. Springfield, Mass.: G. & C. Merriam, 1972.

WECHSLER, DAVID. *Wechsler Intelligence Scales for Children.* New York: Psychological Corporation, 1949.

Wepman Audial Discrimination Test. Chicago: Language Research Association, 1958.

Index